MYSTERIOUS ENCOUNTERS
AT MAMRE AND JABBOK

Program in Judaic Studies
Brown University
BROWN JUDAIC STUDIES
Edited by
Jacob Neusner,
Wendell S. Dietrich, Ernest S. Frerichs,
Calvin Goldscheider, Alan Zuckerman

Project Editors (Project)

David Blumenthal, Emory University (Approaches to Medieval Judaism)
William Brinner (Studies in Judaism and Islam)
Ernest S. Frerichs, Brown University (Dissertations and Monographs)
Lenn Evan Goodman, University of Hawaii (Studies in Medieval Judaism) (Studies in
Judaism and Islam)
William Scott Green, University of Rochester (Approaches to Ancient Judaism)
Ivan Marcus, Jewish Theological Seminary of Americas
(Texts and Studies in Medieval Judaism)
Marc L. Raphael, Ohio State University (Approaches to Judaism in Modern Times)
Jonathan Z. Smith, University of Chicago (Studia Philonica)

Number 50
MYSTERIOUS ENCOUNTERS AT MAMRE AND JABBOK
by
William T. Miller

MYSTERIOUS ENCOUNTERS AT MAMRE AND JABBOK

by
William T. Miller

Scholars Press
Chico, California

MYSTERIOUS ENCOUNTERS
AT MAMRE AND JABBOK

by
William T. Miller

Library of Congress Cataloging in Publication Data

Miller, William T., 1941–
 Mysterious encounters at Mamre and Jabbok.

 (Brown Judaic studies ; no. 50)
 Bibliography: p.
 Includes index.
 1. Bible. O.T. Genesis XVIII, 1–16—Criticism,
interpretation, etc.—History. 2. Bible. O.T. Genesis
XXXII, 23–33—Criticism, interpretation, etc.—History.
3. Rabbinical literature—History and criticism.
I. Title. II. Series.
BS1235.5.M55 1984   222'.1106'09   84-23559
ISBN 0–89130–816–4 (alk. paper)
ISBN 0–89130–817–2 (pbk. : alk. paper)

BS
1235.5
M55
1984

Printed in the United States of America
on acid-free paper

Dedicated to my parents, Mary and William;
  to my sister, Ethel;
  and to the many members of the Society
  of Jesus who helped me persevere, especially
  those at Gonzaga College High School in
  Washington, DC, and at St. Louis University.

TABLE OF CONTENTS

INTRODUCTION

Present day students pursuing graduate studies in the Old
Testament work in a very rich and complex field. Advances in many
related subjects, such as ancient Near Eastern languages, archae-
ology, and history, contribute to the vast amount of information
to be acquired. The exegesis of biblical texts, that is the ex-
plication of their original content, form, and Sitz im Leben, is
the primary purpose of such scholarship.

The exegetical skills and interests gained in graduate study
will be passed on to others, usually through publishing and teaching. However, a certain percentage of these graduate students
become involved in ministry, and find themselves confronted in
varying degrees with the task of hermeneutics, the task of drawing
authentic relationships between the content and contexts of biblical passages and the life situations and systems of thought of
present day congregations or groups of believers.

Training in hermeneutics varies considerably from one denomi-
nation to another, from one faith to another. An individual may
find a congregation or group to minister to without himself having
had any such training at all.

One obvious method of training people in the art of hermeneutics is to present them with some of the history of the art as it
has been practiced over the centuries. Yet this is rarely done.
The reasons are not hard to discover. Much of modern scholarly
understanding of the Bible is so unlike the literal, fundamentalist
understanding of previous generations that their writings are
usually taught in other disciplines such as doctrinal or spiritual
theology, Rabbinics, or Patristics. Further, the press of related
subjects limits experimentation in this regard in OT graduate
course requirements.[1]

In an effort to learn some lessons from the history of hermeneutics I chose to examine ancient writings on specific biblical
passages. By looking at both Jewish and Christian commentary on
two different passages, and by extending the study over as along a
period of time as was practical (to *Yalkut Shimoni* and the writings
of Bede respectively), I hope to discover as many lessons as
possible.[2]

The two passages used in this study, Gen 18:1-16 and 32:23-33,
were not initially selected with reference to modern critical bases.

1

They are, however, very similar narratives. Both are from the
Jahwist and both obviously developed in complex ways before he
used them. Both must be taken within the contexts of their re-
spective patriarchal narrative cycles in order to appreciate the
many subtle notes being raised within them about the relationships
between God and man. These two mysterious encounters, special
moments in the lives of Abraham, Sarah, and Jacob, are provocative
texts for anyone of any time who is called to the task of hermeneutics.

Before going on to examine the two Genesis texts and the
writings about them, I want to mention the reflections of one OT
scholar on the subject of hermeneutics. James A. Sanders[3] observes
that older biblical traditions were often used by the prophets and
other biblical authors and editors in one of two ways. They either
invoked old traditions to bring support and comfort to their audiences or, alternatively, to challenge them in some way.[4]

Starting with these two ways as fundamental hermeneutical
modes, which he calls "constitutive" and "prophetic" respectively,
Sanders goes on to list several rules and principles which can be
useful for current hermeneutics. Most of these rules are essentially aspects of the challenging or prophetic hermeneutic and
need not be reviewed here. The last one, however,[5] is germane to
both the constitutive and prophetic mode.

The rule is that we must be willing to admit that many OT
characters are actually portrayed as sinful, weak human beings.
We cannot minimize or deny the weaknesses portrayed in our efforts
to draw morals from the story for our own time. The two processes,
admitting imperfections in the OT figures and drawing morals while
denying the existence of such imperfections, are respectively
called "theologizing" and "moralizing" by Sanders.

As the comments of the Jewish and Christian writers on the
Mamre and Jabbok stories are examined in the next four chapters,
I would like to see how much of their hermeneutics can be placed
into the constitutive and prophetic categories mentioned above.
It should also be possible to discern whether these ancient writers
admit to human weaknesses on the part of Abraham, Sarah, or Jacob.
These hermeneutical modes and rules are not meant to be criteria
by which to judge the men of former centuries. Rather, we should
look on them simply as aids in our own comprehension of a large
number of citations.

Further, it is obvious that these modes and rules are very
general in nature. In order to examine specific Jewish or Christian

materials for definite spans of time we will need many additional
tools. However, the claim made in this study is that there is a
strong biblical foundation for this system of modes and rules, and
that they should be helpful for anyone doing hermeneutics now. In
applying some elements of Sanders' system to the hermeneutical
work of former generations I am simply trying to see how those
generations were affected by the same biblical foundation.

One might object that I am trying to do two different things
at once--a historical study and an assessment of the results in
light of one article by a modern scholar. The objection is valid,
but there are two additional points to be considered. First, the
time spent in application of these general modes and rules to the
ancient material will be clearly defined. Second, there is always
the possibility that the hermeneutical efforts of the early Jews
and Christians will compel us to reevaluate Sanders' system, which
we shall do in the final conclusions section.

CHAPTER I

EARLY JEWISH HERMENEUTIC OF GEN 18:1-16

In addition to keeping in mind Sanders' general hermeneutical
modes and rules, we shall consider the recent work of Daniel Patte,
who has examined ancient Jewish hermeneutic in particular.[1]

He begins by reviewing current scholarship on different aspects of the use of Scripture in the Synagogue.[2] As is the case
with other scholars[3] who have worked in this area, Patte considers
the study of the Targums to be very important in helping us to see
how biblical passages were commonly understood early on.

He discerns two general norms, two underlying attitudes toward
Scripture as a result of his own analysis of several Targum passages.[4] The first is that since everything is meaningful in the
Bible, any detail can be interpreted by referring to other scriptural passages. The second is that Scripture is meant to be actualized. Let us look at each of these norms more closely.

A Biblical Verse Can be Interpreted by Other Passages

While some Targumic citations of parallel passages are evident
enough, we must realize that, by the very liturgical roles of the
Targums in explaining difficult phrases and in transmitting well
known traditions, they usually present only the *results* of the use
of other biblical passages.[5] Often it is difficult to perceive
the specific text which the Targumist had in mind; but even if we
cannot discover a linking passage by considering the other readings
for the day, other traditions, or the like, we should assume that
in most instances the Targum interpretation was scripturally based.

Such constant comparison of biblical passages can lead to a
"synthetic" view of the relationship between Scripture and sacred
history (i.e., a view that the two are basically identical; that
Scripture contains all sacred history).[6]

Such a conception of the unity of the Scriptures lies behind
Targumic statements which we can only regard as fanciful. The
Targumists often ignored spans of centuries or great distances in
their fusion of biblical identities, e.g., in their saying that
Melchizedek was Noah's son Shem, or that the refugee mentioned in
Gen 14:13 was the king Og of Deuteronomy 3. Locations were also
fused, such as in the tradition that the Temple was built on the

5

exact site where Jacob had had his dream of the ladder and the
angels. The times and dates of certain biblical events were often
said to coincide with feast days or other significant anniver-
saries.[7] Patte calls this process of fusing diverse identities,
locations, or times a *telescoping*.

As Patte observes, "...the result of this synthetic view of
history is to reduce the sacred history to a schematic series of
privileged events."[8] For the Targums this sacred history is, so
to speak, "closed": everything in the Bible is interpreted as
referring to this limited number of sacred events (acts or words
of God).[9]

Major biblical figures also had other biblical passages
telescoped to them or applied to them in more significant ways.
Sometimes these figures were seen as part of a larger series of
closed events (e.g., merit schemes, some of which we will examine
in detail below). Frequently other passages were invoked to help
show that these figures had certain ethical values, that they were
moral examples whom the faithful should imitate. This interest in
the moral example afforded by these major figures is the principal
exception to the lack of reference to present events mentioned
above. Here the circle of interpretation of Scripture by Scripture is broken; the biblical person is interpreted in terms of the
believer's situation.[10]

Scripture is Meant to be Actualized

It was certainly a belief of the Jewish people that the
Scriptures had meaning for the Jewish community of any place or
time. A few Targumic passages, in offering interpretations or
explanations of a difficult text, clearly read current concepts
back into the scriptural account (in addition to reading in ethical
and moral values, as discussed above). These deliberate adaptations often go beyond what we would expect to find in a semi-
official form of liturgical literature such as the Targums.[11]
Patte postulates that Targumic actualizations are few because
Targums were used by the Jewish community *as gathered* in the Synagogue; there people ideally would have the same value systems which
the Scripture readings and other worship forms were celebrating.[12]
Hence, Targumic actualizations would have been redundant in such
situations.

Patte next examines the halakic traditions, which were developed in the School rather than in the Synagogue.[13] There were two
sources for the halakoth: customs or traditions having no biblical

connections, and scriptural rules and regulations. Thus the "oral
Torah" was not closed in the same sense that the written Torah was
to a reading of current cultural influences and events.

A close reading of halakic materials does show, however, that
here also the actualizations which we have were influenced by the
notion that Scripture includes all sacred history. Contemporary
history, contemporary salient events are rarely commented upon.[14]
Instead the subject matter of the halakoth focused on cultural
changes, changes in everyday life, laws, current ideas, ways of
thinking, and folklore.[15]

I am convinced that Patte's analysis of ancient Jewish hermeneutical norms and methods can be of use to us as we examine the
Mamre and Jabbok passages. It provides us with a way to comprehend and subdivide a large body of writings. We can test his findings as we assemble the many individual references in the ancient
literature.[16] We will look for the correlation of other biblical
passages to the two stories we have chosen in order to see how they
helped illuminate them. We will be alert to any telescoping, any
schemata which fuse separate biblical places, times, or persons.
We will note ascriptions of specific virtues to the leading characters in these two passages, and any other deliberate adaptations
or actualizations made by the commentators.

Before examining the ancient translations, Targums, and Jewish commentaries on the Mamre passage, we should review briefly
current analyses of the narrative.

The biblical account maintains an ambiguity as to the exact
nature of the divine and angelic visitations by means of its identifications and enumeration of subjects and speakers. Thus Jahweh
is clearly the subject in verses 1 and 13; it is also possible
that He is the single addressee in v. 3 and the speaker in vv. 10,
14 and 15b.[17] On the other hand, Abraham's term of address in v.
3, אדני, can also be understood as "my lord" or "sir," with just a
slight change in pointing. So it is possible that, in pre-
Massoretic traditions, the principal of the three visitors was
being spoken to in this verse. Since the three visitors continue
to occupy center stage thereafter, the principal visitor might
also be the subject in vv. 10, 14 and 15b.

An examination of the comments of a representative sampling
of twentieth century scholars[18] reveals several common areas of
interest.

Almost all these commentators speculate to some extent on the
possibility that earlier traditions have been worked into the

present Jahwist account. Several assume that the mention of the
gift of Isaac has been grafted onto an older legend which dealt
primarily with hospitality. Parallels from pagan literature (some
of them Canaanite) are often mentioned. Because of the existence
of literary parallels most of these scholars conclude that the
three visitors are meant to be angels rather than Jahweh Himself
in metamorphosis.

Several incidents in the story, such as the sudden appearance
of the visitors, the surprising question in v. 9, and Abraham's
silence in contrast to Sarah's reactions to the message, are seen
as contributing to a gradual awareness on the part of Abraham and
Sarah that their visitors are more than human and that the message
is from God. Most of these commentators propose that the Massoretic pointing of אדני in v. 3 is not in accordance with this motif
of Abraham and Sarah's gradual awareness, and so should be set
aside.

The stress on hospitality in the first half of the story is
seen as a value in itself, a highly proclaimed virtue in the ancient Near East. The literary climax of the second half of the
passage is generally taken to be the question in v. 14. Nothing
is too hard for Jahweh, who will effect His promise to Abraham in
full.

Modern commentators, then, exhibit two primary areas of interest in the Mamre story: many focus on possible antecedents to the
final form as we have it, and several try to establish the main
literary motifs and climaxes in the final form as such. One can
reasonably speak of a consensus among them, perhaps citing von
Rad's work or Speiser's as representative. None of these writers
presents a systematic description of the history of ancient Jewish
or Christian hermeneutic of the passage.

The most notable departure from the general run of modern
commentary on our passage is made by Benno Jacob. In his view
Abraham expects the messengers and is already in 18:1 aware of
God's plans for Sodom and Gomorrah (mentioned later in 18:17-20).
Abraham's hospitality and escorting of his guests are means whereby
he seeks and is encouraged to intercede for these cities. The
whole passage is subordinated to the events concerning the destruction of the cities.[19]

A. Ancient Versions and Targums on Gen 18:1-16

Any study of ancient Jewish biblical commentary and hermeneutical patterns should begin with the principal versions and the

Targums used in the synagogues.[20] A synopsis and a chart of the
variations and patterns found therein will be presented here. A
more detailed description of the refinements of each version or
Targum may be found in Appendix I.

The biblical "oaks of Mamre" is considered to be a specific
location (or valley or crossroad), and not just an unknown stand
of trees. While LXX and *Peshitta* have "oak" in the singular, no
version or Targum firmly identifies any tree in v. 1 with the tree
of vv. 4 and 8.[21] The visit is assumed to follow upon Abraham's
circumcision (Genesis 17) by only a few days. In some of the
Targums phrases such as "the word of Jahweh" or "the glory of
Jahweh" are used in order to modify the impression, which could be
had from the MT, that Abraham had a direct vision of God. Further,
the three visitors are identified as angels in human form by some
of the Targums. In some cases Abraham's bow to them is further
explained so that it may not be interpreted as being a form of
divine worship. In several instances the duties of each angel are
also mentioned.

All the Jewish versions and Targums except the Samaritan
branch agree with the MT pointing of אדני in v. 3. The *Samaritan
Pentateuch* and *Targum* read the plural "lords" throughout the entire
verse. Some Targums refer here to the Shekinah of Jahweh.[22]

In v. 4 some traditions assume that Abraham personally fetched
the water and washed the feet of his guests, while others portray
him as a host whose servants performed these tasks. Targum *Ps.-
Jonathan* makes it quite clear that Abraham had turned his attention
from Jahweh to the three travellers.

In some instances it is noted that the travellers came exactly
in time for the noon meal. In *Ps.-Jonathan* Abraham enjoins them
to pray a grace before the meal.

Different terms are used to explain the עגות of v. 6. They
generally indicate kinds of bread which can be made with little or
no leaven but which need more heat (i.e., scones, flatbreads, or
the like). *Neofiti*'s פטירין most specifically indicates the absence of leaven. Most of the traditions retain the large amount
of flour found in the MT.

Neofiti and *Ps.-Jonathan* deny the plain meaning of the MT in
v. 8 by stating that the angel travellers only *seemed* to eat and
drink.

The LXX and some copies of *Ps.-Jonathan* have a single speaker
in v. 9. In v. 10 only *Ps.-Jonathan* clearly identifies the speaker
as one of the travellers, although *Neofiti* and *Fragmentary* can be

In this chart X indicates the presence of the topic in question; x indicates that the source can be taken as a partial witness, or that inferences can reasonably be drawn from its context. Numbers in parentheses refer to other verses in the same source which apply to the topic.

	LXX	Neof.	Frag.	Onk.	Ps.J.	Pesh.	Sm.P.	Sm.T.
Location is further specified.	X	X	X	X	X	X		X
Abraham's recent circumcision is mentioned.		X	X		X			
God's mode of appearance is specified.		X	X		X			
The three visitors are angels.		X	X		X			
The angels' duties are mentioned.		X	X		X(16)			
Abraham's bow is explained.		X	X					
אדני in v. 3 does not refer to Jahweh.							X	X
The Shekinah concept is used.		X			X			
Abraham personally fetched the water.		X				X		
It was time for the noon meal.	(1)	X			X			
The angels only seemed to eat.		X			X			
The speaker in v. 10 is an angel.		X	x		X			
The return will be in a year.	x				X			
The couple will be vigorous.			X	X	X			
Ishmael is spoken of in v. 10.		X	X		X			
The speaker in v. 14 is an angel.		X			X			
Can anything be hidden from God?		X		X	X			
The return will be at a feast day.					X			
The speaker in v. 15 is an angel.		x			X			

understood to do the same. Some of the paraphrases of כעת חיה
refer to a time one year from the present while others indicate
that both Abraham and Sarah will become more robust in the meanwhile. Many efforts are made to clarify MT והוא אחריו. One tradition was that the הוא referred to Ishmael.

We find many paraphrases of Sarah's reactions in v. 12. Some
of these use the verbs חוך or קטרג, which may intensify the sense
of צחק. Others simply use תמה. Several Targums have Sarah reflect on the days of her youth. The LXX is the most unlike the MT
here.

All the versions and Targums record that Jahweh is the speaker of v. 13, regardless of any prior modifications made in vv. 1
or 3.

The speaker of v. 14 is not identified in the Targums, although *Neofiti* and *Ps.-Jonathan* can be understood to refer to one
of the angels. Several traditions ask if anything is or can be
hidden from Jahweh. The reference could be to Sarah's laughter or
doubt, which is supposedly hidden from the speaker. *Ps.-Jonathan*
explains למועד as the time of "the feast." Presumably those congregations knew which feast was being recalled. Most of the other
Targums do not dwell upon the term at all.

Only *Ps.-Jonathan* clearly identifies the respondent of v. 15
as an angel; *Neofiti* can lend itself to such a reading.

B. Other Rabbinic Traditions on Gen 18:1-16

In the following pages I will attempt to give an overview of
all the significant references to the Mamre story to be found in
rabbinic sources of the first millennium A.D.[23] The reason for
extending the search up to the 11th century *Yalkut Shimoni*, and to
a few excerpts from early medieval sources such as Rashi, Maimonides, and *Zohar* is simple. The state of rabbinic studies is such
at the present time that we are not able closely to correlate the
dates of written manuscripts with the dates of the traditions which
they contain. Thus a 7th century commentary might well have pre-
served statements of a 3rd or 4th century origin. Only by getting
an overall picture of all the citations of a particular passage
can one hope to discern the important trends in the rabbinic hermeneutical traditions.

I have compiled the comments on these verses into sixteen
groupings, but that number is an arbitrary one. I have made no
effort to eliminate all overlapping between groupings since the
logical end point would be a return to a reference list such as

Hyman's. Rather I have tried to be sensitive to the contexts
within which these verses are cited and to present the different
rabbinic written sources in an elementary chronological order only
within these context groupings. I have, therefore, not seen it
necessary to mention the names of the Rabbis and teachers with
whom certain traditions are usually associated, nor to fix a mis-
leadingly precise series of dates to the various manuscripts.

I have made every effort to use the Massoretic Hebrew chapter
and verse numbers throughout, although there are surely points
where I might have confused them with the English enumeration,
which is usually off by one verse when it does differ. If the
English enumeration is quite different, I do mention that fact.

As for the Hebrew sources, they are generally well known.[24]
I provide slightly fuller information than is usual when citing
the *Palestinian Talmud*, and the *Yalkut* references. The *Yalkut* is
usually printed in two volumes--comments on the Pentateuch com-
prising volume 1. Rather than simply indicating the volume number,
I indicate which book of the Bible is under consideration.
Tanhuma B[25] is a variant text of the *Tanhuma*. I have not eliminated reduplications between the two texts. I am reasonably sure
that, in so using the two texts, I have included some real repetitions.

The *Zohar* references were studied only in translation, unless
otherwise indicated.

1. Traditions About the Location

We find some traditions about Mamre in *Genesis Rabbah*.[26] R.
Judah calls it a plain (מישרי) and a place (אתרא). R. Nehemiah
calls it a palace (פלטין),[27] a palace of a man named Mamre. Why
was his name Mamre? R. Azariah, in the name of R. Judah, says
that it was because he argued (הימרה) against Abraham. As the
story goes, Abraham took counsel after God had told him that He
wished circumcision to be the sign of the covenant between them.
Two friends advised Abraham against it, but Mamre reminded him
about all that God had done for him and that he should undergo
this suffering in return. Then God said to Mamre, "You gave him
good advice. By your life, I will reveal Myself to him only in
your palace."[28]

The explanation of Mamre's name as being related to Abraham's
decision to accept circumcision reminds us once again of the serious obligation of circumcision on all Jewish men. Thus even a
place name can be "telescoped" to an important custom.

2. Abraham's Situation

(a) *His Desire for Visitors*

Rabbinic traditions about the hospitality which was shown by
Abraham are very strong and will be taken up in detail later in
this chapter. Here we will simply mention a few of the general
remarks found at the outset of comments on the entire passage.

In *Genesis Rabbah*[29] we read that Abraham was worried that,
now that he was circumcised, no travellers would come to visit
him. God replies that whereas uncircumcised visitors had come in
the past, now "I in my glory will come to you." We also read[30]
that when Sodom was destroyed, wayfarers ceased to come by and
Abraham said, "Why should I permit hospitality to cease from my
house?" He therefore moved to the region of Gerar (Gen 20:1).
R. Abin cites here Job 14:18, "The rock is removed from its
place."[31]

Another reference is made in *Pesikta Rabbati* 42.3.[32] Here,
during a rather compassionate discussion about the sins of Lot's
daughters, we find a consideration about Abraham and how he extended hospitality to visitors and inhabitants in the regions
about Sodom before that city was destroyed. *Yalkut*, Genesis 82
and Rashi also mention that Abraham was sitting by the door of the
tent looking for travellers to invite in.

In these references we see Abraham being presented as a
"moral type" of the virtue of hospitality. The matter of Abraham's
circumcision is again mentioned, but here we have a hint that God's
appearance is to be considered as a *reward* for accepting the cove-
nantal sign of circumcision.

(b) *His Recuperation from Circumcision*

The interest in Abraham's circumcision continues to manifest
itself in our sources. In *Numbers Rabbah*,[33] Lev 9:6 ("And Moses
said, 'This is the thing which the Lord commanded you to do; and
the glory of the Lord will appear to you'") is applied to Abraham.
As soon as Abraham had circumcised himself (Gen 17:26), then God
revealed Himself to him (Gen 18:1). Likewise, the commentator has
Moses demand that any uncircumcised men undergo the ritual right
away.[34]

In *Genesis Rabbah*[35] we have another reference to Abraham's
circumcision, based on Job 19:26, "and after my skin has been thus
destroyed, then from my flesh I shall see God." Abraham said,
"After I removed my foreskin many proselytes came to practice this

sign....If I had not done so, why should the Holy One have
appeared to me?"[36]

There is one more relationship between Abraham and the ritual
of circumcision.[37] Since Abraham is the founder of the faith, in
the world to come he will sit at the door of Gehenna and render
any unworthy Israelite indistinguishable from his non-Jewish fellow
damned. Abraham will do this by grafting on them foreskins taken
from worthy Jewish male infants who die before they are eligible
for the ceremony.[38]

Besides these more general "telescoping" remarks about circumcision, we also find comments, similar to the Targum observations, on Abraham's recuperation from the rite.

In *Baba Mezia* 86b R. Hama says that the appearance took place
on the third day after Abraham's circumcision (the most painful
period) and that God came to inquire after him.[39] More specifically, Abraham had sent his servant out to look for travellers but
he had found none. Abraham then went out to see for himself and
he found God, standing at the door. However, God realized at this
point that Abraham was indisposed (loosening and binding the bandages), and so He went some distance away. The same is true of
the three angelic visitors. At first they were near him but they
saw that he was in pain; so they also said, "It is not proper to
stand here" and moved away.[40]

Another way to describe Abraham's condition is simply to see
him as a *sick* person, in that the operation requires a period of
convalescence. So in *Sotah* 14a, in a discussion of some of the
virtues of Moses, mention is made of works of mercy. God clothed
the naked (Adam and Eve), and so should we. God visited the sick
(Gen 18:1) and so should we.[41]

Thus we see Abraham's continuing interest in hospitality,
despite his pain from the circumcision. God and the angels are
modest during the visit and *solicitous for the sick* in coming to
visit him in the first place. These two virtues are obviously
examples for our imitation as much as are the actions and attitudes of Abraham.

(c) *His Sitting Down*

The fact that Abraham was seated when God visited him lent
itself to several rabbinic interpretations. The first interpretation was simply that God respected Abraham's old age. So in *Pal.
Talm. Rosh Hashanna*[42] God stands before Abraham out of respect.[43]

Another line of thought is that Abraham was taking the posture which is normal in Jewish services and in the Beth Hamidrash.
Genesis Rabbah[44] has a good example of this often made analogy.
Here we are advised to read not יושב (the participle) but ישב (the
simple action), implying a more deliberate action, i.e., Abraham
wished to rise but God said to him, "Sit, and be a sign to your
children that as you sit before the Shekinah, so will your children sit." In other citations of this tradition it is clearly
mentioned that assemblies and houses of Midrash are meant.[45]

Genesis Rabbah[46] mentions a phrase from Psa 18:36, "your
humility has made me great" and applies this to God's humility in
standing before Abraham.[47]

We have seen here more examples of actions taken by God which
are for our imitation. God honors Abraham's old age; He is humble
before the patriarch. Also, justification for the approved posture
when one is in synagogue or school is based on God's wishes, and
not merely on the posture which Abraham happened to be taking at
the time of the visit.

3. The Day and the Hour

The various interpretations of the time of the theophany seem
to be centered on God's involvement.

Some commentators saw significance in the fact that this
theophany took place during the bright part of the day. In *Genesis
Rabbah*[48] the evoking text is Gen 20:3, "God came to Abimelech in a
dream of the night." The Lord deals with pagans as if from *afar*
(e.g., Prov 15:29 and Isa 39:3); whereas when dealing with Israel,
it is as if He comes from *nearby* (e.g., Gen 18:1 and Lev 1:1).[49]

In *Pirke Eliezer* chap. 28 we are told that God comes in night
visions to all prophets but to Abraham He revealed Himself in a
night vision (Gen 15:1) *and* in an actual visit (Mamre).[50]

Many commentators speculate on the exact time of the day or
the amount of heat. In *Berakoth* 27a there is a discussion on
times for prayer. The commentary assumes that כחם היום of Gen 18:1
means the sixth hour of the day.

In *Pal. Talm. Berakoth*[51] Rab Tanhuma thinks that the time is
when no creature has a shadow (i.e., high noon). Along the same
lines, in *Genesis Rabbah*[52] we find the description of no shade, and
another motive: the Holy One poked a hole in Gehenna and heated up
the whole world and its inhabitants for a brief time, saying, "Shall
righteous people be in pain and everyone else be at ease?"[53]

Turning back to look at more instances of God's motives, another idea was that God had made it hot to discourage anyone from travelling at all, so as to spare Abraham any exertion in matters of hospitality. This theme is found in *Baba Mezia* 86b, where the sun is withdrawn from its sheath by God, so as not to disturb Abraham with travellers.[54]

In *Pirke Eliezer*[55] there is another motive attributed to God for making the day very hot—He wanted to try Abraham. Abraham sought the breeze of the day by going to the tent doorway.

4. The Participants

It is understandable, given the tensions of the MT and the variety within the Targum traditions, that there continues to be considerable question in the Rabbinic commentaries as to the precise mode of appearance by God and the angels.

(a) *Divine and Angelic Presences*

I think it would be fair to say that the majority of rabbinic traditions hold for the appearance to Abraham of both the Divine Presence (usually under the Shekinah concept[56]) and three angels. In *Genesis Rabbah*[57] Abraham complains of having no visitors since his circumcision. God replies that "I and my retainers (פמליא) will appear to you." The text then continues, "and he saw the Shekinah and he saw the angels."[58]

In *Tanhuma B* בראשית (§ 4), the proof is a bit more detailed. We know of the divine visit from v. 1, and we know that the angels came afterwards from v. 2. This citation also mentions that the Shekinah had not been at a distance, as Gen 18:22 might lead us to believe. We are told that Gen 18:22 is a Tiqqun Soferim.

Lastly, in *Song of Songs Rabbah*[59] we are told that Abraham was clasped between the Shekinah and an angel. This is supported on v. 2, wherein Abraham *saw* the Shekinah and *ran* to the angels.

The specific problem of how to understand אדני in v. 3 (Lord or lord) is not resolved by what we have mentioned so far in this section. In *Shebuoth* 35b we find the following discussion. There is an opinion that every term of address used by Abraham in Scripture is sacred (i.e., refers to God) except the אדני in Gen 18:3. This term is secular (חול) (i.e., it means "my lord," referring to one of the angels). Two Rabbis think that the אדני of Genesis 18 is also sacred. R. Judah, in the name of Rab, said that hospitality to wayfarers is more important than receiving the Shekinah. Thus

in v. 3, Abraham is asking the Lord to wait until he had entertained the three men. The same is implied in *Ps.-Jonathan*. This
is a very strong endorsement of the virtue of hospitality.

On the other hand, in *Genesis Rabbah*[60] we read that R. Hiyya
taught that Abraham called "lord" the greatest of the angels,
Michael. Several later works mention both sides of this dispute.[61]

(b) *Angelic Duties*

The rabbinic traditions about angels in general and about
their roles in this passage from Genesis in particular are very
rich. Let us first consider God's dominion over the angels.

In *Exodus Rabbah*[62] we come to consider God's power and how He
delegates some of this to angels. Sometimes God has His angels
sit (Judg 6:11), stand (Isa 6:2), appear to be men, and so on.[63]
In a similar listing occasioned by Exod 3:14,[64] God mentions that
He can make angels sit down (Gen 18:4), and the like.

Some of our sources explain the missions of the angels in
great detail; they had much more important mandates than the preceding lists from *Exodus Rabbah* would indicate. As was mentioned
earlier, Targums *Neofiti*, *Fragmentary*, and *Ps.-Jonathan* listed the
duties of each angel: one announced the news that Isaac would be
born (presumably based on Gen 18:10); another came to rescue Lot
(cf. Gen 19:17 and 21); and the third came to destroy Sodom and
environs. In the mention of these duties, we are reminded of some
of the context of our story--the rest of Genesis chaps. 18 and 19.

In *Baba Mezia* 86b the three angels are named: Michael, who
brings the news to Sarah and then rescues Lot; Gabriel, who de-
stroys Sodom; and Raphael, who is to heal Abraham.[65]

In *Pirke Eliezer*[66] we learn a bit more about the sequence of
events. One angel began to tell Abraham about the conception in
Sarah's womb. Another told him about the coming destruction of
Sodom (Gen 18:20). From this we learn that anyone who wishes to
tell his neighbor something which might be repulsive to him should
start off by saying some good words. Here we have a small example
of the actualization of Scripture, or perhaps it is simply a
matter of the angels being "moral types" here.

Some traditions concern themselves with the apparent identities of the visitors. In *Genesis Rabbah*[67] we are told that Michael,
Gabriel and Raphael, who appeared to Abraham, seemed to be of different non-Jewish backgrounds. One seemed to be a Saracen, and
another a Nabatean, and the third an Arab.[68] Abraham looked to see
if the Shekinah waited for them, in order to judge for himself if

they were worthy people. He also wanted to see if they were
polite to each other and, if they were, then he would think them
to be gentlemen. Having been so impressed, he ran to greet them
when he saw them come close.

The related problem of entertaining non-Jewish visitors while
avoiding any pagan practices[69] is addressed in *Baba Mezia* 86b.
When he offers to have water brought for foot washing the travellers ask Abraham, "Do you suspect us to be Arabs, who worship the
dust of their feet? Already Ishmael has come from you." We do
not know when the supposed Arab superstitions about foot dust
would have been known to Jewish people. In any case, this passage
credits Abraham with concern for religious purity and consistently
smooth hospitality[70] in that foot washing was a very welcome aspect
of hospitality.

Abraham's polite scrutiny of his guests and his prudent and
generous washing of their feet are sometimes contrasted with Lot's
more limited actions.

In *Kallah Rabbati*[71] we again have the details of exactly
which angel had which duties, etc., but here a further item is
mentioned. In Gen 19:2, Lot, in his invitation to the two angels,
invites them to spend the night and then to wash.[72] The commentator asks, "why did they not wash at the start, as did Abraham?"
The answer is that Lot feared for his own safety from the towns-
people, if he were found being hospitable. Perhaps in the morning,
if the visitors were seen with dust on their feet, people would
say that they were just coming into the city.

In the same verse in Genesis 19, the angels show their reluctance to accept Lot's offer, whereas those who visited Abraham
accepted his good wishes easily. This teaches us that we may show
reluctance to an inferior person, but not to a great man.[73] In
Yalkut, Genesis 84, Abraham's care in the matter of foot washing
is seen as avoiding any question of idolatry, whereas Lot only
offers it as a customary item of hospitality. The angels who
visited Lot knew that their feet were dirty, but they resisted the
urge to ask for water.

Yalkut, Genesis 82 mentions that Abraham saw the Shekinah as
well as the angels, their names and duties, their reluctance later
on with Lot. Rashi notes their duties, that they were of peaceful
intent in Abraham's eyes, and that Lot was not overly concerned
with possible questions of religious purity such as the dust on the
feet of his visitors. *Zohar* mentions Abraham's running to greet
the guests,[74] the fact that he quickly had their feet washed,[75] and

that his motivation in all this was entirely a great concern for
ritual purity.[76]

In considering the angels, Abraham, and Lot in these passages,
I think Abraham alone emerges as a true "moral type"--his discrete
scrutiny of guests and his concern for religious purity are meant
for imitation by later Jews. The angels' deliverance of good news
first and their reluctance toward an inferior person (Lot) are
small examples of everyday practice--i.e., they are small examples
of the actualizing of Scripture. Lot's lesser interests in matters of hospitality and purity are really only foils to Abraham's
greater example.

(c) *Other Themes Related to Verses 2 and 3*

In v. 3 Abraham refers to himself as "your servant." This
word has deep religious meanings and is used of many OT figures.
For instance in *Sifre*, Deuteronomy,[77] the writer prepares a list
of figures who called themselves servants and were also called
servants by God.[78] The list starts here with Gen 18:3 and God's
use of the term with regard to Abraham in Gen 26:24.[79]

The opening phrase of v. 2, "he raised his eyes and saw,"
came to be listed with other significant instances of seeing. In
Esther Rabbah[80] there is occasion for such a listing. Here evil
men see evil things: the sons of God see the daughters of men (Gen
6:2); Ham sees Noah naked (Gen 9:22); Esau sees unacceptable women
(Gen 28:8), and so on. Good men see pleasant sights: Abraham sees
the three visitors; he sees a ram (Gen 22:13); Jacob sees a well
(Gen 29:2), and so on.[81]

These cross references concerning the titles and actions of
biblical persons would obviously belong to Patte's category of
telescoping to "closed" past events. That is to say, the individuals involved are not really being presented to us as moral types in
any detail.

5. Preparing the Bread

Abraham's generosity toward his guests will now involve his
household in the preparations. He first asks his wife Sarah to
make fresh bread.[82]

In *Genesis Rabbah*[83] we find some comments on Gen 14:13 wherein
we are told that a certain messenger came to Abraham. The tradition is that his messenger was Og (עוג), the same Og who had dealt
with Moses. He was called עוג because he came and found Abraham

working at the prescribed breads (במצות עוגות). The presumption
in calling these prescribed is that they are prescribed for use in
the Passover period.[84]

The flour (קמח) used to make the bread is further specified
to be fine flour (סלת). In *Baba Mezia* 87a it is pointed out that
Abraham had to *demand* this flour since Sarah was less than impressed with his visitors. Rab Isaac said, "A woman sizes up
travellers better than a man does." Rashi also mentions that the
use of fine meal flour is an extra touch on Abraham's part.

A fairly common technique used by the Rabbis is to expand
amounts and numbers when they help to make a point. So here we
find a tendency to elaborate on the already large amount of flour
to be used. *Genesis Rabbah*[85] says that Sarah made nine *seahs*
worth of goods: three for עוגה, and three for חביץ, a kind of
honey cake, and three for other delicacies (מיני סולוטומיה). It
also adds the remark that it was the Passover season.[86]

In the biblical account, at v. 8, it is mentioned that Abraham
took meat and milk and curds (or cheese)[87] and served it to the
guests. The bread is not specifically mentioned here. Any omission such as this is fair game for speculation. In *Baba Mezia* 87a
it is explained that Abraham would eat non-ritual foods only when
they were ritually clean, and Sarah, before the meal had been
served, had admitted to being in a menstrual period. Thus Abraham
would not serve the now unclean עגות.[88] Note that, while he and
Sarah would have been very surprised at her menstruating, Abraham
carries on with his visitors as usual.

In *Genesis Rabbah*[89] this theory (that Sarah admitted her condition and the breads were therefore considered unclean) is mentioned and refuted. The Rabbis said

> Surely he brought the bread to them for he brought to
> them things which he had not promised (e.g., milk and
> cheese); how much the more things which he had promised
> earlier.

Up to this point in this group of traditions about the bread
we have seen telescoping references to the fact that God and the
angels appeared at Mamre at Passover time,[90] and further praise
for Abraham's hospitality. In his wish for fine flour,[91] his
having nine[92] *seahs* of baked goods made, and his concern for
ritual cleanliness, we see Abraham as a moral type of hospitality
and religious purity for others to imitate. Now let us examine
some of the rabbinic comments which concern themselves with
"closed" biblical cross-references.

A purely phonetic connection can be found in Num 33:13-14.
Here mention is made of a place called אלוש where the chosen people
once encamped. This is so because of the merits of Sarah, of whom
we know that Abraham said to her, "knead" (לושי).[93]

The phrase "refresh your hearts" in v. 5 is rare in Hebrew,
and this is often pointed out. Thus, in *Genesis Rabbah*[94] Rab Isaac
says that a bit of bread strengthens the heart; this exact phrase
is found once in the Torah, once in the prophets (Judg 19:5) and
once in the writings (Psa 104:15).[95]

In *Qohelet Rabbah* (on Eccl 1:16) we find a list of actions
which the heart is described as doing in the Bible. The heart can
hear (1 Kgs 3:9); it can walk (2 Kgs 5:26); it can be refreshed
(Gen 18:5).

An orthographic item which the Rabbis commented on was the
fact that the unpointed word for heart was spelled with only one ב
in this verse (לבכם). In *Genesis Rabbah*,[96] Rab observes that "this
proves there is no tempter ruling over the angels." Rashi makes
the same observation.[97] From other sources we know that the word
heart written with two בs was thought to indicate the conflict between good and base desires, which is the more usual state of the
average person.

We have a few instances of a cross-reference between Gen 18:4,
"I will fetch a morsel of bread," and Isa 33:16, "his bread will
be given him." If Mann[98] is correct in proposing Isa 33:17-24 and
35:10 to have been the Haftarah for the Pentateuchal Seder containing the Mamre story, then these citations have a truly liturgical
origin. Thus in *Genesis Rabbah*[99] we have this parallel in a beautiful chain of parallels between Isa 33:15-17 and traditional references to Abraham, ending with Isa 33:17, "your eyes will see the
king in his beauty," paralleled to Gen 18:1, "And the Lord appeared
to him."[100]

6. Preparing the Meat

The main item in Abraham's generous meal was the freshly
killed meat dish.[101] Just as there was a rabbinic tendency to
exaggerate the amount and kind of bread, so too they speculated on
how much meat Abraham served. In *Baba Mezia* 86b we read that Rab
proposed that Abraham had chosen three calves since the phrase
בן-בקר רך וטוב could be taken as a series of substantives in appo-
sition, i.e., "a calf, a tender calf, and a good calf." Other
Rabbis suggested that there might have been two calves, a tender
one and a good one. In either case the only apparent objection

that could be raised is that in vv. 7 and 8 all the references to
the servant and to the animal are in the singular. To answer this
point the theory was advanced that each calf was given to a servant
in turn and each cooked portion was brought out as it was ready.
A possible reason for slaughtering three animals might be so that
each visitor could have a tongue with mustard sauce. In *Genesis
Rabbah*[102] the assumption is that there was one calf. It was not
large but rather a tender calf; even though it was young it was
not tasteless, but very good. The servant to whom Abraham gave
the calf was Ishmael,[103] his son by Hagar. Ishmael was being
trained in hospitality.[104]

There are several rich traditions in rabbinic literature concerning the cave and field of Machpelah (Genesis 23). In *Pirke
Eliezer*[105] we find a connection to Machpelah by means of the calf!
When Abraham went to catch the calf it escaped from him and ran
and entered the cave of Machpelah. Abraham followed the calf into
the cave and found Adam and Eve lying in state, and he determined
to buy the cave at a future time. He then returned with the calf
and went on with his preparations.[106]

Thus in the matter of the meat preparations we again find a
stress on Abraham's generous hospitality. The references to the
cave of Machpelah should be seen as telescoping references less
integral to Jewish appreciation of the Mamre account than those
concerning circumcision and Passover.

In addition to these considerations on the calf theme, we
have about two dozen associations which are almost entirely based
on the mention of the word calf or a synonym such as bull, ox, or
the like. I will mention these closed biblical cross-references
here in some detail simply to show the range of biblical verses
over which such associations can take place.

In *Tanhuma*[107] the commentator is discussing the story of
Dinah (Genesis 34) and Shechem, the son of Hamor. We are reminded
of a nickname for Shechem, namely, "bull," and that Abraham ran to
the herd. In context it is pretty clear that what is meant is that
just as Abraham had quickly dispatched the calf, so too the sons of
Jacob would quickly kill Shechem.[108]

In *Tanhuma B*[109] a young bull must be sacrificed at ordination
ceremonies (Exod 29:1); we use a young bull because Abraham ran to
the herd. In *Leviticus Rabbah*,[110] we read that Aaron must use a
young bull in Temple sin offerings (Lev 16:3), because Abraham ran
to the herd.

Another item in Leviticus has to do with the minimum age of animals for sacrifice (Lev 22:27). This verse is tied to Gen 18:7 in *Leviticus Rabbah*,[111] *Pesikta Rab Kahana*,[112] and *Yalkut*.[113]

Numbers also has several texts involving the sacrifice of bulls. *Numbers Rabbah*[114] alludes to Num 7:15 and that Abraham ran to the herd.[115]

There is even a more phonetic allusion in Cant 7:6, "the king is held in the tresses (ברהטים)." The king is God and the woman is Israel. The king allows himself to be held captive by the merits of Abraham, who ran (רחט) to the herd.[116]

In *Pesikta Rabbati*[117] we find a tale about the patriarchs each begging God to delay destroying the Temple (commenting on Jer 37:1-2). Isaac asks that Nisan, whose zodiacal sign is the lamb, should be spared the disgrace of having the Temple destroyed during that time. Likewise Abraham pleads for his month Iyar, whose sign is the bull.

I would like to end this section on a more spiritual note, so I saved the best of these cross-references till last. In Isaiah 66 we read:

> 2b This is the man to whom I will look, he that is
>   humble and contrite in spirit, and trembles at
>   my word.
> 3a He who slaughters an ox is like him who kills a man;
> 3b He who sacrifices a lamb, like him who breaks a
>   dog's neck.

In *Tanhuma B*[118] and *Yalkut*[119] we have the immediate reference to Abraham running to the herd with regard to the first half of 3a of Isaiah 66. However in *Aggadath Bereshith*[120] there is a much more developed set of parallels. Abraham is the man to whom God looked, when He came to him at Mamre. Abraham trembled at God's word in Gen 17:27, where we read of how quickly he circumcised himself and Ishmael and all his men on the same day. Abraham slaughtered the calf for the three visitors, but he also is the one who sacrifices a lamb, as we know from Gen 22:8 when he had just been spared from killing Isaac.

Aggadath continues to recount how God came to visit the sick man at Mamre, how He told him to stay seated because of his pain, how Abraham would be a sign to future generations to stay seated in synagogue and school, and so on. The angels ask God when He proposes the visit, "O Lord, what is man that thou dost regard him" (Psa 144:3). Psa 25:10 is used to describe Abraham sitting at the door of the tent; "All the paths of the Lord are steadfast love and faithfulness, for those who keep his covenant and his

testimonies."   And when God tells Abraham to stay seated, He says,
"Sit at my right hand..." (Psa 110:1).

7. The Merits of Abraham

(a) *General Merit Framework*
    The rabbinic sense of corporate religious identity can be
very clearly seen in their concept of merit. Put simply, it means
that the good deeds and faith of one person can bring down God's
mercy and love on other people now or in the future.[121] Many
Rabbis saw the totality of Abraham's activities at Mamre as earn-
ing a great deal of merit which God saw fit to apply to Abraham's
descendants. We shall begin by looking at some of the more general
remarks about Abraham's deeds that day and then come to details.
    The essence of Abraham's deeds at Mamre was the virtue of
hospitality. The practice of this virtue is superior to receiving
God Himself. In *Shabbath* 127a the position is taken that in v. 3
of our passage Abraham is asking God to wait while he entertains
his visitors. God does wait, causing the writer to remark that
His patience is very unlike that of men. A man of high rank would
have been slighted to be kept waiting like this.
    In *Psalms Rabbah*[122] we find that God is humble; He waits
while the travellers eat. In *Leviticus Rabbah*[123] we find a list
of people to whom God has spoken in the past. He called to Adam,
His tenant-farmer (Gen 3:8); He called to Noah, His herdsman (Gen
8:15); He spoke to Abraham, His host; so surely He will speak to
Moses, His covenant mediator.
    In *Leviticus Rabbah*[124] the fourfold praises of Psa 18:26 are
applied to Abraham. We find the following on "with the sincere,
You are sincere." Abraham's plea to God, in v. 3 of the Mamre
story, that God wait awhile, was very sincere. Abraham went on to
be most courteous to the visitors. God waited sincerely, as we
know from Gen 18:22.[125]
    In *Yalkut*, 2 Samuel 161, Abraham's request for God to wait is
called an act of piety or kindness.[126]
    These five examples highlight the esteem which the virtue of
hospitality had for the rabbinic audiences. God waits for Abraham
humbly and sincerely and then speaks to His host, because of His
respect for this same virtue. However, God's response to Abraham's
practice of hospitality goes far beyond merely waiting for him and
then speaking to him as an individual. Let us see what God did for
Abraham's descendants.

(b) *More Detailed Merit Parallels*

In *Baba Mezia* 86b we have two groups of Scripture parallels depicting Abraham's actions and later graces given by God to the Chosen People.

In the first group let us consider four things which Abraham did himself and one action which he had his servant do.

Abraham's actions	*God's actions during the Exodus*
Abraham ran to fetch a calf.	A wind went forth from the Lord and brought quails (Num 11:31).
Abraham brought milk and curds.	Behold, I will rain bread from heaven on you (Exod 16:4).
He served[127] (עמד) them under the tree.	Behold, I will stand (עמד) before you there on the rock at Horeb (Exod 17:6).
He *went* with them to escort them.	The Lord *went* before them by day in a pillar of cloud (Exod 13:21)

Abraham's servant	*God's servant*
Abraham had a servant bring water.	God said to Moses, "you shall strike the rock" (Exod 17:6).

The second tradition has a slightly different set of parallels. For Abraham's standing by the tree the second group uses the image of the pillar (עמוד ענן) of Exod 13:21; for the water which was given the guests the parallel is the well of Miriam.[128]

In *Tosefta*[129] we have a longer list of parallels.

Abraham's actions	*God's actions*
Three times Abraham runs or hastens: to greet the visitors, to fetch the calf, and to speak to Sarah.	There are three verbs in Deut 33:2, "The Lord came from Sinai, and dawned from Seir upon us; He shone forth from Mount Paran...."
Abraham *bowed* to the ground.	"Kings shall bow down to you, with their faces to the ground." (Isa 49:23)
Abraham gave them water.	God provided a well at Beer (Num 21:18).
Abraham had them rest under a tree.	God provided seven clouds of glory[130] for His children in the desert.
Abraham provided food.	God provided tasty manna (Num 11:8).
Abraham fetched a calf.	God provided quails (Num 11:31).
Abraham stood and served.	God passed over the marked doors (Exod 12:23).
Abraham escorted the angels.	God escorted His people (Deut 2:7).

On this list from *Tosefta* I would only comment that the example of
God passing over marked doors seems a bit strained as a parallel.
The quotation from Isaiah 49 might point more to a hope for the
future rather than to a past event, although the writer might have
been thinking of David and Solomon.[131]

The lists of parallels which we have seen so far have dealt
mainly with the Exodus events, although they do have a few citations from the Prophets and the Psalms. The number of parallels
apparently grew and eventually came to be put into three general
categories--what God did for His people in the desert, and then in
the Promised Land, and finally what He will do for them in the
time to come (messianic future).[132] Here is the *Genesis Rabbah*
large list.

Abraham's Actions	During Exodus	God's Actions in the Land	In the Future
He gave water.	God gave well at Beer (Num 21:17).	The Promised Land has much water (Deut 8:7).	In the future there will be living waters (Zech 14:8).
He said, "wash your feet."	God washed Israel in desert (Ezek 16:9).	"Wash your-selves" (Isa 1:16).	In that day the Lord shall wash away filth (Isa 4:4).
He offered a tree for shade.	Clouds in desert (Psa 105:39).	They dwelt in booths (Lev 23:42).	Great canopy on that day (Isa 4:6).
He gave bread.	God gave manna (Exod 16:4).	A land of wheat (Deut 8:8).	Abundance of grain in the land (Psa 72:16).
He served a calf.	Quails were provided (Num 11:31).	There will be much cattle (Num 32:1).	In that day a man will keep a young cow (Isa 7:21).
He stood by and served.	The Lord went before them (Exod 13:21).	God stands in the congrega-tion (Psa 82: 1).	The Lord will be at their head (Mic 2: 13).

In *Qohelet Rabbah*[134] we have a similar list.

Confining our remarks solely to the use of the merit framework
with the Mamre account, we can certainly agree with Patte's observations.[135] All these parallel references are closed to the present; i.e., they look to sacred events of the past or to the messianic future. Nevertheless the base to which these parallels are
telescoped remains the generous hospitality of Abraham. Thus a
Jewish congregation of any period, hearing a merit sermon on passages such as these, was being asked to think about a virtue, a
virtue which must in some way be actualized in daily life.

(c) *Related Theme: Abraham's Generosity*

In *Baba Mezia* 87a the contrast is made between the angels'
reluctance to accept Lot's hospitality and their previous willingness to receive that of Abraham. The Rabbis conclude that one may
decline invitations from an inferior but not from a great man.[136]
Abraham was great because he was very generous. He promised to
bring his visitors a bit of bread, but he actually laid out a full
meal, including meat. Rab. Eleazar says that thus we see that
just men say very little and do much.

In *Aboth de Rabbi Nathan*[137] we have this same saying about
saying little and doing much. Abraham is an example of this. He
brought nine measures of flour, and three or four oxen.[138] In
Tanhuma[139] and *Yalkut*[140] we find much the same theme. Rashi[141]
says that whoever does a righteous act does a great thing, even if
it is a small act.[142]

One other tradition about Abraham's generosity might fit in
here. In *Yalkut*[143] a description is given of Solomon's daily food
provisions (1 Kgs 5:2ff.; English enumeration 4:22ff.). The
writer says that, in a way, Abraham did more than Solomon. There
follows the standard way of indicating that Abraham really killed
three calves. I would assume that the *Yalkut* remarks mean that
relatively speaking Abraham's quantities were more lavish for his
guests.

8. Did They Consume the Meal?

The biblical text states clearly that the visitors ate the
meal which Abraham had prepared for them. Two of the Targums,
Neofiti and *Ps.-Jonathan*, indicate that they only appeared to eat.
Eichrodt[144] suggests that the Yahwist has modified a story, originally of Canaanite provenance, having to do with a god actually
eating a meal. The modification was intended to avoid syncretism
in the Jahweh cultus. Could not this avoidance of any hint of
syncretism have been also the conscious or unconscious intention
of later advocates of the visitors only seeming to eat?

There are several other sources which follow the general
trend indicated by the two Targums. In *Baba Mezia* 86b, R. Tanhum
says that when Moses ascended on high he ate no food, but when the
ministering angels came down to Abraham they did eat. Then comes
a remark which may or may not have been part of R. Tanhum's original contributions:

> ...and they ate...do you really believe that? Rather
> consider that they appeared to be eating and drinking.

In *Genesis Rabbah*[145] we find the angels saying, "we do not
eat or drink, but you (for yourself there is eating and drinking),
do as you have said."

Later in the same chapter of *Genesis Rabbah*, the analogy is
again advanced that as Moses refrained from eating when on high
(Deut 9:9), so also the angels really ate when they were here below. The objection which follows includes a little more detail.

> And did they really eat? Rather they seemed to be eating.
> One after the other the courses were removed.[146]

In *Qohelet Rabbah*[147] some cases are mentioned in which a
divine decree is apparently put aside later on. One of these de-
crees is that whereas heavenly beings should not eat earthly food,
nevertheless Abraham's visitors ate. R. Nathan says that they
pretended to eat and the courses disappeared one after the other.[148]

On the other hand there are several sources, in addition to
the Targums, which avoid spiritualizing the matter of the eating
of the meal. In *Pesikta Rabbati*[149] we have a debate between the
angels and God over giving the Torah to mankind. The angels want
it to be kept in heaven. After several rounds of argument, God
offers this rejoinder:

> Are you the ones who fulfill the Torah? A child in
> Israel fulfills it better than you. Even when he comes
> out of elementary school, if meat and milk are both
> there to eat, he never drinks the milk until he has
> washed his hands of the meat. Yet you were sent down
> to Abraham; he brought meat and milk to you at the
> same time and you ate.[150]

This argument silenced the angels momentarily, and at that moment
God gave the Torah to Moses.

In *Exodus Rabbah*[151] we have a more vivid confrontation involving the angels. At the moment of the giving of the Torah, they
wished to attack Moses but God made the features of Moses resemble
those of Abraham. God then asked the angels, "Are you not ashamed
to touch this man to whom you descended, and in whose house you
ate?"

In *Seder Eliyahu Rabbah*[152] an allusion is made to Abraham's
visitors. They sat before Abraham but did not begin to eat. They
did not even speak. But, for the righteousness with which Abraham
was righteous, and in reward for the preparations which he had made,
God opened their mouths for them and they ate.

Whether or not the angels actually consumed the meal, they
partook in some way in honor of Abraham's hospitality. The arguments which God uses against the angels, with regard to giving the

Torah to men, exemplify His love for men and His dominion over the
angels. The mention of the law about not eating meat and milk
together would be another example of telescoping to a specific
Jewish praxis.

9. The Whereabouts of Sarah

Having finished their meal, the angels proceed to their mission of announcing the coming of the son to Abraham and Sarah.
They first ask Abraham where his wife is, and he replies that she
is inside the tent. In the MT this exchange seems to involve only
the three visitors and Abraham himself.

The rabbinic interpretations of this scene vary. In *Baba
Mezia* 87a three opinions are offered. Sarah was modest and kept
from the visitors, as was the proper custom in the Middle East;
the angels asked only in order to make her even more beloved by
her husband as he would reflect on her modesty; or they asked of
her whereabouts so that they could send her the wine cup of blessing traditionally served at the end of the meal.[153]

In *Yebamoth* 77a we find another confirmation of the general
principle that women should stay secluded. The Talmudic context
is the prohibition of marriage with Ammonites and Moabites. Some
Rabbis felt that this restriction applied only to marrying Ammonite
and Moabite men, since in the prohibition, as written in Deuteronomy
23, the men are accused of having refused hospitality to the Israelites at one time in the past. Their women, however, had not the
same obligations to meet men publicly. The text reads:

> It is customary for a man to host; it is not customary
> for a woman to do so. It is for them to host--men to
> greet men and women to greet women.

A few lines later in *Yebamoth* 77a the biblical citations of
Gen 18:9 and Psa 45:14, "All glorious is the king's daughter within"
are used to supplement the remarks about the modesty of women.[154]

By contrast, *Tanhuma*[155] suggests that Sarah was often secluded
in order to hide her shame at childlessness. After giving Hagar to
Abraham, Sarah was secluded in her tent for a long time and she
foresaw that angels would appear to her someday.

In *Yalkut*,[156] we have a discussion on Num 9:10 which specifies
that anyone on a long journey must still observe Passover. How
much the more for anyone near to home. Sarah was very devoted to
her home and when the angels asked where she was they already knew
the answer.[157]

These comments, focusing mainly on Sarah's modesty with regard to male strangers and her devotion to the home, would be
further examples of the use of a biblical person as a moral type.
The references to Passover and the wine cup of blessing would be
other telescoping references; the mention of this query as one of
God's dialogues with Abraham seems to be just a closed cross-
reference. It would also lend a little support to the LXX render-
ing of this line.

10. Puncta Extraordinaria

In the present MT of Gen 18:9 the word "to him" of the opening, "They said to him," has a point superscirbed over each of the
four letters. These points are called extraordinary, for want of
a better term. The Massorah Parva apparatus mentions that there
are ten cases of puncta extraordinaria in the Pentateuch. Their
origin and significance are lost to modern scholars. Sometimes
they call attention to an unusual spelling or usage but there are
not enough cases to make clear categorizations. Here the best
guess is that the tendency would have been for scribes to drop the
entire word "to him" since context indicates very clearly that
Abraham is the only possible addressee. Thus the puncta extraordinaria would have kept scribal attention on the word and it would
not have been lost in copying.

The Rabbis looked for symbolic meanings in these relatively
rare markings. *Masseketh Soferim*[158] simply states that the ו,
י, and א are to be faithfully dotted every time the text is copied,
without question.[159]

However, in *Aboth Rabbi Nathan*[160] we are told that the visitors knew where Sarah was but they asked Abraham out of politeness.
Abraham was pleased to reflect on her modesty. Thus the points
stress that Abraham *alone* was asked.[161]

There is one other possibility. The dotted letters could have
a meaning by themselves. In *Baba Mezia* 87a it is remarked that the
dotted letters spell איו which means "where is he?" It is then
possible that the text contains a shorthand way of stating that
Sarah was also asked the whereabouts of Abraham. Thus it is proper
to ask after a hostess from her husband and to ask after a host
from his wife.[162]

11. The Promise of a Son

In v. 10 the speaker promises Abraham that he and Sarah would
have a male child. In v. 14, after the initial shock of the news

has worn off, he repeats the essentials of the promise. In reflecting on this great grace, the Rabbis naturally considered vv.
10 and 14 to be one expression of God's love and so it will not
matter if we combine comments on both verses here.

This was not the only promise of a son made to Abraham. In
Gen 15:4-5, Jahweh had promised Abraham that his descendants would
be more numerous than the stars. God said at that time, "Look
(הבט-נא) toward heaven." In rabbinic traditions, הבט has the
meaning of looking *down*, so the explanation was that Abraham had
been taken up to heaven to receive that initial promise. The
fulfillment of the promises of Genesis 15 and 18 occurred with
Isaac's birth in Gen 21:1.[163]

In *Genesis Rabbah*[164] on Psa 119:89 ("Your word stands firm in
heaven"), the two promises about the birth of Isaac are recalled.
In the next section of the same source we find Solomon's prayer
when dedicating the Temple, "Lord,...what you did declare to him
with your mouth, with your hand you have done it today." The two
parts of this verse are interpreted as referring to Gen 18:10 and
21:1 respectively.[165]

In *Psalms Rabbah*[166] we study Psa 80:15, "Look down from
heaven...have regard for this vine." God looked down when He made
the promise to Abraham and Sarah, and He had regard when Isaac was
born.

Other places than Gen 21:1 serve to remind one of the gracious-
ness of God toward Abraham. In *Genesis Rabbah*[167] we find comments
on Jacob wrestling with the angel. Jacob says that he will not let
the angel go without a blessing from him. Jacob says, "the angels
who came to Abraham did not leave him without giving a blessing."
The wrestling angel replied, "They were sent for that reason, but
I was not sent for that reason."

The references to Genesis 15 and 21, 1 Kings 8, Psalms 80 and
119, and even to Genesis 32, remind us that God freely promised the
conception and birth of Isaac and freely brought it to pass. The
use of Solomon's prayer from 1 Kings 8 may seem a little strange
but, as we shall see below, this event was telescoped to Nisan
(as also was the Mamre account); so a possible reason for the
connection is uncovered.

As we saw in reviewing the Targums and versions, some of the
paraphrases for כעת חיה can be understood as meaning "at this time
next year." Further, *Ps.-Jonathan* mentions that it will be the
time of a feast.

The feast almost certainly is Passover, a time to which our
passage has been telescoped by many devices. We find in the

rabbinic traditions a telescoping of the Passover season (held in
the month Nisan), the promise made at Mamre, and Isaac's birth a
year later.

Thus, in *Seder Olam Rabbah*,[168] we find a tribute to the month
Nisan. During Nisan the messengers came to our father Abraham to
announce to him that in the same period of the coming year Isaac
would be born.

In *Tanhuma B*[169] we read that God made a mark on the wall for
Sarah and said, "at the return of the sun to this spot, you will
have a child." Much the same account can be found in *Pesikta
Rabbati*:[170] Isaac was born in the same month, Nisan, in which the
Temple[171] was dedicated.[172] We know this because Sarah was making
Passover עוגות. The angels made a mark[173] on the wall and said
that when the sun returned to that spot a year later, Isaac would
be born.[174]

12. The Promise Overheard

As the speaker was talking to Abraham, we are told that Sarah
was listening to their conversation from the tent door. The
Rabbis are inclined to consider this to be eavesdropping or at
least excessive curiosity. The topic comes up either in lists of
womanly shortcomings gleaned from the Bible, or in discussions
about the creation of Eve from Adam's rib.

In *Genesis Rabbah*[175] we are told that God did not fashion Eve
from the head of Adam, lest she be proud or frivolous; He did not
fashion her from Adam's eyes, lest she ogle; nor from his ear lest
she be an eavesdropper. Yet, woman is proud and frivolous and an
ogler (Isa 3:16); she is an eavesdropper, as when we see Sarah
listening to Abraham and his visitors.[176]

In *Genesis Rabbah*[177] the weaknesses of women are mentioned.
Women are greedy (Eve eats the apple, Gen 3:6); they like to eaves-
drop (Mamre example); they are lazy (Abraham *orders* Sarah to bake
bread). Much the same comments are in *Genesis Rabbah* 80.5.[178]

We mentioned earlier that some of the Targums had Ishmael
present with Sarah. In *Genesis Rabbah*[179] the commentator also
understands that Ishmael is present. He was there on account of
"the private meeting." This might refer to social custom which
would not have allowed Sarah to be alone near a guest.

The same section of *Genesis Rabbah* also remarks, "She sensed
that the guest had come." This might indicate that the guest was
behind Abraham, relative to Sarah's position. The only other
comment on this topic is in *Yalkut*.[180] Here Ishmael is mentioned

and also the private meeting. Rashi says that the door was behind
the angel. *Zohar* 103a suggests that one of the parties is the
Shekinah--either God was behind the door or Abraham was behind God.

The attribution of the fault of eavesdropping to Sarah would
be an example of a moral anti-type. The problems with והוא אחריו
remain unresolved, even for Rashi and *Zohar!* Most of the commentaries simply pass over the phrase altogether.

13. The Old Age of Abraham and Sarah

The advanced age of both Abraham and his wife heighten the
force of the promise. In *Genesis Rabbah*[181] this verse is compared
with another mention of Abraham's age in Gen 24:1. Why do we have
a second notice about his age in Genesis 24? It is because the
Lord restored him to a younger condition at the time of the an-
nouncement about Isaac.[182] Thus years later when he was aged a
second time it was necessary to mention this again. In the next
paragraph of the same source, we see that in Genesis 18 Abraham
was still virile, which was not true by the time spoken of in
Genesis 24. Some Rabbis specified that he was virile but impotent.

Other texts are related to the conditions of Abraham and
Sarah. The images of Hab 3:17 apply, "Though the fig tree does
not blossom, nor fruit be on the vine, the produce of the olive
fail, and the fields yield no food." So in *Pesikta Rabbati*[183] the
fig tree is Abraham; he and Sarah are the vines; Sarah is the
olive plant and the field.[184]

In *Pesikta Rabbati*[185] we find mention of the "fruits of
splendid trees" (Lev 23:40). The term הדר can also refer to persons, such as Abraham and Sarah. Their old age is their splendor.
Often the image is applied to Sarah alone. Thus in *Pesikta Rab
Kahana* we see that God made Sarah splendid in her old age.[186]

Another tree image is to be found in Ezek 17:24, "And all the
trees of the field shall know that I the Lord bring low the high
tree, and make high the low tree, dry up the green tree, and make
the dry tree flourish. I the Lord have spoken, and I will do it."
Abraham is the lowly tree which is exalted. The dried up green
trees are Abimelech's wives; Sarah is the dry tree which will
flourish. The Lord has spoken, as in Gen 18:14, and He carries it
out, as in Gen 21:1. This analogy is found in *Genesis Rabbah*[187]
and *Yalkut*.[188]

A comment on God's question in v. 14 ("Is anything too hard
for the Lord?") is found in *Genesis Rabbah*.[189] Here a parable is
told about a locksmith who is asked to fix a quite ruined lock.

He protests that he cannot do it, saying, "Can I create locks from eternity?" *By contrast*, God says,

> I am able to create them (Abraham and Sarah) from eternity; is it not certainly within My ability to restore them to the days of their youth?

Sarah remarks in v. 12 that she is old and can no longer have sexual pleasure (עדנה). In rabbinic Hebrew this word can also mean rejuvenation.[190] So in *Baba Mezia* 87a Rab Hisda explains that Sarah was made young and beautiful again when she was made fertile. The exact words are

> The flesh was rejuvenated (נתעדן הבשר) and the wrinkles were smoothed and beauty came back to where it belonged.

In *Genesis Rabbah*[191] the word עדנה is seen as being very like עדי (ornaments). These ornaments are like the jewelry of fertile women. In the same way Sarah hopes that her עדנה will be עידנין (periods), like the regular periods of fertile women.

In v. 12 we are told that Sarah laughed to herself (בקרבה) when she heard the import of the message. Apparently there was a widely known variant reading בקרוביה, which means "among her relatives."[192] *Megillah* 9a lists major Greek (LXX) translations for the known Hebrew variants and includes this one.[193]

It is not clear from any of these references what significance the act of talking to relatives could have had for Jewish readers. It is possible that making light of such a divine promise *in public* is worse than privately having doubts. After all, Abraham had private doubts (Gen 17:17) and did not incur any rebuke such as Sarah does here.

In v. 11 we read that Sarah was no longer fertile. The phrase is somewhat figurative, but would hardly seem open to doubt--"it had ceased to be with Sarah after the way of women (חדל להיות לשרה ארח כנשים)."

Nevertheless certain verses from elsewhere in the Bible were brought in by the Rabbis. In *Genesis Rabbah*[194] it is pointed out that the verb חדל might mean to *cease*, as in Num 9:13, or it might mean to *not occur* (temporary delay?), as in Deut 23:23.

The word ארח becomes the catchword from the phrase. In *Leviticus Rabbah*,[195] Psa 19:6 ("the sun like a strong man runs its course [ארח] with joy") reminds one of the way (אורח) of which Sarah spoke.[196] In *Yalkut*,[197] Joel 4:15 (English 3:15) is cited: "the sun and the moon are darkened, and the stars withdraw their shining." The commentator remarks that all ways stopped except the way of women, as we read in Gen 18:11. Also in *Yalkut*,[198] the

phrase from Psa 139:3, "You search out my path (ארחי) and my lying
down (ורבעי)," is taken as figurative; the former means *woman* and
the latter noun signifies *man*.

Even Job 6:18, "The caravans turn aside from their courses
(ארחות)," triggers the allusion.[199]

Admittedly, in this section most of the citations are closed
cross-references to other biblical passages. Yet the underlying
theme seems to be that God, who has freely given the promise of
offspring, will do everything needed to bring this about. The
variant בקרוביה evokes comments which might be disapproving of
Sarah's thoughts, but we must look further to be sure.

14. In Praise of Peace

In v. 12, Sarah wonders to herself not only about her own
physical condition but also about Abraham's (ואדני זקן). In the
following verse God recounts her attitude to Abraham, but He depicts Sarah as worrying only about her own condition. Rabbis took
this slight change in wording very seriously. For God to report
ואדני זקן as ואני זקנתי must have been a very deliberate action on
His part. In fact, it was to avoid hurting Abraham's feelings and
so to promote *peace* and *marital harmony* between these two parents
of the faith. In general the theme of promoting peace becomes the
stock occasion for listing this intervention by God along with
other *peace* citations.

In *Baba Mezia* 87a the Lord "changes Sarah's words" and so
fosters peace. In *Yebamoth* 65b, in discussing a mishna on the duty
to beget children, this modification by the Lord is mentioned as an
instrument of peace.[200] In *Genesis Rabbah*[201] we are told that the
Scriptures "made an incorrect statement" to promote peace. In
Tanhuma[202] we are told that God spoke "what was not from eternity";
that He "suppressed" her remarks; that Sarah was "talking foolish-
ly" with her relatives about herself and Abraham.[203] In *Tanhuma*[204]
we see that God "did not tell Abraham exactly why" Sarah had
laughed. *Tanhuma B* also mentions this peace theme.[205]

These closed cross-references practically present God as a
"moral type," a promoter of peace and of marital harmony. The
various ways of avoiding saying that God told a little white lie
do not relieve us of the impression that that is exactly what He
did.

15. Reprimand and Reassurance

While it is true that both Abraham and Sarah were old and
probably overwhelmed by the events taking place, Sarah more fully
acts out her wonderment (or disbelief) in vv. 12-15.[206]

In *Genesis Rabbah*[207] one interpretation is that the Lord says
to Sarah and her relatives:[208]

> You think yourselves to be of the younger set and that
> your companions are the older ones? And am I too old
> to perform miracles?

The Lord is here chiding Sarah for questioning only Abraham's
condition, and He is also playing on her closing words in v. 13
(as if they applied to Himself).

The response to Sarah in v. 15 ("No, but you did laugh") was
considered by many Rabbis as part of the whole spectrum of Divine
messages to women in the Bible. This was apparently the only case
of *direct* conversation between God and a woman. Other examples,
such as might involve Hagar or Rebecca, were thought to be done by
angels or other intermediaries.[209]

In *Genesis Rabbah*[210] we read that the Holy One never condes-
cended to converse with a woman except with the righteous Sarah,
and even that dialogue was roundabout and limited to the very brief
"No, but you did laugh."[211]

In *Ozar Midrashim* (p. 223) the commentator takes a rather
harsh view of Sarah's doubting. He feels that Sarah "feigned
compliance" and by this lessened the greatness of woman in matters
of counsel and harmony. God had told Abraham that he would have a
son by Sarah, but the son would not be born if she did not have
faith.[212]

The fact that the angel of v. 14 promised to return is seen as
significant in *Yalkut*.[213] In contrast, Elisha, in 2 Kgs 4:16 had
made a similar promise of a child for the Shunamite woman without
mentioning that he himself would be there. Presumably Elisha did
so because he knew he was old and liable to die before the birth
of the child.

Rashi says that the angel who spoke in v. 10 was an agent of
God and so did not speak in his own name. Rashi then notes Gen
17:21 wherein God Himself promises to return when Isaac is born.
The intent of Rashi's remarks may be to establish God as speaker
of vv. 14 and 15, but I cannot say for sure. Rashi also mentions
the matter of 2 Kgs 4:16.[214] *Zohar* 102b and 115a says that God
spoke the promise and not an angel.

These traditions include some unfavorable interpretations of
Sarah's doubting. Most, however, are citations of the closed
cross-reference type.

16. The Departure

Having delivered their message and having shared in Abraham's
hospitality, the angels had to get on with their tasks. Abraham
escorts them as they go.

In *Genesis Rabbah*[215] it is pointed out that such escorting is
an integral part of hospitality to visitors. This is done by reminding the reader of an old adage, "I have had food and drink;
escort me."

In *Exodus Rabbah*[216] Abraham's escorting of the angels is
contrasted to Pharaoh's letting go of the Chosen People. This
latter was an act of expulsion and not escorting.[217]

Usually Abraham's act of escorting the angels is considered
part of the group of meritorious actions, which we looked at in
the section B.7 above (see pp. 24ff.). An additional citation of
just the escorting parallels alone is in *Tanhuma* בשלח §4. Abraham
accompanied the angels; God accompanied his children in the desert
for forty years.[218]

Rashi notes that the Hiphil forms of שקף (we have וישקפו in
v. 16) always have a menacing connotation, except in Deut 26:15,
which conerns God's mercy to the poor.

Maimonides,[219] in a list of social obligations, observes that
escorting strangers is a very great virtue. Abraham instituted it
by giving wayfarers food and drink and escorting them. Hospitality
to wayfarers is greater than receiving the Shekinah, and escorting
guests is greater than any other form of hospitality, as it says in
Sotah 46b, "Whoever does not escort guests is a shedder of blood."
This last quote from the Babylonian Talmud is a correct quotation
but hardly for the context in which Maimonides uses it; in the
Talmud the context was criminal actions.

Except for Rashi's semantic note, the thrust of these remarks
is that escorting guests is an integral part of the virtue and
practice of hospitality.

Conclusions to Chapter I

It is clear that most of the variations and additions found
in the principal versions and Targums were maintained and developed
in the later Jewish writings.

For example, while we find new remarks about the Amorite
Mamre lending his name to the place of the visit there is usually
no correlation made between the tree or trees of v. 1 and the tree
of vv. 4 and 8. The Targum references to Abraham's recent circumcision represent a small portion of the range of devices which
connect the divine visit to Abraham with his obedience to this
ritual.

The three visitors are angels who have the appearance of men.
While some attention is paid in later commentaries to Abraham's
bow of v. 2, many other comments are made to assure us that Abraham
does not regard these visitors as divine beings. The concept of
the Shekinah is often used to explain Jahweh's mode of appearance
to Abraham. While there are differences in how to read the singular אדני of v. 3, the Samaritan plural reading is not sustained.

Most of the later sources depict Abraham as the host who has
the supplies provided for the washing of the guests' feet. Besides
being a hospitable act, it also takes on dimensions of religious
purification. Abraham's offer of a meal is central to his hospitality but we do not find many explicit expansions on the Targumic
suggestion that Abraham remarked to his guests that it was exactly
meal time, nor on *Ps.-Jonathan*'s reference to their saying grace.
Some traditions do assume that it was a very hot midday when the
guests arrived.

The tradition that the breads were unleavened was easily maintained since the visit became very firmly associated with the Passover season. Many even speak of nine *seah*s of dough, a prodigious
quantity. The "spiritualizing" of the eating of the meal became a
strong though not unchallenged tradition.

Only *Tanhuma B* שרה (§ 3) has a single speaker (God) in v. 9;
therefore the LXX variation did not receive much support. The
sources vary as to whether God or one of the angels spoke in v. 10.

The Targumic understanding that Abraham and Sarah would be
physically rejuvenated is quite well developed later on. An interval of one year brings us to the birth of Isaac in the next Passover
season. The matter of having Ishmael present with Sarah does not
die out, but neither does it receive much elaboration. Ishmael is
often taken to be the helper in v. 7. As indicated in the Targums,
Sarah's laughter was sometimes taken as wonder or disbelief.

The Lord spoke to Abraham in v. 13. His role as peacemaker
was not delegated to an angel. Traditions vary as to whether God or
an angel spoke in v. 14. The Targumic remarks that nothing can be
hidden from the Lord receive no special development. The feast

mentioned by *Ps.-Jonathan* is surely Passover. Most of our sources
take God to be the speaker in v. 15b.

It should also be pointed out that later Jewish sources do
not always slavishly imitate tendencies found in the ancient versions and Targums. To take one example here, let us review the
question of the precise identities of the speakers. The later
sources understood Gen 18:1-16 as a genuine theophany (groupings 1,
2a, 2b, 2c, 3 and 6) during which angels in human form (groupings 2b,
4a, 4b, 7 and 16) also appear. Many of these sources (groupings
4a and 7) agree with the versions and Targums in seeing God as the
one addressed in v. 3. However in groupings 4a and 4b we also
find a new interpretation--that the addressee was the leading
angel. This interpretation, going back at least to the Babylonian
Talmud, persists up through Maimonides.

In vv. 10 and 14, the MT and most versions and Targums do not
clearly identify the speaker as God. *Ps.-Jonathan* explicitly
understands him to be an angel in v. 10, and a similar implicit
understanding can be derived from other remarks in the *Neofiti* and
Fragmentary Targums. In the later sources, we find both inter-
pretations--that the speaker was an angel (groupings 4b, 11, 12
and 15) or that the speaker was God (groupings 11 and 12). There
are no changes from the MT and Targum understanding that God spoke
directly to Abraham in v. 13. In fact the assertion that God
modified Sarah's words to promote harmony (grouping 14) demands
that He be the speaker here.

On the other hand, *Ps.-Jonathan*, and possibly *Neofiti* and
Fragmentary by implication, identify the speaker of the reprimand
in v. 15 as an angel. All the later sources[220] (grouping 15) assume that God issues the reprimand. So we have one Targumic interpretation *not* being maintained in later Jewish commentary.

We should also evaluate the later Jewish materials in light
of Daniel Patte's hermeneutical norms mentioned at the start of
this chapter. His first was that a biblical verse can be interpreted by other biblical passages. There is no doubt that other passages of Scripture were used in connection with the Mamre story!

One of the results of this use of other Scriptures is that it
helps us to be aware of the *context* of the story. We are often
reminded that God had previously promised offspring to Abraham,
Gen 15:5; that Abraham himself was recently circumcised, Genesis
17; that God continued to speak to Abraham, Gen 18:22; that Lot was
rescued before Sodom was destroyed, Genesis 19; and that Abraham
later moved and had trouble with Abimelech before Isaac was born,
Genesis 20 and 21.

Another result of the frequent citation of other Scriptures
is that the lessons of the Mamre story are carried to other sections of the Bible. The many parallel instances cited in the
merit groupings are in some way enriched by their correlation to
the Mamre account. In the same way other texts such as Lev 9:6,
Ezek 17:24 and 36:36, Hab 3:17, Psa 25:10 and Isa 33:8, 15-17 and
66:2-3 are concretized when one thinks of Abraham and Sarah and
God's dealings with them. This enrichment or concretization (my
terms) is disturbing to us today because in our own exegetical
research we are primarily concerned with the Sitz im Leben of each
text. I think, however, that we must allow for the fact that many
scriptural themes may have consciously or unconsciously been helpful to biblical authors. For example, the citation of Psa 25:10
may seem to be a mere proof text when applied to God's visiting
Abraham as he was recuperating, but certainly vv. 10-14 of that
Psalm may have been unconsciously inspired by traditions about
Abraham present in the Psalmist's own spiritual life.

In addition to citations which help us keep perspective on
the larger contexts of God's dealings with Abraham and Sarah, and
to certain evocative biblical passages such as in the paragraph
immediately preceding, we also find many verbal details of the
story which are cross-referenced with an intensity which we can
hardly imagine prior to seeing specific examples of it. Thus considerations of the exact time of the day when the theophany occurred, of the saying about refreshing hearts, of Abraham as *servant* and as one who raises his eyes and sees good things, of
parallel texts involving the *word* calf or a synonym, of the matter
of the puncta extraordinaria, and the like, certainly lend force
to the hermeneutical axiom that *everything* is meaningful in
Scripture.

The phenomenon of telescoping is much exemplified in our
passage. Principally we are led to set the whole event in the
Passover season and to consider the close relationships which the
story has to the account of circumcision in the previous chapter
of Genesis. Other people (such as Og and Ishmael), places (such as
the cave of Machphelah), and customs (such as the law about not
eating meat and milk together) are telescoped to our study but
only in minor ways.

Abraham is very much presented in these rabbinic traditions as
a moral example for us to imitate. He is greatly praised for his
hospitality, his eagerness to receive guests, his generous table of
bread, meat, and dairy foods. The whole series of merit parallels

are predicated on his actions as host. His escorting is also an
integral part of this virtue. Many of the folk sayings are also
related to hospitality.[221]

There is a certain amount of emphasis on Abraham's concern
for ritual purity, although this is certainly minor in relation
to the moral example he affords with regard to hospitality.

Sarah receives some praise for her helpfulness, her caution,
and her modesty. The commentators are sometimes uneasy with her
for her slower and perhaps doubting responses to the message about
Isaac. Eavesdropping seems to be more of a stock vice.

Lot seems to serve merely as a foil, being either fearful
about hospitality or uninterested in the finer points of hospitality and religious purity.

Patte's second norm was that Scripture is meant to be actualized. He found that such actualizations often dealt with current
cultural changes rather than with salient events.

Our passage bears this out. Besides the virtues of Abraham
and Sarah (hospitality, religious purity, modesty, and so on), we
find very few other actualizations in our research. Circumcision
receives some mention, and also the fact that we should sit during
synagogue services and school. We also see that we may exaggerate
a bit to a groom about the beauty of his new bride in order to
confirm him in his confident love. Certainly these virtues and
practices are important, but they are part of everyday life and
their observation need not challenge us to the core of our beings.

Another set of guidelines which can be helpful in our analysis
of the Jewish material are the hermeneutical modes and rules of
James Sanders, which were mentioned in the Introduction to this
study. We will first look for instances wherein the human faults
and weaknesses of the biblical figures are mentioned. Sanders
called this a theologizing hermeneutic. There is very little of
this sort of commentary in the Jewish material on Genesis 18.

With regard to Abraham, about the only hint of failing stems
from the notion that Mamre had to argue with him in order to con-
vince him to accept circumcision. Abraham's bow to the visitors
was carefully explained as one of greeting rather than adoration:
this simultaneously enhanced Abraham's hospitality and removed any
possible doubt about his understanding of the identity of the
visitors.

Sarah was not quite the plaster saint that Abraham was. She
may have laughed with her relatives about the possibility of her
and Abraham having a child. Her remarks about Abraham's age and

condition had to be covered over by God Himself. The *Ozar Mid-rashim* commentator even wondered how sincerely Sarah accepted the reprimand of v. 15.

On the other hand, to note that Sarah was an eavesdropper or a lazy wife was a much lesser charge. The observation that the Lord spoke to her briefly but without intermediary represented rabbinic thought about the status of women in general much more than it represented criticism or praise of Sarah. Thus there was more comment about Sarah's shortcomings as compared to Abraham's, but the total amount of criticism was still not large.

In addition to these few references to Abraham and Sarah we do have some other considerations about God's love for sinful mankind. In grouping 8 we have three references to traditions about God fending off angelic objections to the giving of the Torah to men. The fuller contexts of the angelic objections (not shown in this investigation) indicate that, before He gave them the Torah, God knew well that men are often weak and sinful. By implication, in the merit parallels based on Abraham's hospitality we may reflect on the lack of faith and perseverance of many who followed Moses out of Egypt, or who settled in the land, or who would be of the generations from then until the final day in the messianic future. Yet for all these, just and unjust alike, God showered down His many blessings.

The rest of the traditions "moralize," to use Sanders' term. They draw lessons, mainly on the virtue of hospitality and the faith which we should have in the word and power of God. Other foci included the observance of circumcision, Passover, ritual purity, visiting the sick, honoring the elderly, and so on.

Granted that the few actualizations based on this passage seem to be mainly cultural ones and that the majority of the Jewish writers drew moral lessons from it, we may reasonably suppose that most of the ancient Jewish commentary on Gen 18:1-16 was supportative or constitutive. Such emphasis on God's love for men and on His special care for the ancestors of the chosen people would, of course, always be a challenge to the hearers in one sense, but does not stand as a demonstrably challenging or "prophetic" mode of hermeneutic as Sanders uses the term.

CHAPTER II

EARLY CHRISTIAN AND ALEXANDRIAN JEWISH
HERMENEUTIC OF GEN 18:1-16

Before we gather together the comments of early Christian
writers, we should try to see how they generally understood and
used the OT. Within such an overall perspective we may then be
more prepared to evaluate their use of the Mamre and Jabbok stories.

Since much of patristic biblical study involved typology and
allegory, we should define these terms at the outset. R.P.C. Hanson[1] defines typology as "the interpreting of an event belonging
to the present or recent past as the fulfillment of a similar
situation recorded or prophesied in scripture." Many NT writers
saw OT persons, events, and situations as types of Christ or of
events in his life on earth. To express the fact that both the OT
situation and the fulfillment in Jesus were believed to be literally true by these writers, we usually call these NT assertions
"historical" types.

The problem with using typology is obviously one of determi-
ning what makes two situations similar. Patristic similarities
which appear to be overly subjective today are sometimes called
"sermon illustration" types or "incidental" types by scholars.

In contrast to typology there is allegory. Hanson[2] defines
allegory as "the interpretation of an object or person or a number
of objects or persons as in reality meaning some object or person
of a later time, with no attempt made to trace a relationship of
'similar situation' between them." There is a rather small amount
of allegory in the NT itself. K. J. Woollcombe points out that
Philo and other ancient exegetes frequently used the language of
typology to describe their own allegorizing. He allows such interpretation to be called "symbolic typology."[3] To avoid confusion I
will avoid using this last term.

G.W.H. Lampe, in an article which sought to establish the
proper bases for a moderate use of biblical typology in our own
time,[4] says that the Jew looked back to the mighty acts of God in
ancient history to find the reality which gave coherence and unity
to all subsequent development. The Christian, in some measure,
reversed this position. The great acts of God in Israelite history
acquired significance because of their character as foretastes of
what was later accomplished in Christ.[5]

43

This Christian *reversal* must be explained. Lampe points out
that typological and allegorical methods of interpreting the scriptures were very common until this century. In fact for many Christians OT events "were not fundamentally important for their value
as literary history, but as types and images in and through which
the Holy Spirit had indicated what was to come when God would bring
in the New Covenant to fulfill and supercede the Old."[6]

Such a way of reading OT events had even been the preconception
of the NT writers themselves. Lampe observes that

> a common belief linked the authors of the New Testament
> books with their readers. This was the conviction which
> they shared; that the whole Bible spoke directly of
> Christ, in prophecy, type, and allegory so far as the
> Old Testament is concerned, and the consequent belief
> that the historical context of a passage and the imme-
> diate intention which the original author had in writing
> it in the circumstances of his own time were of rela-
> tively minor importance.[7]

In the beginning these prophecies, types, and allegories were
often used in apologetical and polemical situations. Lampe points
out, however, that the use of such interpretations "had to be
carried out at least as much for the Church's own sake as for the
purposes of missionary propaganda. It was necessary for the
Christian understanding of the Gospel, and all the indications
show that it was a process initiated by Christ himself."[8]

Lampe goes on to define a legitimate "historical" typology,
wherein there is a real correspondence in history, sense, and context between the type in the past and the fulfillment in the future.
He opposes this to the typology which seeks to establish "not so
much a relation between the past and the future, the foreshadowing
and the fulfillment, as between the earthly and the heavenly, the
shadow and the reality."[9] As an example of this latter kind of
typology Lampe mentions the scarlet cord of Rahab at Jericho, which
was taken by many Fathers to typify the saving blood of Christ.

Lampe also holds that allegory as such is even less valid a
procedure for our times than the second class of typology (which he
calls "sermon illustration" typology).[10] He notes that the Fathers
developed "sermon illustration" typology and allegory to an almost
unlimited extent.

In the companion article to Lampe's, K. J. Woollcombe studies
in detail the origins of patristic hermeneutics. He distinguishes
typology from allegory and also from the fulfillment of prophecy.

He then gives a brief history of Jewish and Christian analyses
of OT prophecies, and a history of pagan, Jewish, and Christian uses

of positive (non-apologetic) allegory. In comparing St. Paul's
allegorical exegesis of Hagar and Sarah (Galatians 4) with Philo's,
Woollcombe sees much greater merit in Paul's approach.

> In the Pauline interpretation, the historical pattern of
> the story of Sarah and Hagar is used as a parable of the
> historical pattern of God's dealings with the Old and
> the New Israel. In the Philonic interpretation, however,
> the historical pattern of the story plays no part at all.[11]

He sees Paul's approach as closer to such Palestinian rabbinic
allegorizing as we have. Woollcombe notes that the majority of
Christian Fathers preferred Philo's allegorical method to that of
Paul. He discusses the differences which eventually developed between the Alexandrian and Antiochean "schools" of exegesis, as
followers of Philo and Paul respectively, and notes that the Alexandrian allegorical approach was more widespread and enduring.

Woollcombe postulates that the primary reason for the rapid
rise of Christian allegory after the example of Philo must have
been Gnostic influence and anti-Gnostic polemics. Thus the *Dialogue with Trypho* of Justin Martyr, which is historical in its
outlook, did not inaugurate a long period of such literature.
Instead allegory and historical typology and "sermon illustration"
typology were gradually fused together in a complex fashion.

Another scholar who has argued for the contemporary use of
historical biblical typology is Jean Daniélou. In *From Shadows to
Reality*, Daniélou examined Christian typological exegesis of certain hexateuchal themes from the second to the fourth centuries.
For each theme he displayed the thematic instances in both testaments, in Palestinian and Alexandrian Judaism, and in the patristic
writings. Daniélou sought for links between NT typological exegesis
and the great doctors of the fourth century, in order to see whether
there was a continuity between the two and on what lines it was
worked out.

He agrees that the dissensions which Christians had with Jews
and Gnostics were influential in Christian development of typology.
Typology helped to show the unity of the two testaments to the
Gnostics,[12] and the superiority of the NT to the Jews.[13] In addition to polemical works, Daniélou reminds us that other sources for
our study of patristic typology include sacramental catacheses,
iconography, homilies, treatises on spirituality, and biblical commentaries. In this survey of sources we see again the value of
Lampe's observation that such interpretations were necessary for
Christians themselves.

In the course of presenting the history of different themes,
Daniélou devoted a chapter to Rahab as a type of the Church. He
notes the oldest Jewish traditions,[14] one of which sets Rahab as
"the type of the pagans who are incorporated into the ecclesia,
the people of God."[15] He then examines several patristic works.
In these Rahab is initially a type of sinful humanity whom Jesus
came to save; in later works Rahab becomes a type of the Church
itself.

Throughout these Christian writings about Rahab the scarlet
cord is taken as a type of Christ's blood. Daniélou admits that
the redness of the cord is only of *incidental* resemblance to the
blood of Christ, as far as we are concerned, but the Fathers
assumed that nothing in Scripture can be fortuitous. He is willing
to accept such incidental types if the thrust of the patristic
typological considerations remains centered on the theological
content of the biblical theme in question.[16]

In a chapter on the typology of the sacrifice of Isaac,
Daniélou notes several patterns of interpretation of the three
patriarchs.[17] In Palestinian Judaism the three were models of observance of the Law and traditions; of the three Abraham was the
preeminent figure. For Philo the three represent stages of mystical ascent. Abraham stands for virtue which comes from study;
Jacob represents virtue acquired by moral effort; at the top of
the ascent Isaac is perfect virtue, which is a gift from God.
Christians continued to see Abraham, Isaac, and Jacob as models
and to some extent they also saw them as types of Christ. Abraham
was usually seen as a model of faith and of withdrawal from the
world. He is *rarely* considered *as a type*. The Mamre incident
"has a theological rather than a typological significance."[18]
Jacob was more often held up as a type--based on the meanings of
his two names, his servitude to Laban, his ladder dream, or his
struggle with Esau in the womb. However it was Isaac who became
the principal patriarchal type for the Christian (as he had for
Philo). The main events of his life were seen to be his birth and
sacrifice.

The insights of these patristics scholars can help us to
comprehend and to order the many individual selections from the
Fathers which we will now examine. Let us fix our understanding
of these insights in the form of eight general principles or
guidelines, and test each guideline again at the end of this chapter.

(1) For Christian writers OT events acquire significance in relation to, or as foretastes of, Christ's later accomplishments.

(2) The immediate literary context of an OT passage need not be as important to the Fathers as typology based on the passage.

(3) Types and allegories based on the OT were considered vital for understanding the life of Christ and the life of the Church. Some of these types and allegories have recognizable anti-Jewish or anti-Gnostic bases.

(4) In addition to "historical" types in which there is acceptable correspondence between an Old Testament event and one in the New, we find much "sermon illustration" typology and spiritual allegory. All of the types of interpretation are frequently mixed together. Some of the sermon illustration typology and allegory is congruent with the theological content of the passage under study.

(5) Philo's allegorical endeavors are much imitated by Christian writers.

(6) There are interpretational differences of some import between the Alexandrian and Antiochean "schools."

(7) Abraham himself is not often considered as a type of Christ; some events in the life of Jacob bring about such typological interpretations.

(8) Biblical passages serve as proofs in discussions of other doctrines or aspects of theology as well as of those directly involving Christ.

Format for Presentation of Christian Hermeneutic of Genesis 18

The nature of the Christian materials is so different from that of the rabbinic materials of Chapter I that we cannot expect to likewise place the Christian findings into thematic groupings.

There is a greater amount of Christian material, and it is much more easily datable and attributable to specific authors. Further, there are at least two schools of interpretation, the Alexandrian and the Antiochean, which should be looked at in their entireties since they differ on the use of allegory and typology. Western Fathers tended to be imitative of the Eastern schools; we shall present them as a group also.

Therefore instead of thematic groupings I have placed the Christian writers as individuals into six chronological groups: (A) early Apologists; (B) the Alexandrian school; (C) later Eastern writers; (D) the Antiochean school; (E) Western writers through Augustine; and (F) later Western writers. Group A represents the earliest writers of all (except Philo); groups B and D

follow in proper time order; and group E more or less covers the
time period of D. Group C is partly out of time sequence but I
didn't want to make too many subdivisions, and the writers by and
large imitate the findings of groups A and B. Group F follows E
chronologically and brings us to Bede in the eighth century.

For the reader who would prefer to choose from among these
many writers, I would recommend Philo, Origen and Chrysostom in
the East, and Gregory of Elvira, Ambrose, Augustine, and Bede in
the West--with Origen and Chrysostom being the most important two
of all.

A. Early Greek and Latin Apologists

Before turning to the writings of Justin Martyr, it is necessary to point out that there are apparently no references to the
Mamre or Jabbok stories in Jewish and Christian Intertestamental
literature. Jean Daniélou, in his study of the writings of Jewish
Christians,[19] examined the theological concepts unique to this
very early phase of Christian history. He points out that Christ
was often referred to as the glorious angel, or the venerable
angel, in these texts. We should take the expression *angel* in a
neutral Semitic sense here--as a supernatural being which manifests
itself. He notes that

> the nature of this supernatural being is not determined by
> the expression but by the context. The word represents
> the Semitic form of the designation of the Word and the
> Spirit as spiritual substances, as "persons," though the
> latter terminology was not to be introduced into theology
> until a good deal later. "Angel" is its old-fashioned
> equivalent.[20]

Daniélou then goes on to show[21] that the image of Michael,
the chief angel in Jewish thought, was at times transformed into
the image of Jesus in Jewish Christian literature. He also makes
a case[22] for a similar process occurring between Gabriel and the
Holy Spirit.

I have personally consulted all the textual citations Daniélou
presents for the above relationships based on Michael and Gabriel
and have found his presentation to be a reasonable one. One would
have to determine the validity of Daniélou's evaluation of each of
the ancient texts he uses *as being of genuine Jewish Christian
origin*. Such a determination is beyond by own competence.

The reason for mentioning Daniélou's study should be clear.
Michael and Gabriel were often identified in Jewish sources as being involved at Mamre. The Christian interpretations which we will

now examine usually assume that the three visitors were the pre-
Incarnate Christ and two angels, or that they represent the
Trinity in some way. Such interpretations may well have origi-
nated in Jewish Christian circles prior to the time of Justin.

1. Justin Martyr[23]

In his *Dialogue with Trypho* Justin makes some use of the
Mamre incident as evidence for the divinity of Jesus. The *Dialogue*
is believed to have been written down between 160-165 A.D., but
the discussions between Justin and Trypho may have actually occurred many years earlier in Ephesus.[24] While we are dependent on
Justin to provide an accurate account of Trypho's opinions and
contributions, scholars are generally satisfied that Trypho has
been depicted fairly.[25]

There are some philosophical presuppositions which Justin
makes which we should mention before going to specific passages.
Quasten notes[26] that "Justin denies the substantial omnipresence
of God. God the Father dwells, according to him, in the regions
above the sky. He cannot leave his place, and therefore he is
unable to appear in the world."[27] Justin postulates that Jesus is
the mediator from the Father; that Jesus is the subject of any
theophany which men may receive.

The Jesus of Justin, however, may be subordinate to the
Father.[28] Justin uses the well-known concept of the Logos in regard to Jesus as mediator, but not in our selections for this
study.[29]

Let us now look at the instances where Justin uses the Mamre
story. The principal line of argument occurs in chaps. 55 to 57.
Perhaps the best way to present the material is in the form of
summaries. In the left margin we will note the chapter, paragraph,
and speaker (Trypho had some Jewish companions with him, and some
of them assist in the dialogue at times).

55.1 Trypho	Let us return to the topic; show us if Scripture speaks of another God, beside the maker of the world.
56.1 Justin	He who appeared to Abraham was God, accompanied by two angels; these three were sent by another...whom we call Creator of the world and Father.
56.3 Trypho & comp.	How does the Mamre incident prove that the Holy Spirit has ever spoken of any other God or Lord?
56.4 Justin	Scripture does speak of another Lord or God, under (ὑπὸ)[30] the Creator of the world, who is also called an angel.

56.5 Justin	Was God one of the three who appeared as men to Abraham?
Trypho	No. God appeared to him before the appearance of the three men. The three men were angels, one of whom was to announce the news to Sarah, and the other two were to destroy Sodom.[31]
56.6 Justin	Note that the one who promised the birth later returned, and the prophetic word calls him God.[32]
56.9 Trypho	Well then, we were incorrect in assuming that the three who visited Abraham were all angels; but you have not yet proven that there is another God.
56.11 Justin	I shall try to prove that He who appeared to Abraham and is called God is different from God the Creator, different in number but not in γνώμῃ.
56.12 Justin	Note Gen 19:24, "The Lord poured brimstone from the Lord out of heaven."
56.13 4th comp.	We must therefore admit that one of these two angels who went to Sodom is called Lord, in addition to God who appeared to Abraham.
56.22 Justin	No. The one called Lord is not one of the two angels who went to Sodom. He is spoken of in Gen 18:22; when the two went to Sodom, He stayed behind to talk with Abraham. Then He went to talk with Lot and He destroyed the city, not the two angels.[33]
57.1 Trypho	If your arguments are correct so far, we are still dubious at the statement that He ate the food which Abraham gave Him.[34]
57.2 Justin	Either only the two angels ate non-human type food, or all three ate but in the mode we would speak of if we were to say that fire consumes all things. We should not understand by this that they ate with teeth and working jaws. There is no difficulty in the interpretation of this verse for those experienced in τροπολογίας.[35]

In 126.4-5, Justin briefly reviews the Mamre story, stressing that it was a genuine theophany. In 86.5 Justin collects many symbols from the OT which prefigured either the cross or some other aspect of the life of Jesus. Even the oak of Mamre is a cross symbol; God appeared to Abraham from (ἀπό) the tree. The use of ἀπό here is surely a bit of calculated imprecision on Justin's part.[36]

If we accept Trypho as an educated Jewish contemporary of Justin's and not simply as a literary foil, we must admit that he goes along with Justin and his Platonic philosophical concepts and Christian exegesis on a fair number of occasions. Barnard describes Trypho this way:

> Trypho was a Hellenistic Jewish layman who combined the
> culture and enquiring spirit of the hellenistic world
> with a knowledge of traditional Jewish exegesis and
> haggadah. He has no knowledge of the Hebrew language
> but knows accurately the Septuagint version of the Old
> Testament. His is not however the Judaism of Philo
> and Alexandrian hellenistic Judaism, nor that of the
> Palestinian Rabbinic schools. Trypho represents a
> mediating Judaism, perhaps having Palestinian roots,
> which cannot be strictly classified. Judaism, even
> after 70 A.D., was not a monolithic structure and had
> a number of facets, as recent discoveries have shown.
> Trypho represents one of these facets. He warns us
> against identifying the linguistic frontier between the
> Greek and semitic worlds with the cultural frontier
> between Hellenism and Judaism.[37]

By the same token Justin has a good deal of familiarity with
Jewish post-biblical milieu. Barnard carefully reviews Justin's
use of the LXX, his acquaintance with Jewish customs, beliefs,
exegeses, sects, etc., and rates it as generally accurate.[38]

The one element of Justin's thought which I would like to note
in ending would be his acceptance of the Mamre story as factual
(except for the consumption of the food). Obviously one cannot
read the pre-Incarnate Christ back into fables. Justin took the
OT accounts to be factual and authoritative, even if awaiting
Christian interpretation to reveal their full significance.[39]
Hanson notes[40] that Justin "does not belittle the sense of history." Justin's use of allegory is rather small; Hanson notes that

> the sources of his interpretation are evidently Rabbinic
> allegory, the example of the writers of the New Testa-
> ment, and traditional typology, partly deriving from
> Jewish liturgy and partly from Messianic and prophetical
> interpretation. All these are acted upon by an eager
> desire to find Christ everywhere in the Old Testament.[41]

Justin's belief in the factuality of OT events can also be
inferred from his lack of dependence on Philo and the Jewish and
Christian Alexandrian schools of allegorical interpretation.[42]

So we see that Justin looks at the Mamre event solely as an
example of the activity of the pre-Incarnate Christ. His interest
is apologetic and theological; he does not dwell on other elements
in the story.

2. Irenaeus

We have a work attributed to Irenaeus, *The Apostolic Preaching*,
but it exists only in an Armenian version.[43] In section 44,
Irenaeus says that the divine visitor at Mamre was the Son of God,
accompanied by two angels, and he uses the Gen 19:24 proof that the

Son rained fire from the Creator of all things. Abraham was a
prophet; he saw the Son of God in human form, who would in the
future speak with men, eat with them,[44] and judge men for His
Father.[45]

Irenaeus also mentions elsewhere that the Son spoke to
Abraham several times[46] but the Mamre incident is not specifically
mentioned.

Thus we have the same desire on the part of Irenaeus to place
Jesus in the OT theophanies (in apologetic and polemic writings
for Christians and Christian heretics), as we found in Justin (who
was addressing himself to Jewish readers). In addition, however,
Irenaeus does refer to the future earthly life of Jesus and his
speaking and eating with men at that time. The reference, however
general and brief, does imply that historical types could be drawn
between the lives of Abraham and Jesus.

3. Tertullian

With the writings of Tertullian we come to the African and
Western Fathers.[47] Quasten reminds us of the great persecutions
waged against Western Christians by non-believers, and of the great
internal dissension caused by heretics.[48] His description of Tertullian will not be contradicted by the few Mamre citations which
we have.

> Except for St. Augustine, Tertullian is the most important
> and original ecclesiastical author in Latin. With a pro-
> found knowledge of philosophy, law, Greek and Latin let-
> ters, Tertullian combines inexhaustible vigor, burning
> rhetoric, and biting satire. His attitude is uncompromi-
> sing. Forever a fighter, he knew no relenting towards
> his enemies, whether pagans, Jews, heretics, or, later
> on, Catholics. All his writings are polemic.[49]

Let us look briefly at Tertullian's use of the Mamre story.
The writings *De Carne Christi* and *De Resurrectione Carnis*,[50]
written around 210-212 A.D., were anti-Gnostic and anti-Docetic in
intent.[51] Tertullian's purpose is to prove the reality of Christ's
Incarnation and of His bodily resurrection and, subsequently, the
future bodily resurrection of all those who believe in Him.

In *De Carne* 3.6 Tertullian observes:

> Sometimes you have read and believed that the Creator's
> angels have been changed into human form, and such a
> realness of flesh have they had that Abraham washed
> their feet.

In 3.7 he compares this temporary[52] but real incarnation with the
greater Incarnation of Christ.

> What therefore is allowed to angels inferior to God--
> that they remain angels even though changed into human
> flesh--you would take from God, who is more powerful.
> Is Christ not able, having truly become man, to continue
> to be God?

Presumably these and other like arguments were directed against
the Docetism of Marcion.

Later, in *De Carne* 6.3-5, Tertullian refutes the objection
(held by Appeles) that Jesus may have been given flesh in the manner of the enfleshment of the angels at Mamre (i.e., *nulla uteri
opera*) rather than within Mary.

Tertullian objects that the motives (*causas*) for the angels'
incarnation were not as exalted as was the motive of Jesus; "No
angel ever came down to be crucified, to experience death, or to
be raised from the dead." A few lines further on, in 6.8, Tertullian suggests that Jesus was at Mamre with the angels in order to
practice dealing with men, learning how to speak with them and free
them and judge them.[53]

In the last section of Tertullian's *De Resurrectione* (62), he
studies the state of our own bodies after resurrection. We will
be *tamquam angeli*, as Scripture says in Luke 20:36 (and Matt 22:30).
This phrase must not be misunderstood.

> Angels have sometimes been as if men, in eating and drink-
> ing and putting forward their feet for washing; they have
> put on a human form without change to their proper nature
> (*substantia*) within.

It follows then that men can become as if angels without losing
their true humanness. This same theme is dwelt on through all of
chapter 62.[54]

In *Adversus Praxean* we find Tertullian dealing with another
heresy--Patripassianism.[55] This is an overidentification of God
the Father and Jesus to such an extent that Jesus really ceases to
be separate in any way. In 10.7-8 we find the heretics asking why
God the Son could not have generated God the Father. Tertullian
admits that God can do all things; He can bring a child to a barren
woman or to a virgin--nothing is too difficult for God. However,
the fact that God can do something does not mean that He has actually done it. The allusions to Sarah and Mary and Gen 18:14 are
only that, and are used no more in the course of the argument.

In *Adversus Praxean* 16.6-7 we are told that all appearances
and direct dealings by God in the OT are actually experiences had
by Christ. How could the unbounded omnipresent Father have come
down and rested at Abraham's camp under the oak? The heretics are

unaware that from the beginning the whole order of divine dealings
has been channeled through the Son.

We have seen this problem with the omnipresence of the Father
before, in Justin and in Irenaeus; here also it can lead to subordinationist tendencies concerning Christ, even in a writer who
did so much to initiate classical Trinitarian formulae.[56]

Tertullian's considerations concerning the nature of Christ's
incarnation in Mary, and of our own resurrection after death, are
theological ones and do not really use much of the Mamre story.
His remark that the pre-Incarnate Jesus was "learning how to deal
with men" at Mamre could have been the basis for drawing out types
involving Jesus' earthly life.

4. Novatian

Novatian,[57] like Tertullian and other early apologists,
assumes that Jesus, as subordinate to the Father, performs all the
actual OT visitations.

In *De Trinitate* 18 Novatian tells us that, by these appari-
tions, men are learning how to gradually approach God the
Father.[58]

> For Christ is the image of the invisible God, that the
> weakness and frailty of the human condition might get
> used to seeing the Father someday in the image, that is,
> in the Son. For gradually and by stages human frailty
> had to be built up by the image to the glory of someday
> being able to see God the Father.

At Mamre, Abraham saw three men, but he called one of them by
the name Lord. Novatian points out that if one were to object that
Abraham could just as easily be calling the chief angel by the
title Lord, it is clearly stated in vv. 1 and 14 that *Deus* is involved. This is a title not properly given to an angel. This
Lord, then, is Christ.[59]

Novatian then mentions the washing of the feet of the disciples
by Jesus in a beautiful passage.[60]

> He was acting in symbol (*in sacramento*) by being Abraham's
> guest; He would be among the sons of Abraham again someday
> and He would wash their feet to prove that it was He; He
> repaid to the sons the law of hospitality which father
> Abraham had once extended to Him.

Note that the concept of Christ repaying Abraham's descendants (the
Apostles) for Abraham's good deed is similar to the rabbinic "merit"
concept.

Novatian's remark that at Mamre Abraham, as a representative
of mankind, was learning to deal with God is simply the opposite

side of the idea of Irenaeus and Tertullian that there God was learning to deal with men. It too could have been a basis for discussing events in the life of Jesus.

The first firm example of a historical type involving Mamre is certainly Novatian's linking of the footwashing with Christ's similar action at the Last Supper.

B. Alexandrian Hermeneutics

1. Philo

At this point in our study, we should turn our attention to Alexandria and to the Jewish writer Philo.[61]

Hanson offers a good summation[62] of the Hellenistic and Alexandrian Jewish antecedents to Philo, such as Aristobulus and Pseudo-Aristeas, focusing primarily on the use made by these writers of allegory. Hanson is interested in the practical effects of such Alexandrian Jewish allegorizing on Scripture. He notes that the allegorizing of certain Mosaic laws in the *Letter of Aristeas*

> presents us with unmistakable allegory and the biblical texts are allegorized, not into Messianic prophecies nor types of the Law, but into moral examples and exhortations. We shall find exactly the same treatment of the Law in Philo, and later still in the Epistle of Barnabas, in Clement of Alexandria and in Origen; but this is the first known appearance of such an interpretation, and it is remarkable that in effect it empties the regulation of its literal force, making this merely the outward pretext for an inner moral meaning.[63]

The influence of Greek allegorical methods upon the Jews of Alexandria seems to have been stronger than rabbinic hermeneutical methods. Hanson remarks:

> It is obvious that the allegorizing of Scripture is a firmly established tradition in Philo's milieu by Philo's day, and it is interesting that those allegorizations tend to transmute the words of the biblical text into either philosophy or natural science, not into references to the Law and the chosen people, or into Messianic prophecies, as we should expect had Philo and his predecessors been influenced by the Rabbinic, presumably Palestinian, tradition of allegorizing.[64]

Hanson then examines[65] Philo's own extensive use of allegory, noting his sharing in "many traits in biblical exegesis with the Palestinian Rabbinic tradition."[66] These traits would include a great reverence for every word in Scripture, the method of collecting together all the instances in the Pentateuch of a certain word or phrase, and the juxtaposition of texts.

Philo usually allegorizes the text into moral or psychological lessons and frequently carries over the main allegorical
attributes of a person or place into many of the different biblical passages where this person or place is mentioned. Thus Abraham
will often be taken as representing wisdom gained by divine teaching.[67] Sarah represents virtue; Isaac stands for joy or for
natural (self-taught) virtue.[68]

These moral or psychological allegorical meanings, whether
drawn from persons, events, or places, are not types by Hanson's
definition--the interpreting of an event belonging to the present
or recent past as the fulfillment of a similar situation recorded
or prophesied in Scripture. Philo's lack of interest in typology
is a reflection of his lack of interest in eschatology or Messianic
expectation.[69] Hanson also notes that Philo "is not even much interested in historical events, for his attitude to history is
ambiguous."[70]

Let us now look at Philo's comments on the Mamre story. The
longest commentary is to be found in *De Abraham* 22-25 (§§107-32).
In the first part of his study, Philo briefly recounts the story;
the following is a summary.

107   Philo speaks of Abraham's kindliness (φιλανθρωπία);
        he saw three travellers in the form of men, whose
        more divine nature was not perceivable. He invited
        them to enjoy his hospitality and they quickly agreed,
        impressed more by his intentions than by his words
        alone.

108   Abraham's soul was full of joy at their coming and
        he and his family rushed to prepare the meal.

109   Indeed, no one is slow at kindness in the house of a
        wise man such as Abraham.

110   The three visitors feasted, not so much on the food as
        on the good will and great unbounded generosity of
        their host. They promised him a son in the time to
        come. This promise was made by the one of the three
        who was the chief, since it would have been unrefined
        for all three to talk at once.

111   Abraham and Sarah at first did not believe the message,
        because of their old age.

112   In fact Sarah laughed at the message, but afterwards,
        when they[71] said that God can do all things, she was
        ashamed for she knew that they were correct.

113   This serious thought after her initial laughter brought
        Sarah to a deeper appreciation of what was going on

                Then, it seems to me, was the first moment that
                she apprehended their more grand essence (unlike
                what they had first seemed to be), either of

prophets or angels who were changed from their
spiritual and soul-like selves into human form.

114   Really, Abraham's greatest virtue was not hospitality,
       but rather fear of God (θεοσέβια).

115   The angels would not have thought so much as to peep
       into the tent if they had seen any deep-rooted passions
       in the souls of those who were dwelling inside.

116   They only allowed the feast to take place because
       they regarded Abraham as a relative and fellow servant
       of the same God. Abraham and his whole house made
       more advance in virtue as a result of the arrival of
       the visitors.

118   Philo thinks that the angels only seemed to eat; even
       more significant is the fact that they took on the
       form of men, being incorporeal by nature, to do a
       good deed to the courteous Abraham. The whole miracle
       of the coming of the three visitors had as its purpose
       to assure Abraham that the Father had not failed to
       notice that he was such a man (i.e., wise).

At this point Philo declares that he will look for deeper
(allegorical) meanings in the text, having already presented the
literal sense (τῆς ῥητῆς ἀποδόσεως).

119   Whenever the soul is illuminated by God, as at
       noonday...the underlying object presents to the soul
       a triple vision; one vision is real while the other
       two are shadows cast by it.

120   Neither of the two shadows could be God.

121   Rather the middle figure, the underlying one, is the
       Father of the universe, He who is. The two shadows
       are the senior and nearest powers, the creative and
       the kingly. The creative power is called θεός because
       He made (ἔθηκέ) all things and the kingly power is
       called Κύριος since He who makes also has the right
       to rule and control (ἄρχειν καὶ κρατεῖν).

122   Thus God and His two powers can appear to those
       favored with visions in either a single or a triple
       mode. The single mode is reserved to the most vir-
       tuous. The triple mode is for those who can only
       comprehend the deity either through His creative or
       ruling activities.

124   If we assume that there are three classes of men, and
       that only the most virtuous are favored with the single
       mode of appearance by God, then the creative power
       stands to the Father's right and can appear as bene-
       ficient to the middle class of men, and the least
       virtuous men may see the ruling power on the left.

126-30 Digression on God's love for all three classes of men.

131-32 Philo notes that the change to single modes of address
       in Gen 18:3 and 18:10 reminds us that Abraham is really
       dealing with He who is, the underlying one. Therefore,
       Abraham belongs to the most virtuous class of men.

Philo's other, briefer, comments can be put into the following four groups.

(a) *The Theme of Theophany*

In *De Migratione* 165 we have an etymology for Mamre as a place name; it means "from seeing" or "from vision,"[72] and symbolically refers to a life of contemplation.[73]

In *De Cherubim* 106 Philo says that if we prepare our soul with much learning and study, then the divine powers will descend bringing laws and ordinances for our salvation. They will dwell with us, sowing roots of happiness, just as they gave Isaac to Sarah in gratitude for their stay with Abraham.

In *De Sacrificiis* 58-60, the topic is eagerness to serve God. Cain was not eager; he delayed offering sacrifices. Abraham, however, hastened to have Sarah (virtue) make ἐγκρυφίας. Thus the soul which has seen God and His two highest powers, sovereignty and goodness, will "knead" and "blend" this gracious manifestation within itself. The story of these mysteries must be buried (κεκρύφθαι) and kept from outsiders.[74]

(b) *"Masculine" Virtues and "Feminine" Vices*

Philo frequently refers to virtues and vices as being represented in Scripture by the categories of male and female, respectively. Thus, in *De Cherubim* 8, we read of Isaac being given to Abraham and Sarah. They were older and more virtuous now; they had both died to the emotions and to the "ways of women." In *Deterius* 28, Sarah alone leaves the ways of women (passions) and so should we also go over from these to the "masculine" traits of good desires.[75] Sarah (virtue) is returned to the rank of pure virgin (higher virtue) when she ceases to have periods; this note is found in *De Cherubim* 50 and, similarly, in *De Posteritate* 134.

In *De Ebrietate* 59-62, Philo talks about the claim that many make that they will not be affected by riches, honors, or the like. He says that this claim often fails when we actually come within reach of such riches or honors. So we still follow the ways of women. Sarah was able to abandon such ways; having done so she exulted in the joy given by God, and she counted as laughable the cares which most men have.[76]

In *De Migratione* 126, Philo discusses the merits which a righteous Noah or Abraham or whoever can bring upon his fellow men. Philo muses, citing Gen 18:10, that virtue will always be around in some form

> which the undue seasons of men can probably overshadow,
> but the time which is an attendant on God can reveal again.

> In a time such as this the "male" thought (Sarah) blossoms, not according to the temporal hours of the year, but according to untimed zeniths and seasons.

(c) *Sarah's Laughter*

Philo takes a benign view of Sarah's laughter. In *De Mutat. Nom.* 166, he speaks of the deep spiritual joys which righteous people can have in the graces to come. For example, Sarah laughed when she heard of her blessed son to be, this carefree, self-sprung good, saying "He who promised is my Lord and is older than all creation; it is necessary to believe in Him."[77]

In *De Abraham* 206, the topic is that joy and sorrow are both ingredients in our lives.

> It is on account of this fact, it seems to me, that Sarah (virtue) first laughs and then denies the laughter to the one who questions her. She was afraid lest she be appropriating joy proper to God alone and not to creatures. Therefore the holy word encouraged her, saying, "Do not be afraid; indeed you laughed, and there is a share of joy for you."[78]

(d) *The Final Escorting*

In *De Migrat.* 173-75, we have a brief allegory on Abraham's escorting of the angels as they left for Sodom. The context of the remarks has to do with the pitfalls involved in seeking after wealth, honors, etc. We should desire to stay close to God at all times and not to venture out on our own.

> ...he who follows God of necessity will have the words (customarily called angels) which attend on God as his fellow travellers.

Abraham did this sort of following at Mamre and was rewarded.

> O excellent parity, by which the escorter is escorted. Being the giver, he instead receives.

Another work attributed to Philo[79] contains almost all of the observations and allegories which we have mentioned on these pages. Here I will just mention briefly two new items peculiar to *Questions and Answers on Genesis*, which later Christians echo.[80] Loeb page numbers are on the left.

268   Abraham's seated posture represents "a state of tranquility and peace of body."

269   Our virtue should "watch" our senses as Abraham "watched" at his tent door.

Conclusions Concerning Philo. The contrast between Philo's use of the Mamre account and the rabbinic traditions which we collected in Chapter I is striking, but I am inclined toward caution in stressing the differences between them.

Admittedly we find no references to other OT passages in
these excerpts from Philo, but this is possibly due to the fact
that Philo was writing at least some of his commentaries for Gentile audiences.[81]

We find almost no elaboration on the details of the meal and
the hospitality involved. There is also no direct parallel in
Philo to the "merit" lessons of the Rabbis. However we must recall that Philo's writings are possibly older than a good deal of
the rabbinic traditions.

We could even say that, with regard to §§107-18 of *De Abraham*,
Philo is in effect interested in the account along basically Jewish
lines; the principal allegory of §§119-32 (the vision of God and
His two powers) is meant to explain the same problems in the text
which the Rabbis will explain by interpretative use of the Shekinah
concept.[82]

Although he is Jewish and may well have appreciated the structure of the Pentateuch, Philo obviously uses some hermeneutical
principles from his Greek background. In addition to his analysis
of Philo and other Alexandrian Jewish allegorizers, Hanson gives a
brief history of Hellenistic allegory up through Plutarch.[83] Hanson concludes:

> By the third century at latest it (Hellenistic allegory)
> had become almost part of the intellectual atmosphere in
> which educated men moved, in a position perhaps comparable
> to that held by the theory of evolution in our day.

> This Hellenistic allegory was characterized by being en-
> tirely unhistorical; it took no account at all of the
> historical situation, and very little of the original
> meaning, of the material allegorized. It was not only
> arbitrary; it required no sense of history at all; the
> results of its allegorization were general statements
> of a philosophical or psychological or scientific nature.
> What we have called typology was wholly unknown to it.

> In spite of the remarkable historical accident that the
> first extensive examples of this allegory are found, not
> in Hellenistic, but in Jewish writers, Aristobulus,
> Pseudo-Aristeas, and Philo, it is clear that we must
> conclude that Alexandrian allegory was derived from
> Hellenistic.[84]

The process by which Alexandrian Jews "derived" their use of
allegory from Hellenistic influences must be spelled out very carefully to include those positive influences from their Jewish reli-
gion, but Hanson emphasizes once again that the lack of interest in
history is not modified in the process.

> But Alexandrian allegory has in all its forms one feature
> in common with Hellenistic allegory; it is unhistorical.
> It does not use typology. Its ultimate aim is to empty

the text of any particular connection with historical
events. Even in the matter of allegorizing the Torah
we can safely conclude that the Alexandrian allegorists
saw no profound significance in its literal meaning,
however cautiously they may have expressed their conviction. Philo can see no point in history as history; to
him it is simply so much material to be allegorized into
philosophy.[85]

We will conclude our consideration of Philonic exegesis by
noting, with Hanson, that Philo was imitated by Alexandrian Christians, but apparently not by his coreligionists.

Philo's use of allegory, then, marks him and the tradition in which he stands as taking an attitude to the Old
Testament Scriptures in several important points quite
distinct from that of Palestinian Judaism. Philo used
allegory not only to emancipate himself from the literal
meaning of the text, but also from its relation to history, and also to some extent from the obligation to
observe the Jewish Torah in full. We know of almost no
direct successors to Philo; with him, as far as we know,
the line of Alexandrian Jewish thought ended. Pharisaic
Judaism took over the direction of Jewish thought after
the fall of Jerusalem, and in its schools a speculative,
Hellenistic Judaism was impossible. The heirs of Philo's
system--in its own way a noble and admirable system--were
the theologians of the Christian Church.[86]

2. Clement

The first Alexandrian Christian to use Philo's approach to the
Scriptures was Clement,[87] who died in 215 A.D. Clement was not
merely an imitator; he was capable of making his own interpretations,[88] and many of these were of a very practical sort. Hanson
notes that Clement "does not indeed show quite the same tendency to
undermine historical narratives by allegory as Philo does."[89]

In *Pedagogus* 3.10, Sarah and Abraham are praised for their
personal physical effort in hosting the visitors at Mamre.[90] In
Stromata 4.19, Sarah is praised for her humility in that she herself baked the bread for the angels. In 6.12 the topic is how
women also may grow in knowledge and virtue. In so growing, a
woman is becoming more "man-like," to use Philo's image.[91]

I think these remarks of Clement's[92] are too few in number for
further comment, except to agree with Hanson that Clement seems to
accept the literal facts of the Genesis account.

3. Origen

We come now to Origen (c. 185-254), the leading representative
of the Alexandrian Christian school of biblical commentators.[93]
Origen's life was one of intense intellectual and church activity,[94]

involving him in controversies on biblical questions with a broad
range of Christian heretics, Alexandrian Jews, and pagans.[95]   Unfortunately, many of his works are available to us only in Latin
translations by Rufinus, Jerome, and others. Rufinus, at least,
was capable of modifying statements of Origen's for doctrinal
reasons.[96]

Origen's writings include commentaries on specific books of
the Old and New Testaments, and collections of homilies. Quasten
regards the homilies as more pastoral than the commentaries and,
by implication, less scholarly.[97]   Hanson has a higher opinion of
the scholarly content of Origen's homilies.[98]   On the Mamre passage, we have about equal amounts of material from both homilies
and commentaries, with the longest excerpt being from a Genesis
homily.

The biblical student who wishes to understand Origen's exegetical and hermeneutical presuppositions would do well to read
Hanson's analysis at the outset.[99]   While Hanson is often dis-
tressed at Origen's specific allegories, he does provide us with a
historical and analytical overview which can help anyone wishing
to study Origen's use of a particular passage from Scripture.

(a) *Origen's Use of Scripture Texts*

Origen, like Philo, relied usually on the LXX, although he does
seem to have known some Hebrew. A case can be made for the propo-
sition that Origen did not value the LXX above the Hebrew text.[100]

Hanson describes the format Origen uses when commenting upon
a verse.[101]   Origen tries to see the text in context of the whole
Bible, but he often ignores the context of the particular book in
which the text was found. He seeks some immediately edifying meaning from the passage and so sometimes cuts his own work short. He
handles phrases and words in detail, referring to many other parts
of the Bible, and then replies to objections and difficulties.[102]
Many times Origen evidences a correct grasp of the intent of a
passage, even if he is perhaps too rational in working with it.

This tendency toward the rational and the intellectual is
pervasive and occurs in the homilies as well as in the commentaries.

> Origen began as a philosopher and never ceased to be a
> philosopher, though as a Christian priest he saw the
> necessity and usefulness of applying his philosophy to
> the personal problems of ordinary men and women. We
> must not forget that Origen and Clement of Alexandria
> formulated and openly professed a doctrine of Reserve;
> there were certain mysteries of the faith which could
> not be publicly declared to the unintelligent and unedu-
> cated, but only to the cultured Christian intelligentsia.[103]

(b) *Origen's Theory of Biblical Inspiration*

Origen has a very strong concept of biblical inspiration--that every verbal detail was directly inspired by God. Hanson remarks that "Origen's theory of inspiration very often drives him into exasperatingly atomistic exegesis, just because he is determined to believe that every verse, and sometimes every word, is an oracle in itself, independently of its context."[104]

We must reflect too on the fact that Origen regards both Testaments as equally referring to Jesus. His exegesis passes back and forth between the two Testaments with regularity. Hanson points to the problem that this approach engenders.

> A conception of inspiration such as this one rested
> necessarily upon a conviction of the inspearable unity
> of Scripture, and this is a theme of which Origen never
> tires. In fact what he is contending for is not so much
> the unity as the uniformity of Scripture. A modern
> theologian might think of the unity of the Bible as like
> the unity of a tapestry in which there are a multitude
> of different strands, and different colours and patterns
> woven by these strands into a single theme or picture.
> Origen's conception of the unity of Scripture is more
> like that of the steel shell of a ship, in which a number
> of different but uniform plates of steel are welded into
> one.[105]

One way, which we have seen used before, to express the inseparable relationship of the two Testaments is the reading of a pre-Incarnate Christ back into scenes in the OT. Origen, however, carries this approach very far; so far in fact that Hanson finds it unjustified.

> It in fact consists in turning the Old Testament into an
> intellectual dress rehearsal for the New, not in the sense
> that in the Old Testament are found conceptions of God
> which achieve at once their focus and their embodiment in
> the New, but in such a way that the Old Testament contains
> the whole gospel contained in the New--Christology, minis-
> try, sacraments, everything--only presented in the Old as
> a number of intellectual propositions apprehended by the
> enlightened, instead of enacted on the stage of history
> and associated with an historical figure, as in the New
> Testament. This seems to me not only a superfluous and
> indeed misleading piece of speculation but a complete
> misunderstanding of what the Old Testament, and indeed the
> the whole Bible, conceives to be the method of revelation,
> the way in which God meets man.[106]

Origen's view of the unity of the two Testaments was coupled with a desire to use any passage as an aid to an allegory or a proof. The Bible was thus used as if it were "a vast series of oracles which might or might not have some connective with each other, but which each in its own right had some divine or mysterious truth to convey."[107]

Hanson notes that Origen's theory of biblical inspiration was essentially a defense of the Bible.

> It ought to be obvious that Origen's doctrine is not founded upon any secure foundations. It was very largely a theological expedient resorted to in order to justify his particular "oracular" treatment of the Bible, and to place it securely beyond the reach of Marcionites, Gnostics and Literalists; and it was made possible only by the unlimited use of allegory. It is totally unscriptural, totally uncritical, totally unreal.[108]

(c) *Origen's Theory of Accommodation*

While Origen consistently holds for an "oracular" approach to the inspired Bible, he tempers his actual exegesis by his rationalistic categories. Thus he downplays any hints of predestination, transmigration of souls (although he has a similar concept of the preexistence of souls), God's foreknowledge of events, and so on. One other rationalizing tendency which must be mentioned is his studied disinterest in detail. Hanson refers to details as the "particularity" of Scripture.

> ...rationalism is inevitably suspicious of what modern theologians call the particularity of God's revelation in the Old Testament, that is, its involvement with local, ephemeral, and often apparently trivial or even improper details and situations, and Origen accordingly strives to dissolve this particularity into general truths and abstract principles.[109]

The end result of Origen's reliance on human rational powers as a counterbalance to his view of biblical inspiration was his theory that the Bible itself contained expressions which were meant to convey ideas to immature and imperfect men in a simpler way. In other words, Scripture accommodated its message to men.[110] Hanson credits Origen for his effort, which comes near to explaining our modern theory of progressive revelation, but he points out that Origen felt compelled to assign this immaturity to the audience to whom the Scriptures were addressed rather than to the human writer of the passage.[111]

(d) *Three Senses of Scripture*

In his theoretical discussions about Scripture, Origen frequently expressed his belief that there were three meanings in Scripture--the literal, moral, and spiritual (or intellectual);[112] in practice he often failed to develop the moral sense. Hanson postulates that the two categories of moral and spiritual meaning were simply not distinct enough for consistent application to sequential biblical passages, and that the moral sense became absorbed in the spiritual.[113] Further, when we examine the

methods and results of Origen's allegorizing we find no systems;
Hanson calls the spiritual allegory "protean"[114] and "unchartably
subjective."[115] He even refers to its use by Origen as sometimes
reducing the Bible to "a divine cross-word puzzle the solution
to whose clues is locked in Origen's bosom."[116] The material is
often handled with psychological and ethical allegories of the
Hellenistic type which Philo used;[117] even the material which was
traditionally seen as typological of Christ was often reduced to
"a timeless analysis of good and evil impulses warring within the
Christian's soul."[118]

(e) *Origen's Approach to the Literal Sense of Scripture*

We come now to the most important aspect of Origen's thought
system and the one which separates him most decisively from our
own time. Origen chooses in each case whether or not to concede a
literal, historical sense to the biblical passage.[119] One reason
for his belief that historicity could be questioned in an individual case was his theory (presumably based on Philonic material)
that there were divinely inspired deliberate inconsistencies in
the Bible, which were intended to clue the reader that allegory
was needed to understand the passage.[120]

Let us now look at Origen's exegesis of the visit at Mamre.[121]

In *In Cant. Cantic.* 2,[122] we learn that Abraham was granted
great wisdom by God, who came to him often to teach him. Thus the
references in the opening lines of the Mamre story are allegorical.
Noontime signifies the high level of virtue which Abraham had.
Mamre means a place of visions; Abraham sits because he has the
time and inner peace for such visions. "At the door" means "outside," i.e., Abraham's mind was outside his body, far from bodily
considerations or desires.

The principal example of Origen's work on Mamre is found in
his *Genesis Homily 4*.[123] We will summarize here, with paragraph
numbers on the left margin.

§1 Origen begins his comments by contrasting Abraham's experience
at Mamre with the visitation given to Lot in Genesis 19. Three men
came to Abraham and they stood *super eum*; only two came to Lot and
they delayed *in platea*. Lot is very inferior to Abraham; he had
parted from Abraham (Genesis 13) and he had chosen to live in
Sodom. Abraham's three visitors came at midday; Lot's two came in
the evening. Abraham could stand the full glory of the light; Lot
could not. Abraham received the Lord and two angels--the Savior
and two destroyers; Lot only received the two destroyers.[124]

Who made the greater show (apparatus) of hospitality? Abraham exhibited alacrity in his courtesies; he ran to the men, hurried to the tent, and bade Sarah to hurry. The cakes which Sarah made from fine flour are called *subcinericias*[125] (ἐγκρυφίας) and signify secret or hidden or spiritual bread.[126] Lot does not use such fine flour, nor does he make three measures, nor does he make the spiritual breads.[127]

Abraham chose a good and tender calf, not simply taking the first calf he came across. Everyone moved with speed, even the servant boy. No one is lazy in the house of a wise man.

§2   The men appear "above" Abraham because he had indeed submitted himself to God's will. Abraham gave *three* measures of baked goods to the *three* men; Origen observes that everything Abraham did was "spiritual" and full of mystery (*sacramentis*)--an apparent allusion to the Trinity.[128] A calf was served--another mystery (*sacramentum*). How tender and good was he who humiliated himself for us even unto death, and who gave up his life for his friends. This is the fatted calf, killed by the father of the prodigal son; this is the only son offered by God who so loved the world.

Abraham knew that his guests were not ordinary men (Gen 18:2-3; he adored one and spoke to one), yet he had water brought for footwashing. This was not only thorough hospitality on his part (which we should imitate) but also a sign about Jesus' remarks, in Mark 6:11 and Matt 10:14-15, about shaking the dust off the feet. Abraham wanted no dust left to be a "testimony of unbelief" against himself on Judgment day.[129]

§3   Origen notes that Abraham served the Lord[130] and the angels "under the tree," the tree of Mamre. There must be an allegory here.[131] Mamre means *visio* or *perspicacia*; the Lord was delighted with the vision and sensitivity of Abraham, who was clean of heart. In such a heart the Lord and his angels can have a true feast.[132]

§4   Abraham and the visitors were overheard by Sarah, who was standing behind the tent door "*post Abraham.*"[133] We should learn from the example of the wives of the patriarchs that women should follow their husbands--follow them "to the Lord." Our manly senses and intelligence lead us to God; our womanly aspects are carnal.[134]

There is another meaning to Sarah following Abraham. At the Exodus God, in the column of smoke by day and in the column of fire by night, preceded and the people of the Lord followed behind.[135]

Abraham and Sarah were old, not in the sense of age but in the sense of maturity and virtue;[136] before them no one, no matter how old, had ever been called a *presbyter* with regard to his age.[137]

Conclusions. Many of Origen's allegories are clear imitations
of Philonic material—the idea that Abraham was taught by God; that
Mamre signified a place of vision; that Abraham's seated posture
signified his inner tranquility; that his mind "watched" his body.
The "hidden secrets" theme, based on the "hidden" breads, shows
Origen using the additional LXX Greek semantic meaning just as
Philo did. Other imitations include the dictum that no one is
lazy in the house of a wise man; that manly and womanly attributes
compete within our souls; that the patriarch, his wife, and their
son represent wisdom, virtue and joy respectively. The attempts
to allegorize the eating of the meal are also imitative of Philo.
The overall thrust of Philo's exegesis, as seen in his statement[138]
that the whole miracle of the coming of the three visitors had as
its purpose to assure Abraham that the Father had not failed to
notice that he was a wise man, is substantially the same as Origen's.
His statement[139] was that the Lord was delighted with the vision
and sensitivity of Abraham, who was clean of heart, and that within
such a heart the Lord and His angels can have a true feast.

There are, of course, some peculiarly Christian interpretations
in Origen. Twice he sees in the number three a type of the Trinity,
although these are brief. The pre-Incarnate Christ is assumed to
be one of the visitors, as is needed in Origen's theory of salvation
history. In other instances the calf signifies Christ, as Origen
fuses together active and passive images of Jesus as the willing
calf and the calf offered by the Father.

Origen's view of the unity of the two Testaments is well shown
in his remarks about the footwashing. While he may allude to the
Mandatum (and briefly does so in *Comm. in Joannem* 32.4), his comments in *Genesis Homily 4* concern Mark 6:11 and Matt 10:14-15. Origen explains that Abraham wanted to anticipate (*praevenire*) and
wash their feet so that there might not be any dust left to be
shaken at him on Judgment day, as a testimony of his unbelief. This
is indeed a complicated type. Abraham, by washing their feet and
so not leaving any dust for his visitors to shake against him (as
the disciples of Jesus are to shake off the dust from their feet
against those who will not accept their message), stands for those
who will accept the message of Christ someday from His disciples—
but Abraham's visitors are the pre-Incarnate Christ and two angels!
To put it another way, what was there for Abraham to not believe or
not accept? What relationship is really there between the two
passages, Genesis 18 and Mark 6:11? For Origen the relationship
may be strictly a verbal one.

In the early sections of *Genesis Homily 4* several legitimate
contrasts are drawn between Abraham and Lot. As far as I can tell
from a quick survey, Philo does not concern himself with the same
contrasts, although we did find some of these contrasts occasionally
mentioned in the rabbinic materials. Perhaps the clue to Origen's
thinking lies in the *Leviticus Homily 13*.3. Here Origen sees Abraham and Lot as representative of those who know of religious mysteries and of those who only know the common rules for salvation,
respectively. There is no indication here, or in the other places
where Lot is mentioned, that one can work oneself up to the higher
class of men.

While Origen does recall the Mandatum scene once, his references to the calf as a symbol of Christ, to the footwashing as a
reminder of Mark 6:11, and to the Trinity can at best be called
"sermon illustration" types. The contrasting of Abraham and Lot
can be seen as an example of ecclesial sermon illustration typology.

C. Later Eastern Writers

Before coming to the Antiochean school, I will mention briefly
ten Eastern writers later than Origen. These ten usually repeat
points we have already seen. Many of them focus on the question of
the pre-Incarnate Christ or the Trinity at Mamre, or use the matter
of the consumption of the food in various theological arguments.
By the early part of the sixth century we find Catenae of biblical
knowledge being produced by Procopius of Gaza.

1. Eusebius of Caesarea (writing 303-312), in his *Church History* 1.2.7-8[140] explains that Jesus had to be present at Mamre,
since God the Father cannot be limited to a physical space or to a
human form. Briefer remarks to the effect that Christ appeared at
Mamre can be found in *Church History* 1.4.6-8[141] and *Life of Constantine* 3.53.[142]

2. Athanasius (writing 358-359) also holds that Jesus was the
divine visitor at Mamre and other occasions in the OT.[143]

3. Cyril of Jerusalem (writing ca. 350) also briefly mentions
that Abraham received Jesus at Mamre.[144] Context indicates that
Cyril is explaining the reasonableness of the Incarnation of Jesus,
in that He had already come often to men in a pre-Incarnate mode.
Cyril accepts the fact that Jesus ate the food at Mamre, since he
mentions that later the Incarnate Jesus also ate with his fellow
men.

4. Gregory Nazienzen (writing 369-374) speaks of the patriarchs who recognized God in a theophany or great work. Abraham

received a man and gave him food; then he realized who his visitor
was, and reverenced him.[145]

5. Cyril of Alexandria (writing 433-441) in *Contra Julianum*
1.20[146] sees the visit of three figures to Abraham as a type of
the Trinity.

6. Eutherius of Tyana (writing ca. 431), an ally of Cyril's
enemy Nestorius, denies that the angels really ate the food which
they were served.[147] His concern was to point out that the visitors were angels and not men; context indicates that his main aim
in this section was to discuss the human nature of Jesus, who truly
needed food when He lived among men after His Incarnation.

7. Hesychius of Jerusalem (writing 430-450) notes that *simila*
is the word used in Gen 18:6, and in Lev 2:1, while *farina* is used
in Matt 13:33.[148] The Matthew citation, the parable about hiding
yeast in three measures of flour, must certainly indicate the
Trinity. In the OT, the word *simila*, as when Sarah is told to
make three loaves of bread from *simila*, can serve at least as a
partially effective indicator of the same mystery of the Trinity.
This allegory seems to be new with Hesychius, who was a follower of
the Alexandrian school of exegesis.

8. Baradotus (writing ca. 451) relates the three measures of
flour which Sarah must use to the image in Luke 13:21. Thus the
Mamre story is a foreshadowing of Christ's life on earth.[149]

9. Procopius of Gaza (d. 520) was the first to assemble
catenae of patristic comments into verse by verse commentaries on
some of the books of the Bible. The following summary is subdivided according to the Migne column numbers.[150]

364   He begins by discussing the identity of the visitors.

> Some say that the three men are angels; some, following
> Jewish patterns, say that one of the three is God and
> the other two are angels; some say that it is a type
> of the holy and consubstantial Trinity.

Procopius maintains that however God chose to come, He moderated
the mode of appearance to our human limitations.[151]

365   Mamre means "from vision"; the participants were worthy of
the vision. The bow Abraham made was as to a close friend; it was
not an act of worship. Abraham rushes about like a young man. The
angels were above him (i.e., not on the ground); this indicates
that their status was above that of men. In the house of a good
man everyone works quickly. Abraham served but did not eat with
them, out of respect. He acted as host not in the traditional
sense of fellow diner, but rather as a servant.

<u>368</u>   Abraham was modest; his hospitality was cheerful, eager and
generous.   Sarah's laughter seems to be an innocent reaction to
the thought of her own age as well as Abraham's condition.   God
questioned her to deepen her faith, so that the birth of the son
who was promised might be all that greater a miracle.   Abraham's
escorting is an integral part of his hosting duties.

    I think that Procopius' evaluation of the Mamre account
focuses often on factual details.

    10. Maximus the Confessor (d. 662) offers a Trinitarian ex-
planation of the Mamre theophany in *Quaestiones ad Thalassium* 28,[152]
and in his *Letter on Charity* 2.223.[153]

                        D. Antiochean Hermeneutics

1. John Chrysostom

    We are fortunate to have a great deal of material on the Mamre
passage in the writings of John Chrysostom, a leading member of the
Antiochean school of exegesis.[154]

    The development of another approach to exegesis, represented
by certain Christians of Antioch, can be traced to Origen's own
scholarly example.   His interest in grammar and textual exactness
influenced Lucian of Antioch and Pamphilus of Caesarea.[155]   Later
members of the school continued to be interested in literal, non-
allegorical interpretations, although they did not advance textual
study as much as they might have.

    Chrysostom himself was, as Chase notes,[156] a "scholarly pas-
tor" more than an "accurate, conscientious commentator."   Despite
the extensive pastoral and polemical challenges to him, Chrysostom
did not marshal scriptures as proof texts in his main works; he
preferred instead to write continuous biblical commentaries.   Chase
speaks favorably of his priorities.

> Chrysostom was the founder of no school of theologians.
> No critic can trace to his teaching or influence any
> shadow darkening the page of later theology.   No General
> Council has anathematised him.   No controversy is spe-
> cially connected with his name.   No bigots have ever
> claimed him as their own.   Speaking generally, there is
> a breadth about his Biblical work, the freedom of one
> who was not pledged to support a favourite doctrine
> from every passage or every book.[157]

    After Chrysostom, the Antiochean school lost much of its mo-
mentum.   Chase[158] follows its traces through the influence of
Chrysostom and Theodoret upon later generations; through Greek
writers such as John Damascene, Photius, Oecumenius, and

Theophylact;[159] through the Syrian schools of Edessa and Nisibis;
and through individual Western Fathers.

We should get some idea of how John dealt with the whole
range of the Bible, rather than just confine ourselves to these
two Genesis passages.[160]

Given the tradition of Christianity up to his time, and the
pressure of many heresies such as the Marcionites, Arians, and
Manicheans, Chrysostom firmly believes in the unity of Scripture;
the Old and New Testaments speak of the same God and of the same
Jesus. This unity, however, is not a uniformity; the reading of
the NT is not veiled, as was that of the Old. The old law was a
tutor, preparing us for Jesus.[161]

Chrysostom had two principles which applied to both Testaments. The first is that all Scripture exists because of God's
condescension (συγκατάβασις). The second is that the Scriptures
are minutely accurate.

The first of these principles means that revelation came
gradually during the development of the Bible,[162] and was conditioned by the powers of those to whom it was given.[163] Thus we
must understand that anthropomorphic expressions are legitimate
attempts to convey attributes and intentions of God. We cannot
allow ourselves to be led astray by such expressions into excesses
of allegorism or literalism. Further, a particular passage in
Scripture may have been given in order to correct previous human
weaknesses and we may have in our possession a passage from later
still which corrects the previous correction.[164]

Secondly, we must not confuse this gradual revelation, this
conditioned series of revelations, with inexactness of language.
The minute details and wordings of Scripture have a plain meaning
which should not be put aside.[165] Nor should the actual texts of
Scripture be diminished or expanded in any way.

In sum, those books of the Bible which relate history are
meant to expose us to God's gradual revelation, His gradual and
growing moral education of all men. Unlike secular history, which
may have no morally educative purpose, biblical history has a moral
aim. Chase summarizes:

> Here the ruling aim is not literary or artistic, but moral
> and spiritual. Thus two principles are involved. In the
> Bible we have real history. Again, there is that in it
> which makes it yield to the touch of the seeker after
> spiritual wisdom. But here we reach a principle of in-
> terpretation which became the distinguishing mark of the
> School of Antioch. If the histories of the Bible are
> not fictions or fairy tales, their genuine historical

character must be honestly recognised, or their spiritual significance will surely be missed or marred.
This superstructure of doctrine must be built on the
rock of historical interpretation; otherwise the floods
of heresy and the shifting winds of theological fashion
will overwhelm it. And because it will drag down with
it, to be buried at least for a time, some of the true
and solid treasures of Christianity, its fall will be
great.[166]

Let us now look at the specific use Chrysostom made of the Mamre
account, in many works from his years as a preacher in Antioch,
and in a few works from his later years at Constantinople.[167]

(a) *Hospitality and Charity*

The longest single passage of Chrysostom's on Genesis 18 can
be found in *Homily 41 in Genesim*.[168] In the brief outline of the
homily given here, the Migne column numbers will be on the left.
The opening sections of the homily deal with the Gospel parable of
the servants who invest five, two and one talents; one type of
spiritual "investing" we could do would be to be hospitable.

378   God appeared to Abraham at Mamre because he had obeyed His
wishes in the matter of circumcision.[169] Abraham was very eager
to have guests; he himself sat outdoors to watch for visitors. He
did not take a nap or relegate this duty to a servant or otherwise
excuse himself from this task. Noon would be a good time to find
travellers.

When the three first came, Abraham did not know who they were
and, while being attentive to their needs, he was not overly inquisitive. Thus, because of his hospitality, the Lord God of all,
and His angels, visited him.

379   Abraham himself *ran* to greet them.

380   Abraham acts almost as if a young man, so motivated is he by
diligence. His bowing to the ground is a hospitable act (*not* one
of worship); he does not want to seem to be acting merely because
custom prescribed it. The entreaty "If I have found favor in your
eyes..." makes the guest feel like the master; it is as if Abraham
had said, "You, oh guest, are giving the favor, not receiving it."
Perhaps one of the visitors seemed to be the chief but, even if
this were the case, Abraham did not recognize him as divine.

381   When Abraham tells Sarah to rush, he is not being critical
of her usual pace.[170]

382   Since there were three visitors, he had three separate
measures of flour prepared, in order that the bread would be

finished that much faster. Abraham and the boy *rush* to dress the calf. Abraham's joy and eagerness actually invigorated his body. He was not in any way condescending to his guests.

383   Abraham, standing under the tree waiting on them, is the very model of a host. When the men ask for Sarah by name, this is Abraham's first clue that his visitors are not ordinary men. The mention of the age of Abraham and Sarah in v. 11 helps us to excuse her subsequent laughter.

384   *Abraham*, in v. 15, said to Sarah, "No, you did laugh." Abraham said this to hush Sarah and so keep her from compounding an already tense situation. It was also his duty as a host to help in ways such as this. Indeed, true hospitality is

> not the needing of a vast array of courses, nor a costly display, but rather a cheerful atmosphere. Not a service rendered with some words but rather with love from the heart, and noble thoughts.

Another instance of Chrysostom's understanding of the Mamre account is his *Homily 23* Περὶ 'Ελεημοσύνης καὶ Φιλοξενίας,[171] which we will summarize briefly here.

When we speak of hospitality we are really considering not wealth, but willingness. Abraham was a rich man but that is incidental to his hospitality. The Lord and three men appeared to him; he arose and bowed, not realizing that God was present. Abraham had been "spreading the net" of hospitality by himself and not through his servants. If he had known that God was there, naturally he would have been generous. His not knowing better demonstrates just how genuinely kind and hospitable he was.

Sarah also shared in the work herself. She "snapped at commands." In doing all this, Abraham increased his understanding of philosophy. Even the calf was made lighter by his understanding and willingness. Isaac would be the reward which Abraham and Sarah would receive for all this.[172]

In *Homily 45 on Acts 20:32*[173] the context is the greater value of private charity over public church almsgiving. The following is a summary.

Let us help the poor as Abraham did; he did not know that he was hosting Christ and angels. To the travellers he showed liberality as regards food, eagerness in personally working, and modesty in greeting them and asking them to stay. We too should also have eagerness, joy, and liberality when we help someone. The soul of a stranger blushes and is ashamed, and, unless one shows an excess of joy as Abraham did, the stranger will depart feeling disregarded.

Therefore, come to the church door; do something extra; take home
a poor person or at least give him an alms. *Beat* the church; *beat
us out* in generosity.

The above excerpt from the homily on Acts shows a shift which
is new to us with Chrysostom--Abraham's hospitality has now become
Abraham's almsgiving or charity.[174] Let us look at three aspects
of the Mamre story which Chrysostom considers to exemplify standards
of proper almsgiving.

(1) *Abraham used his wealth to aid the poor.* In *Homily 34 on
First Corinthians*[175] the topic is the proper use of material
wealth. John distinguishes "self-made" rich people and those so
endowed by God; Abraham was one of the latter. He gave all he had
to strangers and the poor. To the three visitors he offered much
food and personal care. He was a "harbor" for strangers and those
in need. Abraham acted as if he possessed nothing exclusively for
himself.

In *Ad Populum Antioch* 2.5[176] we hear of the truly rich--those
who give to others. Abraham was rich but not fond of money. He
searched for travellers; he used a mobile tent rather than a house.
This tent was deemed worthy of a visit by angels, who seek not
beauty of dwelling but virtue of soul; to express it another way,
they seek not only simplicity of dwelling but richness of soul.[177]

(2) *Abraham and Sarah were personally involved.* In *Homily 21
on Romans 12:13*[178] John speaks of how we should seek chances to
help others. Abraham looked for guests as if they were "prey"; we
knit the brow and try to avoid such encounters. Abraham set a
table for his guests because he was full of an ingrained disposition to be hospitable.

Homily 35 on First Corinthians[179] mentions Abraham's humility
and personal involvement. He was humble; he took in the travellers.
He was not conceited; he ran, bowed, called them lords, presented
Sarah in the role of a servingmaid.

In *Homily 14 on Timothy*[180] we see that Abraham and Sarah were
involved personally at Mamre, and not just financially. So too we
should pitch in ourselves, since the personal touch is needed to
make guests feel at ease; "we have to show in words and deeds that
the doer is not doing good but receiving it, and is being shown
kindness more than he is showing kindness as host."

Homily 35 on Matt 10:34[181] notes that if one donates money to
charity he only gets one reward; if he does the work himself, he
gets an extra real return. Thus Abraham got his own calf, ignoring
his 318 servants.

(3) *Abraham was not overly inquisitive.* In his *De Lazaro,* *concio* 2.5[182] the question is asked why the Lazarus of the Gospel parable went to "Abraham's bosom" when he died.[183] The answer is that Abraham is a rebuke to the rich man's inhospitality. Abraham had received "men," whom he did not know were angels; he thought they were human travellers and no more. So also we earn more grace when we take in the common, abject, and truly poor. Like Abraham, we should not be overly curious about the identities of guests or their itineraries.

(b) *Further Remarks Concerning Sarah*

In the following citations from Chrysostom we shall concentrate on new remarks concerning Sarah. In *On Psalm 48:17* (English Ps 49:16)[184] the visit at Mamre is recounted at length, along the lines of *Homily 41 in Genesim.* In col. 509 Sarah is depicted as keeping her modesty even though she helps to serve the visitors outdoors

> ...using a tree instead of a chamber; having the shade
> of the leaves for a chamber, she was not ashamed to be
> seen in public. Sarah stood, displaying the proper
> domestic attributes, and earning the reward for service.[185]

In *Homily 23 on Hebrews 11:11*[186] Sarah's laughter is briefly mentioned. Her laughter was prompted by a lack of faith, but the ensuing fear was motivated by faith. In *Homily 6 on Matthew 2:1,*[187] Sarah's laughter in Genesis 18 is said to have been blameworthy.

In *Homily 20 on Ephesians 5:31,*[188] in a discussion on "spiritual" marriages, Sarah's lack of monthly periods is considered praiseworthy. Further,[189] we find approval of her submission to Abraham (she called him "lord" in Gen 18:12), and praise for the domestic harmony in all of Abraham's household.

In *On Galatians 4:20ff.,*[190] and *Homily 16 on Romans 9:9,*[191] Sarah is taken as a type of the Christian Church. The analogy drawn from the Mamre account emphasizes the life-giving power of God's promise (Gen 18:14) and ignores Abraham's physical cooperation in the conception of Isaac.

(c) *Further Remarks Concerning the Identity of the Visitors*

Chrysostom does not generally concern himself with lengthy speculation on the exact mode of theophanic visitation at Mamre.[192] In most of the citations which we have seen so far the angel visitors receive more attention than God the Father or Jesus. The most specific reference to Christ appearing at Mamre is in *Contra Theatra* 3,[193] summarized here.

The tent was open to all; it was situated on a main road
and not in some remote place. Christ and two angels
appeared to Abraham; he knew this with the eyes of faith
even though all three visitors had strictly human forms.
They ate with him on account of his hospitality. Sarah
was his co-worker. The bread was unleavened so that it
would bake faster. All the procedures were done as
respectfully as if for religious rites. Then Abraham
receives from the only begotten God news of Abraham's
only begotten son, Isaac.[194]

On the other hand, in *Homily 42 in Genesim*[195] we read that
the angels and their Lord had come to Abraham at the same time;[196]
the angels then went on to Sodom but He remained behind and talked
with Abraham[197] about things to come. The "Lord" in this context
seems to be God the Father.

Conclusions. The contrast between Chrysostom's use of the
Mamre story and Alexandrian use of it could hardly be more striking.
Chrysostom, convinced of the factual history of the event, employs
no allegory at all in his exegesis. He makes no effort to find
types of Christ in the footwashing or in the calf; he draws no
Trinitarian types from the fact that three visitors are spoken of
or that three measures of flour are baked. He has no trouble with
the idea that the visitors ate the food provided.

On the other hand, his comparison of God's word of promise to
Sarah in Gen 18:14 with God's later bringing forth of the Christian
Church is a rather weak use of type, since it so patently ignores
Abraham. Also, Chrysostom's inclination to see the travellers as
poor men is not based on any internal biblical evidence, nor did we
find any such inclination among the Rabbis. Further, Chrysostom
seems to exhibit little interest in vv. 9 to 16 of the Mamre story.
One would not get much of the religious force of v. 14 if one relied only on Chrysostom's comments. Chase speaks of Chrysostom
sometimes being "too realistic";[198] perhaps that is why his interpretation of the story, for all its welcome literalness and pastoral
intensity, might seem a bit pale.

Unlike most of the Fathers we have seen so far, Chrysostom does
pay attention to the details of the Mamre passage. Thus he makes
telling observations on Abraham's recent circumcision, his hospitality, his assumption that his visitors were human, and so on. The
sum total of his commentary certainly constitutes an interpretational difference of import from the Alexandrian tradition. His
evaluation of Abraham and Sarah as models of charity for our own
imitation is entirely new and quite intense.

2. Theodoret

Theodoret (writing 450) was the last major writer of the Antiochean school.[199]   His few remarks on the Mamre account deserve attention.

In his commentary on Daniel 10:16-17,[200] Theodoret notes that use of the word *lord* does not imply that the speaker is necessarily aware of his addressee as divine. Thus Abraham used the term in Gen 18:3, thinking them to be men only.

In *Questions on Genesis* 69,[201] Theodoret admits that the text says that the men ate the food which Abraham gave them. However, they were angels who have no bodies. Thus they seemed to be eating, but they were not putting the food in their mouths and stomachs; we should not wonder too much as to how they got rid of it.[202]

The visit at Mamre is briefly mentioned in his commentary on Heb 13:2.[203]

E. Western Writers Through Augustine

Western Christians developed no schools of interpretation as such, but tended to borrow and adapt Eastern methods. We have for the Mamre passage the writings of six Western Fathers for the period up to Augustine's death.

1. Hilary of Poitiers

We have a doctrinal work of Hilary[204] (writing 350-365) in which he uses proof texts from the OT to show the presence of Christ among men before His Incarnation and to prove His divinity. Hilary's Christology is not subordinationist. A summary follows with paragraph numbers on the left.

25   In invoking the Mamre account, Hilary assumes that Abraham saw Jesus and two angels, all three of whom were similar in their human appearance. Abraham knew by faith which one was Jesus.

26   Jesus spoke the promise (Gen 18:10 and 14), which earlier had been attributed to an angel of God (Gen 16:10); Jesus is indeed God's "angel,"[205] and He is also God.

27   In adoring just the one visitor, Abraham saw the mystery (*sacramentum*) of the future Incarnation. Christ later mentions this in John 8:56.[206]   Christ remains with Abraham while the two angels go on to Sodom.

<u>28</u>   We know that only angels came to Lot from the texts them-
selves.

> Here (19.2) a simple appearance of angels merits a
> plural expression; there (18.3) the faith of the
> patriarch gives honor to one. Here (19.1) the history
> of Scripture indicates that two of the three were only
> angels; there (18.3) Scripture proclaims the Lord and
> God....Lot called them lords (19.2) but Scripture
> identifies them as angels (19.1); there (19.2) it
> was the courtesy of the man, here (19.1) the procla-
> mation of the truth.

In commenting on our Psa 119:132,[207] "Turn to me and be
gracious to me," Hilary is reminded by the word *aspice* of the fact
that God *looks on*[208] the punishment of the wicked as He did at
Sodom; the word *miserere* reminds him of the mercy with which God
looked on Abraham.[209]

2. Zeno of Verona

Another Western bishop, Zeno of Verona (writing before 372)
has left us one brief literal sketch of the Mamre story.[210]

> 1. Abraham heard an exile ordered for him by God, that
>   he give up his family as well as his homeland....
>   Then Abraham, looking with his eyes, saw three men,
>   and adored flat on his face, and offered hospitality.
>   "Refresh yourselves," he said, "under this large
>   tree." He made bread and killed a calf.
> 2. After this he was promised a son of faith, not of
>   age, from his legitimate marriage. Sarah conceived.
>   She who was hardly able to walk bore her burden
>   without any effort of the womb; she learned to be a
>   mother when she did not flow. Her drooped breasts
>   gave an abundance of milk, and from her weak old
>   age the stronger boy was nourished. Nothing is
>   difficult for faith, which receives as much as it
>   believes.

Zeno sees Abraham and Sarah as models of faith, because they
believed the message given to them. Daniélou noted that Abraham
is generally considered as a model of faith. In relation to the
Mamre story, however, most of the Fathers have focused on the fact
of the theophany rather than on the actual promise to Abraham and
Sarah.

3. Gregory of Illiberia

The bishop of Elvira, Spain (writing 360-392), has a Mamre
commentary in his *Tractatus Origenis 2*,[211] consisting mostly of
short allegories.

1. His citation of Gen 18:1 reads "...ad ilicem Mambre
   juxta exitus viarum."[212] Abraham was noble and
   admirable; he pointed to many things which are to
   come, not only by words but also by actions.

2. Abraham represents four different meanings which
   are great mysteries of the divine dispensation.
   He stands for the law and the prophets, the people
   of Israel, our Saviour and ourselves who are the
   future sons of Abraham in Christ, and lastly Abraham represents all nonbelievers.

4. The fact that wayfarers could rest at Abraham's camp
   is a *figura* that from every part of the world, from
   the ends of the earth, men will be led to believe in
   God by the apostles, who will be the future sons of
   Abraham.

5. Jesus himself enriched this symbol-for-the-future
   in Matt 22:8-9, where he speaks of the king who sent
   servants out to the roads (*exitus viarum*) to seek
   new guests.

6. And so we may consider the Jews to have been the
   originally invited wedding guests; when they de-
   clined, the Lord sent out His apostles to gather
   in new believers.

7. The tree at Mamre also functions clearly as a symbol
   of the Cross, which by others has been seen as if
   of hard and rough wood.

8. The tree offering shade could also be a symbol of
   Christ, in whom believers are protected and refreshed from the heat and passion of persecutors.

9. Abraham dwells in his tent at any one place only for
   a time. The tent stands for Jerusalem, where the
   law and the prophets, and also Jesus and His apostles,
   were for a time; now, since they are all gone, the
   earthly Jerusalem is worth nothing.

11. The two angels or men who accompanied Jesus *might*
12. symbolize Moses and Elias, who were together with
    Jesus at the Transfiguration.

13. At the end of the world, Abraham will accompany Jesus
    on His Second Coming, since he was our father in the
    faith.

14. Gregory comments on John 8:56
    Then indeed he saw the day of the Lord coming,
    and he knew the mystery of its aspects. He ran
    to the one coming to him in cheerful joy; he
    prepared the feast, and those things which go
    with the wonder of a feast he prepared, made
    very joyful by the spirit of prophecy; he washed
    the feet--all this to show a full and perfect
    submission at His coming.

15. So too Jesus washed his apostles' feet (children of
    Abraham), to purify them spiritually for their tasks.

17. Gregory adds *azimos* in v. 6 and reads *saginatum* for
    bonum in v. 7.

18. The *fatted* calf symbolizes Christ, who is most
    excellent in the *fulness* of good works.

19. The milk is like the law, which is not solid food
    for the spiritually mature.

20-23. The butter is like the stricter life style urged
    upon us by John the Baptist; i.e., there is more
    "churning" to rid us of sin.

24. The three measures of fine flour stand for the three
    post-flood sons of Noah--Shem, Ham, and Japhet, from
    whom the whole human race now descends. From out of
    all mankind the just will one day eat at the heavenly
    banquet.

25. The just are like the purified (baptized) grains
    which are put in *simila*.

26. The unleavened bread is a symbol of being without
    sin. It is baked in the ashes, which are a symbol
    of penance and mortification. Thus sinless and
    purified, we shall be able to enter into *panem
    Christi corporis*.

29. Sarah is a figure of the Church, which administers
    the mysteries (*sacramentorum*) and is obedient.

30. As Sarah conceived Isaac in her old age, and he
    was heir to the promises, so the Church conceives,
    by the word of God, many children, heirs of heaven,
    in the world's old age.

In *Tractatus Origenis 3*[213] Gregory discusses Sarah's laughter:

11. ...which laughter has a twofold meaning: one is that
    the Christian people will be laughed at by unbelievers
    in this age; the other is that, in the future,
    laughter and joy will come, as Jesus told His dis-
    ciples (Luke 6:21, John 16:22). Whence also Isaac
    has the name "laughter."[214]

While Gregory asserts that Abraham may represent four different meanings in scriptural accounts, the main focus of Gregory's
remarks has to do with the Christian Church. Gregory is interested
in the role of the larger community of believers, in the holiness
to which we are called as individuals, in the role of the Holy
Spirit, and in the Jews as a community which continues not to
accept Jesus.

Many of his brief allegories touch new themes--the univer-
sality of the Church, the tree as Cross, its shade as Jesus, the
present worthlessness of Jerusalem, the law as milk and the Bap-
tist's message as butter, and so on. However, in *form*, his allegories are similar to those of Origen.

4. Ambrose

Perhaps the Western Father who best exemplifies the Western
tendency to pick and choose exegetical points from the various
Eastern schools is Ambrose, the dynamic bishop of Milan in the last

quarter of the fourth century. His major commentary on our passage is found in *De Abraham* 1.32-44, which we will summarize here.[215]

32   We should note Abraham's hospitality, a virtue in which
      he was not average.[216] He sat alert at the door of his
      tent at noon (while others would be resting) in order to
      look for the arrival of guests. God rewarded his eager
      longing to be a host with an apparition.[217]

33   God appears to him and he sees three beings; this is a
      mystery of faith. Whomever God shines on, sees the
      Trinity.
          Let us look at some of the ethical meanings of the
      text. Abraham rushed to greet his guests; it is not
      enough to do good--you must also do it quickly.

34   Hospitality earns one first the gratitude of the guests
      and then divine reward. We are all guests in this life;
      if we have not been gracious to our fellow men in this
      life, when we travel on to the next life we shall not
      be hosted by the saints. We have a tendency to look
      down on travellers, but all of us at some time have
      either the desire or the need to travel. Would you
      want a poor traveller to rest with animals in their
      dens rather than with humans? Do you use your own
      poverty as an excuse?

35   A guest will be satisfied with pot-luck (*cibum obvium*).
      Thus Jesus speaks of how blessed one will be who gives
      just a drink of water in His name, and so on.

36   As hosts we need willingness and eagerness. Abraham
      demonstrated these virtues when he served all three
      visitors, even though he regarded only one of them as
      chief.

37   Abraham allowed Sarah to share in the duties and rewards
      of hospitality. A good husband will not be selfish in
      this regard; nor will he be loathe to join in when his
      wife has initiated a similar action. At Mamre, while
      decency demands that Sarah not meet the guests herself,
      nevertheless she truly participates in the deed and
      she can hasten as well as Abraham can.

38   The cakes are hidden under the coals; this reminds us
      to be secretive on sacred topics. Also, in using three
      measures of the one substance of flour, Sarah was pre-
      figuring the trinity of persons and the oneness of
      divinity.

39   The fine flour is more "spiritual." The calf is a sign
      of Christ's passion.[218] The boy who dresses the calf
      is pure and innocent, and so worthy to handle the
      mystery of the calf.

40   So this calf is sacrificed at noon in purity of faith;
      Passover calves are sacrificed at eventide, with blood.
      This good calf will atone for sins; this tender calf
      will not refuse to shoulder the Cross.

41   Abraham stood and served the visitors; he was humble.
     You, however, sit at the main place at table.

42   God knows where Sarah is when He asks after her, but
     He wants to stress her decency and modesty. Adam also
     now reflects on the great task which God wants her to
     perform in having a child at her age.[219]

43   Sarah laughed in anticipation of the laughter that would
     accompany the news of her having a child. Her laughter
     was not a deliberate act of disbelief.[220]

44   The fact that Abraham escorted his visitors when they
     left adds just that much more intensity to the punish-
     ments for Sodom and the other cities.[221]

As §§33 and 38 of the *De Abraham* selection above indicate,
Ambrose was inclined to consider the Trinity as having been typi-
fied at Mamre. In *De Excessu Fratris* 2.96[222] we read that at
Mamre Abraham saw a type of the Trinity; he saw three and adored
one.

>   ...and the distinction of persons being observed,
>   Abraham called only one Lord; to three he offered the
>   honor of his gift but he indicated power to one.
>   Doctrine did not move him but grace; he believed
>   better what he had not learned than we do who have
>   been taught. No one had falsified the type of the
>   truth, so he saw three but worshipped one. He gave
>   three measures of flour and cooked one calf. He
>   believed one sacrifice enough, a triple gift; one
>   victim, a triple service.[223]

Occasionally, however, in discussions on Christ's divinity and
His relationships with the Father and the Spirit, Ambrose will use
the Mamre account as a proof that the pre-Incarnate Christ alone
appeared at Mamre.[224] In *On Luke* 1.25[225] he even implies that
Jesus had to be the divine visitor at Mamre since God the Father
can never be seen by men. Generally, however, Ambrose does not
espouse a subordinationist Christology.

Conclusions. I think it is clear that Ambrose often borrowed
"sermon illustration" types and allegories from the Alexandrian
traditions. Some of the themes common to Ambrose and Origen, for
example, would include allegorizing the *noon* visit with God's *full*
revelation of Himself, that the cakes signify the secrecy which
should surround spiritual matters, that no one is slow in the house
of a wise man, that the calf in some ways is a type of Christ, and
that the three measures of flour are a symbol of the Trinity. Also
common to both churchmen is the contrasting of the humility of
Jesus with the hospitality of Abraham in the matter of footwashing,
and the allegorizing of Sarah's "womanly" inclinations as evil,
and Isaac as representing joy.

On the other hand, Ambrose is personally interested in ex-
horting his flock to hospitality and almsgiving, and so he stressed
the actual hospitality afforded by Abraham and Sarah in a manner
reminiscent of Chrysostom.[226]

Ambrose is responsible for the exegetical mixture which he
makes. His effectiveness as a preacher and church leader could
not have come from the mere imitation of other exegetes.

5. Jerome

St. Jerome (writing 380-415) was one of the outstanding
Christian Scripture scholars of the early Church. His new Latin
translation of the OT from the Hebrew represented a significant
advance in accuracy and style.[227]

Aside from his translation work, however, we have only a few
references to the Mamre account. In *Letter 66*.11, to Pammachius,[228]
Jerome mentions that Pammachius had started a hospice and had
"planted a twig from Abraham's tree."[229] He then proceeds to recall the Mamre story, here summarized.

> Abraham and Sarah did the hosting themselves; they did
> not dilute the merit of their service by using servants.
> Abraham himself[230] washed their feet. He brought the
> fatted calf from the flock on his shoulders; he stood
> by the travellers as a waiter does, and he placed before
> them the food which Sarah herself had cooked. He in-
> tended to abstain from eating.

Elsewhere[231] Jerome advances the allegory[232] that the bright-
ness of noontime is the proper time for God the Father to come in
His full glory to someone worthy like Abraham. He returns to this
theme again[233] in speaking of Lot, who had less faith because of
his long dwelling in Sodom. Lot therefore received a lesser vision
than did Abraham at noon.

Jerome had a high regard for virginity and apparently considered post-menopausal women to be more capable of virgin-like
spiritual progress than their sisters in the child-bearing years.
He often mentions Sarah's aged condition in this regard.[234]

In *Against the Pelagians* 1.34[235] Jerome speaks of our interior
dispositions, which are as important as our actions. As an example
of an interior disposition that was not acceptable to God, Jerome
mentions Abraham and Sarah, who had laughed in their hearts at
Mamre; this indicated a bit of unbelief or lack of confidence, and
was properly rebuked. After the rebuke, they believed and they
received the palm of justice.

In his commentary on *Daniel* 2,[236] on Dan 8:15b, Jerome notes
that at Mamre Abraham saw the three angels whom he thought were
men, and he adored one of them as Lord. This one was Jesus, who
later said that Abraham had seen His day and had rejoiced (John
8:56).

The majority of Jerome's scholarship and commentary on the
Mamre story is literal, after his own and the Antiochean manner.
His understanding that the pre-Incarnate Christ was the subject of
the theophany, and his few spiritual allegories, show his connections with the more dominant patristic traditions.

6. St. Augustine

Augustine (writing 395-427) makes some use of the Mamre passage in his doctrinal works.[237] The most interesting theological
application he makes is to assume that the Trinity appeared at
Mamre, rather than the pre-Incarnate Christ alone. This preference for a Trinitarian explanation fits in with his assumption
that the Trinity can be known from creation, rather than from the
Incarnation of Jesus.[238] The argument is laid out most clearly in
Contra Maximinum 2.26.5ff.[239]

5   It is not stated in Gen 18:1 whether the Father or the
     Son appeared to Abraham at Mamre. In any case, we are
     told that these three men appeared to him; in these
     three we should more probably understand the Trinity,
     which is one God. It is clear from the story that
     Abraham regarded them simply as men. In v. 16 we must
     realize that the number of men whom Abraham escorted
     is not specified. It could have been all three who
     had been with Abraham.

6   The customary explanation has been that Christ and two
     angels had come to Mamre; but what if we also find one
     Lord in the two angels who went on to Sodom? Augustine
     argues from God's intention (18.21), Lot's bowing down
     (19.1), and Lot's singular address in 19.18 (my Lord),[240]
     that the encounter Lot had was a true theophany and not
     just a visit by angels.

7   Abraham did not favor any one visitor. He washed their
     feet and fed them as equals, and so he saw God in all
     of them. Lot dealt in a similar way with his visitors.
     Therefore both Abraham and Lot understood that God was
     in the angelic visitors, whether they were three or two
     in number. In the case of Abraham, the three might be
     the Father, Son, and Holy Ghost, but we know that this
     is one God. In the case of Lot, the two who were sent
     might be the Son and Holy Ghost, since the Father is
     never described as being sent.[241]

Augustine's other uses of the Mamre account utilize literal
elements of the story. The angels who appeared at Mamre had real

flesh. *Letter 95.8*[242] asserts that Abraham washed their feet and
fed them. In *Sermon 277.9*[243] we are told that Abraham did not
merely wash their feet, but actually gripped their feet and ankles
in the process.[244] They were good angels, even though they then
went on to destroy Sodom and the other cities on God's orders.[245]

The miracle of Sarah's conceiving and bearing at such an age
is commented upon occasionally by Augustine. For example, in
Contra Julian 3.11.22[246] we read that God restored fertility to
Abraham and Sarah (especially Sarah) in order to emphasize the
wonder of the miracle. Abraham was sterile relative to an old
woman (even were she fertile), but he could possibly have had
children by a young woman.[247]

Several of these literal comments are repeated in *Quaestiones
in Genesim*, 33-37 and 41,[248] summarized here.

> We should say that God was in all three angels; these
> angels seemed to be men and so Abraham offered them
> food. Abraham might have been able to father offspring
> by a younger woman. Sarah's laughter came from her
> doubt. The fact that she was bold enough to deny
> having laughed makes us wonder when she and Abraham
> realized that their guests were not merely men. It
> could even have been the case that Abraham and Sarah
> first learned this when the angels ascended to the
> heavens at the end of the visit. Lot was also slow
> to comprehend who his visitors really were.[249]

Augustine's precision in explaining how Mamre was a mediate
theophany of the full Trinity (involving three enfleshed angels of
equal appearance) is welcome, since it clearly stresses God's
ability to appear to anyone in any fashion that He wills. His
other observations should also be looked upon as attempts to take
the story literally.

F. Western Writers After Augustine

To conclude our survey of Western Fathers, I include sixteen
writers who worked after Augustine. They are arranged by geo-
graphic region and only then chronologically, starting with African
churchmen close to the time of Augustine and ending with Venerable
Bede.[250] Perhaps the single most interesting feature of this group
is the growing consensus that the visit at Mamre was a visit of the
Trinity.

Africa

1. In *Liber Genealogus* (anon. c. 427)[251] Isaac's name, which
means joy, is related to Sarah's laughter at the promise made at
Mamre. Gen 21:6 is *not* cited.

2. Quodvultdeus (writing c. 440-450) mentions[252] that the
divine majesty appeared *in* the three men at Mamre. This use of
the phrase "appear in" is reminiscent of Augustine, whom Quodvultdeus is known to have imitated.[253]

3. Vigilius of Thapsus (writing before 484) also prefers to
see the Trinity at Mamre.[254]

4. Pseudo-Fulgentius of Ruspe (6th cent.) uses Augustinian
phrasing to explain that the Trinity appeared in the visitors.[255]

Italy

5. Maximus (d. 428) held that Christ alone visited at Mamre.[256]

6. Gregory the Great (writing 595-601) in *Moralium* 9.66.106,[257]
allegorizes Sarah to represent our bodily impulses and Abraham as
our spiritual motivation. Abraham went outside to greet visitors

> because clearly our intellect, as man and lord of our
> spiritual house, should go beyond the door of the flesh
> in knowledge of the Trinity.

Sarah waited in the tent since

> the concern of the flesh, like a woman, should not
> appear outdoors and she should blush to seem to be
> boastful; she should be intent only on necessary
> things as if behind the back of the man, under the
> direction of the spirit. In no way should she know
> how to be boldly uncovered but rather she should know
> how to be shyly restrained.

Sarah's lack of monthly periods and her miraculous rejuvenation
and child bearing can also be taken symbolically to mean that we
grow in faith as our carnal self confidence fails us.

France

7. Cyprian of Gaul (early 5th cent.) rendered much of the OT
into poetic form. The Mamre story received some noteworthy
nuances.[258] The three men were of equal rank (598, 621) and God
was represented by all of them (611). Cyprian puts more terms in
the singular than does the Bible (e.g., v. 4, 602-603). The calf
is described as having no blemishes (609); otherwise Cyprian uses
no allegories in this part of his poetry.[259]

8. Eucherius of Lyons (writing 428) mentions that the cakes
which Sarah baked in the ashes signify humility.[260]

9. Evagrius of Gaul (writing 430) sees the Mamre account as a
Christophany in his Jewish polemic *Altercatio* 2.1.[261]

10. Pseudo-Hilary of Arle (writing 450) notes Sarah's obedience to Abraham (she called him lord in Gen 18:12).[262]

Christian Comments on Mamre   87

11. Faustus Reiensis (d. 480) expresses the Trinitarian interpretation of the Mamre theophany by saying that "from the one, three miraculously appeared to his eyes."[263]

12. Caesarius of Arle (d. 542) was the author of several sermons which eventually were attributed to St. Augustine. The longest of these which refers to the Mamre story is *Sermon 83.* 2-5.[264] This is very clearly imitative of Origen's *Genesis Homily 4*.1-3. In addition, in §5, we find the flour divided into three units as an allegory of the Trinity.[265] In another sermon[266] we find the stress on the hospitality and kindness of Abraham. No allegories are used; the Trinity appeared in the visitors.[267] Food is really eaten and Sarah is really rejuvenated.

Germany

13. Avitus of Vienna (writing c. 516) explains[268] that any OT passage which suggests plural aspects about God is referring to the full Trinity. Thus at Mamre all three visitors were equal in every way and Abraham understood the mystery of the undivided Trinity.

Spain

14. Isadore of Seville (writing c. 624) in *Quaestiones in Genesim* 14[269] finds many allegories in the Mamre story. In general he allegorizes in much the same fashion as his fellow Spaniard, Gregory of Elvira, who wrote over 200 years earlier. Like Gregory, Isadore makes no mention of Trinitarian allegories, although he does find several christological ones. We will mention here those items which Isadore has that Gregory does not have.

> The feet of the visitors stand for *novissima*; therefore the washing of the feet represents the resurrection of all at the end of the world. The butter which Abraham served represents the Gospels, which are the richer law. The wetting of the flour by Sarah signifies Baptism. Sarah's laughter represents the laughter which Jesus will direct at unbelievers or that which He will direct at all His enemies at the Last Judgment.

England

15. Anon. Monk of Lindisfarne, *Life of Saint Cuthbert* (written 698-705). In Book 2, chap. 2 we read that Cuthbert, while guestmaster at Ripon monastery, was visited by an angel in the form of a man. Cuthbert went to prepare an adequate meal but the guest disappeared while he was doing so. As a heavenly reward three fresh loaves of bread were then miraculously found by Cuthbert in the storeroom. The author mentions that angels in the form of men had likewise come to Abraham at Mamre.[270]

16. Bede (674-735) has an extensive commentary on the Mamre
story,[271] which borrows often from writings of Augustine, Ambrose,
Gregory the Great, and others. I will summarize the work here,
mentioning new material, but not identifying his sources.[272]

Verse 1
Mamre and his family were allied with Abraham; so too we,
although of Gentile lineage, also have Abraham as our
spiritual father. This should stir sentiments of humility within us. Abraham and Sarah saw what they thought
were strangers and performed many hospitable acts for
them. Abraham, and all of us, are pilgrims, citizens
of another world; we are tent dwellers in this time,
not permanent residents. However, we have to deal with
secular matters at times and, like Abraham, we look to
a future reward. The heat of the day signifies love
of virtue, and also hope for Christ's coming, and
contemplation of divine love.

Verses 2-3
The Trinity was in the three men; as Abraham spoke to
and adored one, this reminds us of the equality of
worship which the Trinity merits. Abraham lifted his
eyes as a sign for us to contemplate higher things.
The meal reminds us of the later time when Jesus ate
and drank and accepted the hospitality of others.
Jesus, of course, was more interested in evangelizing
and in healing the sick than in the actual meals
themselves.

Verses 6-7
The flour means the inner sweetness of the word of God;
the three measures stand for the three kinds of scripture interpretation--historical, allegorical, and
anagogical. The loaves are packed under the coals;
so also truly spiritual people must come in close contact with the Holy Spirit before they can become "food"
for their fellow Christians. The calf is Christ,
offered by the Father in joy at the return of the
prodigal son (the Gentiles). Christ, in whose blood
the world is redeemed, is the especially chosen one of
all mankind.

Verse 8
The milk stands for the Mosaic laws; the butter for
evangelical perfection. The milk stands for the literal
sense of Scripture; the butter for the mystical sense.
The milk represents the beginning of faith; the butter
for the perfection of faith. As Abraham placed the
food before the visitors, we sons of promise should
place spiritual food before other people. The bread is
the Scriptures; the calf is the message of the Incarnate
Christ. The milk is the perfecting of faith and history;
the butter is good attitudes and good works. We should
remember that we always stand before the Lord in all
of our actions.

Verses 9-10
Sarah rejoiced not only for her own motherhood, but
also for the blessings to be poured out on many nations
through her child. When we receive the Lord with faith

and good works so too will grace come to us. The
angels seemed to eat,[273] in order to prefigure Christ's
Incarnation; they do eat invisible food--the joy of
contemplation. Thus the food which Abraham served was
evaporated as if by a flame and did not serve for
nourishment in any conventional sense.

Verse 12
Sarah was undecided; Abraham did not display any lack
of confidence himself.

Verse 13
Actually Sarah was doubting and overjoyed at the same
time; her doubt was eliminated by the angel's remark
in v. 14.

Verse 14
Bede tries to explain the Vulgate's *vita comite* by
rewording it as *si vita comes fuerit*; a higher interpretation is that the angels are always accompanying
Vita in heaven or on earth, and later on so will the
saints. Bede notes many contrasts between Adam and
Eve and Abraham and Sarah. Adam hid in the bushes
and avoided the light; Abraham ran in the noonday sun.
Adam ate forbidden fruit and had to go away from the
tree of life; obedient Abraham hosted God under a
tree. Eve spoke to the serpent, ignoring God's command, and she got herself and Adam in trouble; Sarah
stayed in the background, fearing God, and she helped
her husband and received an equal reward. Through
Adam and Eve all have suffered; through Abraham and
Sarah we are all blessed by Christ, the new Isaac, who
saves us all.

Verse 16
Abraham escorted his visitors as part of the hospitality
which he offered; blessed are they who so walk through
life that angels will come to escort them to heaven.

It should be clear from the above overview that the Trinitarian
explanation of the Mamre theophany begins to dominate. Of the
twelve writers who touch on the question, nine hold for the Trinity.

Bede refers to meals which Jesus had during his earthly life.
This theme was last alluded to clearly by Irenaeus. He also makes
comparisons between Abraham and Sarah and Adam and Eve. This has
not appeared in any other of our patristic sources.

Excursus

In addition to written works, we should examine ancient
artistic representations of the Mamre story. Perhaps they will be
additional indicators of the popular understanding of this biblical
passage.

There is a mural panel of three young men (usually understood
by art historians to be the three visitors at Mamre) on the north
half of the west wall of the third century Dura-Europas synagogue

in Syria. The central man's robe is of a ligher color than that
of his two companions.[274] There is no representation of Abraham
or Sarah nor any scenery from the story in this mural.

The earliest Christian representation of the visit is from
the Via Latina catacomb in Rome.[275] This mural shows three men
approaching a seated Abraham. The central man is somewhat shorter
than the other two. Abraham is raising his right hand in blessing,
and next to him is a very young calf.

We have literary references to and archaeological remains of
a basilica at Mamre. This building was planned and financed by
Emperor Constantine as part of a series of commemorative churches
in the Holy Land.

Eusebius of Caesarea gives an account of the founding of the
shrine at Mamre in his *Life of Constantine* 3.51-53.[276] Several
remarks in these three chapters indicate that Constantine believed
that the theophany involved Christ and two angels. In his *Demonstratio Evangelica* 5.9,[277] Eusebius mentions an artistic representation of the Mamre scene, presumably at the shrine. This context
also indicates that Christ and two angels were the principal
subjects of the work.

The site of the basilica was excavated by E. Mader. Remains
indicate that originally the church was on one side of a courtyard
which contained an old well and the large oak tree supposedly used
by Abraham.[278]

Opinions vary as to the Emperor's motive for building this
shrine. G. Armstrong reminds us that church building was a meritorious act of philanthropy expected of the wealthy in the ancient
Byzantine world.[279] Further, Constantine himself stressed the
this-worldly aspects of the Christian faith and he may have wished
to embody the emerging alliance of church and empire with these
Holy Land shrines. W. Telfer[280] postulates that Constantine may
have wished to foster unity among Christians by enabling Holy Land
pilgrimages to take place. There may also have been a desire on
his part to function independently of Rome. Massey H. Shepherd[281]
points out that Constantine's deepest grasp of the Christian faith
was in terms of *theophania* rather than of *parousia*. He goes so far
as to suggest that Constantine's interest in theophanies may have
stemmed from his own experience on the eve of the Ponte Milvio.

From the fifth century there is extant a bold mosaic in the
Church of Santa Maria Maggiore in Rome.[282] This mosaic, which is
under an upper level window, is subdivided into three sections.
Across the upper area we see Abraham bowing to three young men with

halos; the central figure is also outlined with a mandorla. On
the lower left we see Sarah preparing three round loaves of bread
at a worktable and Abraham extending his right hand in a blessing
over the bread (the last two fingers of the hand are clenched).
To the right we see the three men seated at a table with the bread
on it. Abraham is presenting them a platter, which holds an entire
miniature calf. In this lower right scene the central guest does
not have the mandorla. In front of the table one can see a wine
jug (mostly restoration).[283]

The sixth century Church of San Vitale in Ravenna has a much
larger mosaic on the north wall of the sanctuary which depicts the
Mamre scene.[284] Here three men with halos are seated at a table
holding three quarter-creased round loaves, and Abraham serves
them a miniature calf on a platter. Sarah is also present. The
right third of this mosaic space contains a depiction of Abraham
sacrificing Isaac.

On the opposite sanctuary wall there are representations of
Abel and his offerings and of Melchisedech with his bread, wine,
and a table. The two mosaic panels taken together, and in relation
to the main altar in the church, carry the theme of eucharistic
sacrifice.[285] Abraham is a type of Jesus in his placing of bread
and wine upon a table. His act of blessing the bread in the Maria
Maggiore panel may have been intended to convey a similar impression. We found no such allusions to the eucharistic liturgy in
our written sources.

The next extant Mamre art works are from the eleventh or
twelfth centuries, according to Reau, and are therefore beyond the
scope of this investigation.[286]

In conclusion, I want to take a stand on just one aspect of
the Via Latina mural and the mosaics in Maria Maggiore and San
Vitale. I think these three works should be considered as *possible*
symbolic representations of the entire Trinity, with Jesus as the
central figure.

These artists subtly take advantage of the ambiguity of the
biblical account. The three visitors are equal in some respects,
such as age, appearance, dress, and halos (often used). Yet one of
the three can seem to be set off by his stature, location, gesture,
or, as at Santa Maria Maggiore, by a mandorla (in one of the two
scenes). Except for this last case, the other ways of setting off
a chief visitor can hardly be said to be clear indicators of mere
angelic status for the two remaining figures.[287]

Just as the energies of Christian commentators focused primarily on theological and spiritual levels of meaning in the Mamre
story, so also early Christian art is primarily interested in the
divine. One looks in vain for artistic scenes wherein Sarah prepares really large quantities of bread, milk, and the other dairy
products. The only calf of decent size is in the Via Latina panel.
There are no extant art examples of any members of Abraham's household being involved in the event. The footwashing could well have
been a worthwhile subject for some artisan or patron.

Conclusions to Chapter II

Let us review the patristic commentary on Mamre in light of
the eight guidelines which we established at the beginning of this
chapter.

1. We proposed that OT events acquired significance for
early Christians in relation to, or as foretastes of, Christ's
later accomplishments. Most of the Fathers up to Jerome considered
the theophany at Mamre as an activity of Jesus. Given the brevity
of many of their comments on this specific biblical passage, it is
fair to suppose that for many of them the Mamre story had no other
major significance.

2. We assumed that the literary contexts of an OT passage
need not be as important to the Fathers as typological considerations of it. Indeed, few Christian authors showed much interest in
the Mamre story's immediate literary context. Chrysostom spoke
favorably of Abraham's acceptance of circumcision as being the
reason for the theophany. Bede mentioned Mamre as being an ally of
Abraham. The Emperor Constantine, and his biographer Eusebius,
were the only ones to concern themselves with the actual site in
the Holy Land. Ambrose and a few others contrasted Abraham's virtue with the sinfulness of Sodom. Chrysostom, Jerome, and Augustine tried to contextually explain Sarah's laughter. Augustine's
remark on Abraham's physical state, while speculative, is another
rare example of Christian interest in the context.

3. In addition to looking for types and allegories which
related OT passages to the life of Christ, we also planned to look
for ones which helped to explain the life of the Church. In fact
some of the Mamre commentary was directed toward church life.
Origen saw his theory of Reserve reflected in Abraham and Lot.
Gregory of Illiberia and Isadore of Seville made many ecclesial
allegories on the passage, some of which were unfortunately very
anti-Jewish. Some of Bede's remarks were also exhortatory.

The outstanding commentators on how the Church should respond to Abraham's example at Mamre were certainly John Chrysostom and Ambrose. Their call to almsgiving was deeply personal and inspiring, even though we do not hold today that the three visitors were necessarily poor.

4. We expected the early Fathers to mix together historical types, sermon illustrations types, and allegories. Given the patristic tendency to search for types in the OT, it is surprising that parallels were not drawn between the meal at Mamre and later meals of Jesus during his earthly life. Irenaeus, Tertullian, Novatian, Cyril of Jerusalem, and Bede made very brief observations as to Christ's future dealings with men, including his eating with them. Novatian, Origen, and Ambrose mentioned Christ's washing of feet at the Last Supper. In the latter set of remarks Novatian is outstanding. After him none of the Fathers ever hinted that Christ at the Mandatum was *repaying* the descendants of Abraham in any way. Nor do we find the Mandatum related to the Mamre foot washing in art works.

As we saw in the Excursus, the mosaic at San Vitale (and possibly the one at Maria Maggiore) had eucharistic overtones to it. This similarity or type is not present in our written sources, unless one wishes to argue over context in the work of Cyril of Jerusalem.[288]

5. We held that Philo's allegories were frequently imitated by Christian writers. This was clearly the case with the Mamre story. Origen and Ambrose were the two leading imitators.

6. We anticipated differences in interpretation between the Alexandrian and Antiochean schools. The Antiochean Fathers clearly avoided allegory on our passage. Chrysostom's interest in Abraham's hospitality in all its ramifications, down to how fast the bread could be baked, was very unlike the majority of patristic material on Mamre. Some writers, such as Jerome, avoided allegory and typology part of the time.

7. We mentioned that, of the three patriarchs, Abraham was rarely seen as a type of Jesus. In the ancient Christian understanding of the Mamre account this proved to be the case. For some, he and Sarah functioned as representatives of mankind, or at least of believers. For Zeno they were models of faith in God's promise concerning Isaac. For Chrysostom and Ambrose they were models of hospitality *qua* charity. But these are not types involving Jesus as such. We saw in guideline number four above how little development there was of any Last Supper or Mandatum motifs, which would have involved Abraham as a type.

8. We assumed that biblical passages served as proofs in discussions of other doctrines or aspects of theology as well as of those directly involving Christ. There were obviously doctrinal uses made of the Mamre passage. For several reasons many Fathers saw Jesus as divine and preexistent at Mamre. Thus the later Incarnation of Jesus was a reasonable act of divine love. The Church's continuing conflict with Arianism eventually led to a deemphasis on any biblical interpretations which could cast doubt on the equality of Jesus with the Father.

Other writers used Mamre in discussions on the nature and role of angels.

The explanation of the visit as Trinitarian grew from being a minor allegory in Origen through Augustine's full and free theophany to become the dominant opinion of the Eastern and Western churches into the Middle Ages.

As with the first guideline, here also it seems clear that patristic preoccupation with angelology, Christology, or Trinitarian theology diverted energies which might have been put to better use in analyzing this story as part of Abrahamic and Genesis cycles.

Turning to the hermeneutical modes and rules mentioned by James Sanders at the beginning of this study, we find that the Christian material follows the same general tendencies as does the Jewish material.

We were able to find a few instances in the rabbinic writings where the human faults and weaknesses of Abraham and Sarah were mentioned, but there were not many such cases. In the Christian and Alexandrian Jewish commentary Sarah's faults received some attention, but Abraham seems to constantly have been a model of great faith--whether in Philo's *De Abraham* 118 or in Origen's *Genesis Homily 4*,3 or in Chrysostom's *Homily 41 in Genesim* 378 or elsewhere. Thus the theologizing hermeneutic spoken of by Sanders was largely absent.

Rather, much of the material studied in this chapter can properly be said to draw lessons for the reflection or for the faith of the audiences. It was a moralizing method of hermeneutic.

Given the Christian and Alexandrian Jewish interest in theophany and in the use of different sorts of typology and allegory, the majority of the resulting commentary was supportive or constitutive,[289] as was the quite different rabbinic commentary. The only major exception to this was the use made of the Mamre

account by Chrysostom and Ambrose. These two bishops often
challenged their urban congregations to assist in alleviating the
very real poverty and destitution to be found in their cities.

CHAPTER III

EARLY JEWISH HERMENEUTIC OF GEN 32:23-33

The Massoretic Text of the Jabbok story presents relatively
few difficulties.[1] The opponent, who first appears in v. 25, is
called simply a man and is never more clearly identified. The
most difficult section is v. 29. שָׂרִיתָ (from שׂרה) is used only
here and in Hos 12:4-5.[2] Here it has two objects, אלהים and
אנשים.[3] The final word in this verse (וַתּוּכָל) refers to both objects.[4] The form פְּנִיאֵל of v. 31 is a variation of the more common
פְּנוּאֵל of v. 32. The yod may have been used to relate the name in
v. 31 more clearly to the phrase פָּנִים אֶל-פָּנִים.

At this point we shall review the work of a representative
number of 20th century scholars to see whether they exhibit common
areas of interest.[5]

Some commentators endeavor to put the Jabbok story in its
proper relationship to the larger series of Jacob traditions. Such
efforts usually serve to anchor later remarks about the effect of
the event upon Jacob. Most scholars of non-Jewish background seem
to be willing to consider the Jabbok event as a genuine theophany,[6]
while Jewish scholars are much more inclined to consider the opponent to be merely an angel.[7]

A good deal of the effort of recent scholars has been centered
on various supposed elements of the pre-literary Jabbok traditions.
Thus, some examine geographical inconsistencies in the account,
possible alternate sequences in the roles and fortunes of the two
wrestlers, or pagan dawn-spirit or river-spirit parallels to the
mysterious opponent. Other topics frequently discussed include
possible earlier etymologies for the name Israel, remote origins
behind the prohibition against eating the thigh nerve, and possible
origins for the place name Penuel.

While there is a relative amount of agreement on many of these
pre-literary elements, other aspects of the story have proven to be
more difficult. There are at least four different current proposals
as to the nature of the blessing received by Jacob: that it is the
name itself or the promise of it; that it is a legitimation or a
confirmation of the blessing of Isaac; that it is a sharing in some
sense in divine vitality; or that it is the wound itself and the
effect it has on Esau. The few who comment on Jacob's question to

97

the angel in v. 30 disagree as to its import. For example, von
Rad looks upon it as a primitive boldness on Jacob's part with
regard to what is holy, while Benno Jacob sees it as an indication
that Jacob wished to be able to send the man a gift when the promise would later come true (cf. Judg 13:17).

There are two basic opinions as to the main theme of the
story. Some commentators are impressed by the psychological and
moral struggles which Jacob experienced at Jabbok. They see him
as being a better man afterwards. On the other hand, many scholars
find little evidence of Jacob's inner conversion. For these the
two principal lessons are the initiative of God throughout this
entire encounter and the mix of human qualities of Jacob precisely
as our ancestor in faith. Morgenstern and von Rad respectively
can serve as representatives of the two camps.

Benno Jacob's remarks on our passage are a fascinating amalgam
of the two schools of thought just mentioned. He also dwells extensively on Esau's later reactions at his meeting with Jacob, and
on the justice of Esau's grievances. His reflections on the way
in which we should model our lives on that of our ancestor Jacob
are perhaps best summarized by saying that we must fight for God
with God's help.

Recent analysis of the Jabbok story, then, has not come to as
much of a degree of consensus as has recent scholarship on Mamre,
but the general outlines are clear. I would recommend von Rad's
and Elliger's presentations as very comprehensive. As with the
Mamre commentary, none of the writers mentioned presents a systematic description of the history of ancient Jewish or Christian
hermeneutic of the Jabbok passage.

A. Ancient Versions and Targums on Gen 32:23-33

We turn now to the principal Jewish versions and Targums and
their treatment of our passage.[8]

Some Targums supply the expected definite article on the הוא
of v. 23, though its omission in the MT is of little consequence.[9]
Several Targums explain in v. 24 that Jacob took across *everything*
that he had.[10]

Many Targums take the wrestler to be an angel; some even
identify him as Michael or Sariel. Many of the Targums record a
dialogue in v. 27 wherein the angel explains that he must leave at
dawn in order to join the choir of praising angels in heaven.
Jacob's remark in v. 31, that he had seen God face-to-face, is
modified in several Targums to refer to an angel or angels.

In this chart a capital X indicates the presence of the topic in question. A small x indicates that the source can be taken as a partial witness, or that inferences can be reasonably drawn from its context.

	LXX	Neof.	Frag.	Cairo	Onk.	Ps.J.	Pesh.	Sm.P.	Sm.T.
Def. art. with הוא of v. 23.		X		X				X	X
Addition of *all* in v. 24.		X		X	x		X	X	X
Opponent is an angel; name is included where found.		X Sariel	x	X	x	X Michael			
Dialogue in v. 27 about angelic choir.		X	X	X		X			
Explanation of name Israel is modified.	X	X		X	X	X	X		X
V. 31 is modified about seeing God.		X			X	X	X		
MT Peniel/Penuel sequence is maintained.	X				X	X			
Peniel is in both verses.		X							
Penuel is in both verses.							X	X	X

The mysterious opponent's explanation of the name Israel in
v. 29 is frequently changed. Some Targums refer to angels rather
than to God; one refers to angels and drops the reference to men;
and the *Peshitta* speaks of one angel and one man. The LXX separates the two objects by means of the two verbs. Some LXX manuscripts even add a future sense to the latter part with "you will
be strong with men."

The two spellings, Peniel and Penuel, evoke no speculation.
The versions and Targums either retain the MT sequence, or spell
both as Peniel or Penuel without comment.

Three additional traditions are to be found only in Targum
Ps.-Jonathan. There is an incident in v. 25 wherein Michael challenges Jacob to tithe from his goods and from his children. Levi
is selected for special duties as a result of this tithe. In v.
32 the sunrise is held to be earlier than usual, and reference is
made to the sunset of the day when Jacob had left Beersheba. That
sunset had been later than usual. Thirdly, in v. 33 *Ps.-Jonathan*
speaks of the nerve in *cattle* and *wild animals*, as well as in
Jacob's *right* thigh.

B. Other Rabbinic Traditions on Gen 32:23-33

Major rabbinic writings on the Jabbok story include *Genesis
Rabbah* 77-78 and *Canticles Rabbah* 3.5-6. I have assembled the
rabbinic material into ten groupings, starting each time with these
two sources and then presenting related material. After the last
grouping (on the nerve prohibition), five more sources will be
studied individually.

1. Dinah

The mention of Jacob sending across his wives and sons prompts
an inquiry as to the whereabouts of Dinah.[11] She was hidden by
Jacob in a chest to keep her from Esau. There is a question as to
whether Esau might have turned out to be a better man if he had
been allowed to marry Dinah.

2. Jacob the Ferryman

The Jabbok current is strong and difficult to cross. Jacob
took his family and possessions across by boat. Indeed, he himself
acted as ferry(man) (גשר), taking them from one side to the other.[12]

3. Jacob Alone

The Rabbis dwelt often on the fact that Jacob was by himself
when the trial came at Jabbok. *Gen. Rab.* 77.1 cites Deut 33:26,
"There is none like God, Oh Jeshurun." Jeshurun means the finest
and most praiseworthy among you. In fact, you will find that all
which God plans to do in the time to come He has anticipated and
done by means of holy people in this world. Thus God will raise
the dead, make rain to cease, and so on, as Elijah raised the dead,
made rain to cease, and so on. Israel is another such holy person;
at Jabbok he was left alone, and so also we read in Isa 2:11, "The
Lord alone will be exalted on that day."

There are several short remarks on the solitary figure of
Jacob to be found in *Ozar Midrashim*.[13] Jacob is "alone" in God's
favor; He says, "I put My name on Abraham and Isaac, and again on
you will I confer it; from now and forever I confer My name because of Jacob's strength." Another possibility was that Jacob
was "alone" in a hiding place (cave?) with his ancestors. In
another sense, he was "alone" in righteousness. Indeed, his children are a "people dwelling alone."[14] Another tradition is that
the Lord is often "alone."[15]

Another scriptural verse which reminds us of Jacob at the
Jabbok is Isa 40:31, "They who wait for the Lord shall renew their
strength."[16]

3a. Jacob the Self-reliant

The main *Canticles Rabbah* commentary was initiated by Cant
3:6, "What is coming...with all the fragrant powders (אבקת) of the
merchant?" In contrast to Abraham and Isaac, Jacob was the more
self-sufficient. Indeed, his business success came from the dust
under his feet. In fact, all the business success with which
Israel prospers in this world is due to the merit of the dust of
Jacob our father.[17] That dust was taken by God and put under the
throne of His glory, as it says in Nah 1:3, "...and the clouds are
the dust of His feet."[18]

4. The Encounter

There are several traditions concerning the opponent of Jacob.
One[19] is that the angel came in the form of a shepherd, with flocks
of sheep and camels. He and Jacob agreed to each take their own
animals across the river. Jacob took his flock across and then
returned to see if he had left anything behind.[20] It was on
Jacob's return that the wrestling took place.[21]

Another tradition is that the angel came as a robber chieftain with flocks.[22] He encouraged Jacob to cooperate in moving their combined cattle. He himself took across all of Jacob's flocks in the wink of an eye; Jacob then had to make several trips to move the robber chieftain's flocks. Eventually Jacob became suspicious at the need for more trips, and he called the man a sorcerer. He took a clump of wool and stuffed it in the robber's throat and called him a sorcerer again, saying, "Witchcraft is not allowed to succeed at night."[23] The angel decided to let Jacob know with whom he was involved. He touched the ground and fire shot forth. Jacob was not afraid; he said that he was made of fire himself, as it is written in Obad 1:18, "The house of Jacob shall be a fire."[24]

Another tradition is that it was Esau's guardian angel who wrestled with Jacob.[25] We know this from Jacob's remark to Esau in Gen 33:10, "...to see your face is like seeing the face of אלהים." Here the commentator wishes us to understand אלהים not as God but as an angel, specifically Esau's guardian.

Cant. Rab. has roughly the same exegesis. The angel is the guardian of the wicked Esau, and the import of Jacob's plea in Gen 33:10 is that Esau's face resembles his guardian's face. Because Jacob wrestled so well with Esau's angel, in the future, when other nations come to attack Israel, God will say to them, "Your angel could not stand up to their father Jacob; shall you overpower them?"

In *Tanhuma B*[26] we have a compound scene. Four bands of angels were sent to keep Esau occupied that night. The first band said, "We are sons of Isaac," and Esau fought them furiously. The second band said, "We are sons of the son of Abraham," and Esau also fought them. The remaining bands then said, "We are brothers of Jacob," and on account of Jacob they were not opposed by Esau. Meanwhile, Jacob was by himself; he did not know what trials the Lord had in mind for him. He was very afraid of Esau. God sent Michael in the form of a shepherd to have a contest with Jacob, in order to ease his fear. Eventually Jacob escaped from Michael. The whole trial was meant to encourage Jacob.

The fact that Jacob was involved in a contest which lasted all night should teach us not to go out at night.[27]

5. Jacob is Wounded

In the opening words of Gen 32:26, "He saw[28] that he could not overcome him," we do not know who is who. *Gen. Rab.* 77.3 says

that the angel, who at that point was covered with dust, was the
one who could not prevail. Jacob is characterized as one who came
against his opponent with five "amulets"; these were his own merit
and the merits of Abraham, Sarah, Isaac and Rebecca. God remarked
to the angel, "You cannot even prevail over his own merit!"[29]

Another opinion offered in *Cant. Rab.* 3.6 is that Esau's
angel saw the Shekinah standing over Jacob. When he saw the
Shekinah, he knew that he could not win, and so he surrendered to
Jacob.[30]

The injury inflicted by the angel is a mysterious one. *Gen.
Rab.* 77.3 suggests that the angel "touched" the holy ones who were
destined to come from Jacob, i.e., the generation of persecution.[31]

The verb ותקע in v. 26 is given some further explanation in
Gen. Rab. 77.3. It could mean that the angel flattened the bulge
of the thigh, or that he split the muscle as one splits a fish,
or that he moved it aside. This last possibility finds some support from a phrase in Ezek 23:18, "My soul turned (ותקע) from her."[32]

The contest lasted all night. *Gen. Rab.* 77.3 notes that "the
two of them kept struggling all that night, one on top of the other;
the shield of one at the shield of the other."

6. The Opponent Asks for His Release

The angel's request to be released and Jacob's bold refusal to
do so offer opportunities for rabbinic development. In *Cant. Rab.*
we are reminded that up to this point in the story the reader is
not sure who is in control of whom, but v. 27 indicates that it was
the angel, who had to go at dawn to sing praises to God, who was
losing the contest.[33]

In *Gen. Rab.* 78.1 the nature of angels is dealt with. Citing
Lam 3:23, "God's mercies are new every morning," the theory is advanced that heavenly angels do not praise a second time. Every day
God creates a new band of angels and they sing a new song and then
depart. An obvious objection to this theory is that the angel who
wrestled with Jacob was not new that morning after the match. The
reply is that this was a chief angel such as Michael or Gabriel,
and chief angels do not depart or get replaced.[34]

Gen. Rab. 78.2 continues by recalling that Jacob was not impressed with his opponent's need to sing. He told the angel that
the choir would not miss one singer; then Jacob said, "Those angels
who came to Abraham did not go away from him until they had blessed
him." The angel replied, "They were sent to do that; I was not."[35]

Another objection was brought up by the angel. He said,
"Because the ministering angels revealed the mysteries of God,
they were exiled from their regions for 138 years. Shall I heed
you and be exiled from my region?"[36]

Finally, the angel told Jacob, "In the future God will appear
to you at Bethel and He will change your name; I will be standing
there also."[37]

7. The New Name and Its Meaning

Gen. Rab. 78.3 addresses itself to the problem that, after
receiving the new name of Israel, the patriarch is often called
Jacob in other places in the Bible. One opinion put forward is
that the name Jacob was not to be abolished entirely but would
have a second place to Israel. The opposite opinion is also mentioned, namely that the name Jacob should continue to dominate and
the name Israel be second in use.[38]

Another scriptural passage often linked with Gen 32:29 is
Isa 44:26, "The Lord confirms the word of his servant." The servant angel performed his task in renaming Jacob at the Jabbok,
and the Lord confirmed that when He gave Jacob the name Israel in
Gen 35:10.[39]

The phrase "...you have striven with God and with men, and you
have prevailed," evokes only a few comments. *Gen. Rab.* 78.3 takes
אלהים to mean gods (angels). The sense then is "you have striven
with heavenly beings (העיליונים) and you have beaten them; with
dwellers here below (התחתונים) and you have beaten them." The
heavenly being[40] was the angel--perhaps Esau's guardian angel.[41]
The earthly beings were Esau and his chiefs.

Yalkut, Hosea 528 (on Hos 12:5) mentions that Jacob prevailed
over the angel, and that Jacob was beseeched and then blessed by
the angel. The phrase from v. 29, "You have striven with gods and
with men," is explained as referring to the Princes in Israel and
the Rulers in exile in Babylon respectively.[42]

According to *Gen. Rab.* 78.3, an alternate rabbinical understanding of שרית in v. 29 was to read שַׂר אַתָּ. The sense then is,
"You are a prince with God."[43]

In *Mekilta Yohay* יתרו 19.3, Moses is compared to Jacob; Moses
is also deemed worthy of "receiving" the great name Israel, for he
also had "striven with God" in his lifetime.

8. The Opponent Leaves

When Jacob asked the angel what his name was, his question
was not answered. The Rabbis saw this reticence as part of the
ordinary way in which angels act. In *Gen. Rab.* 78.4, two scriptural verses are cited: Psa 147:4, "God gives all the stars their
names (שמות)," and Isa 40:26, "God calls them all by their name
(בשם)." The change in number from שמות to שם implies a change in
name. This teaches us that angels have no permanent names; their
names may not be at a later time what they are now. Therefore,
the angel who spoke to Jacob was reluctant to give his name. A
similar case occurs in Judg 13:18. There to Manoah's question the
angel replied, "Why do you ask my name, seeing that it is wonderful (פלאי)?" By this answer the angel meant that he did not know
if and when his name would be changed.[44]

The blessing which the angel gives in v. 30 caused little
comment from the Rabbis. It is usually numbered in a standard set
of five blessings which Jacob received in his lifetime.[45]

9. The Sunrise

The rising of the sun upon Jacob became the focus of several
traditions. *Gen. Rab.* 78.5 says that the sun had healing effects
upon Jacob, but only cast light for other people. In fact the sun
healed Jacob but burned Esau and his men. God said to Jacob, "So
shall your children gaze at the sun and it will heal them, and it
will burn the nations." Mal 3:19-20[46] speaks of the bright day of
the Lord which will burn evildoers and heal the just.[47]

In *Gen. Rab.* 68.10, we read that in Gen 28:11 God had caused
the sun to set early.[48] Thus Jacob "lost" some hours of daylight
when he left the Holy Land. God "gave it back" to him when he
reentered the Holy Land, in Gen 32:32. In all this Jacob is a
sign to his children. They would later go into exile[49] and later
return.[50]

Jacob's limping is involved in a few traditions. In *Gen. Rab.*
79.5 a story is told of a Rabbi who travelled to Rome and back.
On his return trip he began to limp and another Rabbi said to him,
"You resemble your ancestor (Jacob)."[51]

In *Exodus Rabbah* 30.11 there is a parable about a king who
"brings wood" near to a high official. The king stands for the
all-powerful God who "brought wood" near to Jacob, as a result of
which Jacob limped.[52]

10. The Sciatic Nerve Law

The word גיד in rabbinic literature can mean a tendon, blood vessel, or a nerve.[53] Many translators also use the English "sinew" for it. The common understanding of the term גיד הנשה in this passage from Genesis is that it means the sciatic nerve. Since we have a fair amount of legal material about this regulation, I have divided it into three parts: the Mishnah, the Talmud, and other sources.[54]

10a. Mishnah *Hullin*

In the *Mishnah*, tractate *Hullin*, chap. 7, we have six regulations dealing with the גיד הנשה. We shall briefly summarize them here.

Mishnah 1
The prohibition of the thigh nerve is operative inside and outside of Israel; before and after the destruction of the Temple; for sacrificial and table fare, whether wild or domestic; and for both thighs, right and left. It does not apply to birds, which have no כף. It does apply to embryos (Rab. Judah denies this). Its fat is allowed to be eaten. Butchers can be trusted to remove the nerve properly (Rab. Meir denies this).

Mishnah 2
One may sell meat with the nerve not removed to a Gentile since the location of the nerve is well known. When removing the nerve, one should remove it completely. Rab. Judah says that one need only remove a symbolic part of it (a part adequate to fulfill the law about removing it).

Mishnah 3
If one eats an olive-sized portion of the nerve, he is liable for forty lashes; if he eats less, he is still guilty. If he eats an olive-sized portion from two thighs[55] he is liable for eighty lashes (Rab. Judah holds for only forty).

Mishnah 4
If one were to cook a thigh containing the nerve and the meat was affected by the nerve as to taste, then the leg is not to be eaten. In cases like this we should consider the leg meat as if it were made of turnips; i.e., the nerve would have to give a taste to a comparable amount of turnips. The rabbinical custom is to assume that there must be sixty times as much bulk of meat as nerve in order to assume that a taste is *not* imparted.

Mishnah 5
If the sciatic nerve were cooked with other nerves, and was still distinguishable, it should be removed and the previous taste standard would then be applied. If it was not distinguishable, all the nerves should be removed and the previous taste standard applied.

Mishnah 6
The prohibition applies to clean animals but not to
unclean ones. Rab. Judah extends it to unclean animals
since the Genesis prohibition would have included all
animals before the Judaic period (i.e., Sinai). Others
reply that the law is from Sinai, but was written of
in this place in Genesis to show the origin of the
custom.

10b. Talmud *Hullin*

These six laws are greatly expanded on in the Babylonian
Talmud, tractate *Hullin*, chap. 7, pp. 89b ff. I will summarize
these Talmud remarks here, noting the page on the left margin.

Mishnah 1
89b Dispute over the application of the law to unborn
     sacrificial animals. This is tied into the question
     of whether or not the sciatic nerve imparts a taste.

90a Dispute continues, involving the question of the time
     needed for development of nerves in a foetus, and the
     fact that the law was binding on the sons of Noah
     (i.e., before Sinai). Attempt is made to restrict
     discussion to born animals. Distinction is then made
     between animals which will be offered and then eaten,
     and animals which will be entirely burnt. Several
     Rabbis dispute the application of the law in these
     ritual cases.

90b Rab. Judah seems to be in favor of at least allowing
     the nerves to be burned in whole-burnt sacrifices.
     Discussion continues on disposition of sciatic nerves
     in various types of offerings. Rab. Judah says that
     only the *right* thigh of an animal must be stripped of
     its nerve (the custom is for one hip, and reason de-
     cides for the right hip). There follows a discussion
     on why Rab. Judah was so sure about this.

91a There seem to be two nerves in question: one near the
     bone and one near the flesh.[56] There are fewer regu-
     lations concerning the latter. Dispute turns to whether
     there should be forty or eighty lashes for eating both
     sciatic nerves of a single animal. Further discussion
     on if two animals are involved. Rab. Judah consistently
     holds for the more lenient punishment.[57] He notes that
     the text in Gen 32:33 speaks of *the* leg, which must
     mean the stronger one; this would be the *right* one.
         The Rabbis specify that the verse refers to the
     nerve which is spread like a bundle over the whole leg,
     to the exclusion of the outer nerve. Rab. Joshua
     agrees with Rab. Judah that only the right leg is in-
     volved. He says that the wrestling match was as when a
     man grasps another person and his hand touches the
     hollow of the other's right hip.
         Another Rabbi said that the angel appeared to Jacob
     as a pagan (as a worshipper of stars כעובד כוכבים).
     The custom is for Jews to keep pagans on their right
     when walking with them, so Jacob's own right leg was
     the more easily hurt. Another tradition is the opponent

appeared as a wise man. The custom is for Jews to walk
on a scholar's left, so Jacob's own right leg was the
more easily hurt.

The Rabbis say that the angel came up behind Jacob
and dislocated both thighs. They explain בהאבקו עמו
of Gen 32:26 as meaning that the two sent up the dust
of their feet to the throne of glory, as we see in
Nah 1:3. In so doing, the Rabbis seem to be stressing
the dust and not the grasping actions in the wrestling
bout, since they wish both sciatic nerves to be removed.

The nerve is called הנשה because it slipped from its
place and went up (שנשה ממקומו ועלה); a similar phrase
can be found in Jer 51:30, "...their strength has
slipped away (נשתה)." Another Rabbi cites Isa 9:7,
"The Lord sent a word to Jacob and it will fall upon
Israel," as referring to the nerve injury to Jacob and
the fact that all Israel observes the nerve prohibition.

Another tradition is that in Gen 43:16, "...slaughter
an animal and prepare it," *to prepare* means to remove
the sciatic nerve, since the law was operative among
all the sons of Noah.

Another tradition explains why Jacob was alone; he
had gone back to get some small jars. We know that
Jacob valued all his hard-earned possessions. The man
then wrestled with him all night. This teaches us
that an important individual should not go out at night.

91b   Gen 32:32 notes specifically that the sun rose on Jacob.
A Rabbi asks, "Did the sun shine on him alone? Did it
not shine on all the world?" Rab. Isaac replied that
the sun which had set early on his account now rose
early on his account. For in Gen 28:11, "He came to a
place" means that since he had resolved to go back and
pray, the earth contracted for him and he came to the
place immediately. Then he prayed and the sun set
early so that he would rest exactly on the spot (site
of the future Temple).

Digression on Jacob's ladder dream. The angel tried
to explain why he had to be released to sing praises.
His time to sing had been scheduled for that day since
the beginning of creation. Digression on the exact
duties of praising angels.

92a   Remarks on Hos 12:5, "He strove with the angel and
prevailed (ויכל), he wept and pleaded with him." The
subject of ויכל may be unclear, but we know from Gen
32:29 that Jacob became stronger than the angel.
Similarly, we may not know who wept and pleaded in
the Hosea verse, but by looking at Gen 32:27, we know
that the angel wept unto Jacob. Gen 32:29 also brings
the following comment,

The angel hinted to Jacob that two princes were
destined to come from him; the Ruler in exile in
Babylon and the Prince in the land of Israel.
Thus he hinted to Jacob about the exile.

92b   Dispute over the meaning of the "fat" of a foetus.
It means either the fat of the animal or of the sciatic
nerve. Dispute over the application of the law to a
foetus taken alive from a slaughtered dam. Rab. Judah
is always lenient; e.g., he advises one merely to cut
the nerve near the hip bone cap, rather than to remove
the entire nerve. Continuation of dispute over whether
a sciatic nerve imparts a taste.

93b   Return to the matter of there being two nerves in
        question: the one near the bone and an outer one near
        the flesh. It is noted that at certain places along
        the leg the inner nerve is actually nearer the flesh
        and the outer one nearer the bone. Question arises
        again about inspecting the work of butchers.

        Mishnah 2
        Question of whether we may send a whole thigh or just
        a segment to a Gentile. In general the nerve would
        be harder to identify in a segment.

94a 94b Questions about buying from and selling to Gentile
        butchers, in matters relative to the sciatic nerve
        prohibition.

96a   The question of removing all the sciatic nerve or
        only a symbolic portion of it. Further discussion
        of Rab. Judah's view towards a symbolic part.

        Mishnah 3
        Guilt incurred by eating the nerve. Dispute over
        whether we are speaking of nerve only near the hollow.

96b   Further dispute over the quantity to be consumed to
        incur guilt.

        Mishnayoth 4 and 5 combined
        Problems arising from the roasting or boiling of
        sciatic nerves. Disputes on roasting.

97a   Conversation turns to forbidden fats and other
        substances.

97b   Problems with salted and marinated thighs. Review
        of the sixty-to-one rule. Mention made of an older
        standard which equated forbidden substances to onions
        or leeks.

99b 100a Further disputes on the taste standard.

        Mishnah 6
100b   Dispute on overlapping prohibitions about sciatic
        nerves and uncleanness in applying the law to unclean
        animals. Did the sons of Jacob observe the law?
        Taste standard and law on foetuses reviewed.

101a   More questions on the taste standard and multiple
        prohibitions.

101b   Digression on Sabbaths. The law was given on Sinai
        because Gen 32:33 speaks of the children of Israel.
        The Jews were not called children of Israel until
        Sinai; thus the law was given at Sinai but written
        down in this place to indicate why it was given to
        them. Rab. Judah objects that they are called the
        children of Israel in Gen 46:5, so the prohibition
        should date from that point (entry into Egypt).

10c. Other References

In addition to the *Hullin* section of the *Babylonian Talmud*, we have several references to this prohibition.

In *Antiquities* 1.20.2, Josephus notes that Jacob refrained from eating thigh nerves in meat in honor of his own injury, and that Jews observe this custom also in honor of Jacob's experience.

In *Gen. Rab.* 78.6, it is also mentioned that the nerve is called הנשה because it slipped (שנשה) from its place. The opinion is advanced that the fat of the sciatic nerve is allowed, but that it is avoided out of devotion. Rab. Judah's preference for only the right thigh is mentioned, as well as the alternate possibility that the left thigh could be the prohibited one. Custom favors avoiding both nerves.

In the *Jerusalem Talmud*, tractate ערלה 3.1, the topic is grain and vegetable harvests prohibited by Lev 19:23ff. A review of multiple prohibitions leads to a citation of the sciatic nerve prohibition as an example of a *partial* prohibition (i.e., against *eating*, but not against other uses of the nerve).[58]

In *Yalkut*, Leviticus 536, mention is made of the non-prohibition of the nerve in the thighs of birds.[59] In *Cant. Rab.* 1.16 (on Cant 1:2), and *Pesikta Rab. Kahana* 12.1, we find catalogs of divine commands to the patriarchs, and the sciatic nerve prohibition and Gen 32:33 are specifically mentioned. In *Yalkut*, Leviticus 445, both opinions are given on the matter of sciatic nerves in whole-burnt offerings. A brief restatement can also be found in *Yalkut*, Leviticus 505, on guilt offerings, which are also whole-burnt.[60]

The preference of Rab. Judah for the prohibition of the nerve only was used as a legal analogy in other cases. Thus, in *Hullin* 134b, the *right* shoulder should be used in certain sacrifices. In *Kiddushin* 21b, on piercing the ear of a slave about to be freed, *the* awl used must be a great awl (borer); *Horayoth* 12a speaks of *the* anointed priest, which must mean the high priest. All of these conclusions depend on the use of the definite article, just as Rab. Judah had noticed the definite article on הירך in Gen 32:33.[61]

The *Mishnah* and *Babylonian Talmud Hullin* opinions on dealing with Gentiles recur in other Talmud tractates. In *Sanhedrin* 59a, Rab. Jose b. Hanina observes that any law given to the sons of Noah and repeated at Sinai is meant for both Jews and Gentiles. If a law was given to the sons of Noah but not repeated at Sinai, it should apply to Israel only. We Israelites have no such case of

the latter except for the sciatic nerve law. In *Peshahim* 22a and
in the minor tractate *Kallah Rabbati* 9.8,[62] it is mentioned that
one may sell thighs containing sciatic nerves to Gentiles.

There are several mentions[63] of a five-fold prohibition
involving the sciatic nerve; obviously the case was an aid to
memorizing legal material. A man cooks in milk and eats a thigh
containing the sciatic nerve on a festival day. He is guilty of
unnecessary work on two counts--lighting the fire and cooking. He
is also guilty of cooking meat in milk and of eating the same forbidden combination; and he should be punished for eating the
sciatic nerve.[64]

C. Later Traditions

In Chapter I above, I entered all the rabbinic materials
under sixteen thematic groupings. Here I would like to present
five ancient commentaries as an appendix to the ten thematic groupings of this chapter.

My reasons for doing so are simple enough. The passages from
Pirke Rab Eliezer and *Midrash Abkir* evidence a further stage of
exaltation of Jacob and should be presented in their entirety.
Rashi has several new observations on linguistic and exegetical
aspects of the passage, and can also be best appreciated in a full
summary. The *Zohar* has many more citations of the Jabbok material
than it had of Mamre, but few of these are properly within the
scope of our study; I thought it best to explain my selection of
Zohar citations in a unified analysis of all the *Zohar* material.

1. *Pirke Rab Eliezer*

Chapter 37 of Rab Eliezer's commentary deals with the Jabbok
incident. It starts by citing Amos 5:19, "The day of the Lord
shall be as if a man fled from a lion and a bear met him."

> The lion is Laban; the bear is Esau, who wished to slay
> Jacob. Esau had no shame within himself. Jacob prays,
> citing Gen 31:3, about his obedience, and says, "...and
> I fear him (Esau)." Thus we have the popular saying
> that one should not fear a leader or ruler, but rather
> one in whom there is no fear of heaven.
>   God sent an angel to save Jacob from Esau. He came
> as a man and they wrestled all night. In the morning
> the angel begged to be released, explaining that he
> had to go to chant praises. Jacob did not want to let
> him go, so the angel began to sing from on earth. The
> angels above heard his voice and said, "We hear his
> voice in honor of the Righteous One." Concerning Him
> we read in Isa 24:16, "From the ends of the earth we
> hear songs of praise, of glory to the Righteous One."

Jacob demanded and received the angel's blessing.
Then Jacob wanted to know the angel's name, which
turns out to be Israel (the same as Jacob's new name).
Jacob wanted to overpower the angel and to throw him
down. So the angel dislocated Jacob's thigh nerve,
making it like the fat of something dead (i.e., numb).
   The angel reminded Jacob of his promise to tithe,
in Gen 28:22. So Jacob then tithed 550 animals. The
angel said, "Don't you have sons?" So Jacob set aside
the first-born sons and counted until the tithe fell
on Levi. Michael then brought Levi to heaven and God
blessed Levi, and so instituted the priesthood. He
also decreed concerning their income.[65]

2. *Yalkut Shimoni* and *Midrash Abkir*

The principal comments on our passage can be found in *Yalkut*,
Genesis 131-133. The author incorporates substantially all of *Gen.
Rab.* 76.9 and 77-78. The only exception is 78.3, §3, involving
comments on Isa 44:26, and a discussion on whether Jacob or Israel
would be the patriarch's more prominent name after Jabbok.

The *Yalkut* comments on the sciatic nerve law, taken mainly
from *Bab. Talm. Hullin*, have already been mentioned. In addition
the *Yalkut*[66] adds excerpts from the *Pirke Eliezer* passage mentioned
above (chap. 37). The author of *Yalkut* drops most of Eliezer's
comments on the Jabbok story itself, but does mention the matter
of tithing the cattle and then Levi. Levi's divine approbation is
recounted.[67]

The other significant commentary to be found in *Yalkut*,
Genesis 132 is a dialogue between Michael and God; this is identified by Ginzberg as part of a work known as *Midrash Abkir*.

The "man" who wrestled with Jacob was Michael, who
said, "I am one of the chief praising angels; thus you
have striven with me, and do you still fear Esau?" One
opinion is that Michael was destined to lose his
chiefhood only when he yielded it to Jacob.
   Jacob asked Michael why he feared the dawn. Meanwhile bands of angels encouraged Michael to ascend for
praising, but they also speculated, "...or will Jacob
be our leader?" In spite of his pleading, Michael was
not released until he imparted a blessing. He said,
"Happy are you, born of a woman, who entered the heavenly
palace and escaped."[68]
   Another tradition is that while they were wrestling
a band of Michael's angels came to assist him, but God
held them back, saying, "Michael's strength is failing."
Indeed, Michael saw that he could not overcome Jacob,
so he touched his thigh nerve. God said to Michael,
"You have given my priest a blemish." Michael replied,
"Am I not your priest?" God said, "You are my priest
in heaven, and Jacob is my priest in the Holy Land."
   Michael asked Raphael to heal Jacob, so that men
would say, "The sun of the future shines on the just to
heal them."[69]

God asked Michael why he had wrestled with Jacob.
Michael said, "I did it for your glory." God said, "Be
with Jacob now and protect him."[70] God said, "You are
great, and Jacob will be great...you are a fire and
Jacob will be a fire (Obad 1:18)...you are the chief
of all the serving angels, and Jacob will be chief of
all the faithful." When Michael blessed Jacob, he
said, "It is the will of God that your sons be holy,
as you are."

3. Rashi

Rashi's remarks on our passage are worth looking at; perhaps
a verse-by-verse summary would be the best format to use, with
verse numbers on the left.

23   The text does not mention Dinah. She was hidden in a
     chest, so that Esau would not see her. Rashi agrees
     that Dinah might have had a good influence on Esau if
     he had been allowed to marry her.

24   Jacob himself acted as a ferryman for his family,
     cattle, and possessions.

25   Jacob was left alone because he had gone back for
     some small jars. One meaning of the verb ויאבק might
     be that one gets covered with dirt (dust). Rashi pre-
     fers the meaning of a man entangling himself (ויתקשר),
     which is an Aramaic word. He cites two examples from
     the Bab. Talm. of this meaning for the root אבק.
     Another meaning could be grappling (עניבה), as is
     done in wrestling.
        The opponent might have been Esau's guardian angel.

26   The hollow of the thigh is the flesh of the upper
     thigh, which is shaped like a ladle. ותקע means that
     the nerve was strongly pushed from its place. Such
     usage can be found in Jer 6:8, "My soul is removed
     from you," and in the Mishnah title לקעקע ביצתן which
     means to root out.

27   The angel had to go at dawn to sing praises. Jacob's
     demand for a blessing can be taken in the sense of
     "grant me the blessings with which my father blessed
     me, which Esau now claims.[71]

29   The angel, in renaming Jacob, intends that Jacob shall
     no longer be honored for deceiving and superceding,
     but for rulership and openness. The angel says that
     later God would officially change his name at Bethel,
     and that there the angel would also acknowledge
     Jacob's right to his father's blessings.
        The angel wanted Jacob to wait until Bethel; but
     Jacob would not wait. So the angel, against his will,
     granted his rights.
        The "men" with whom Jacob strove were Laban and
     Esau.

30   The angel remarked that he and his companions did
     not have permanent names, but names which changed
     according to their assignments.

32   A Midrash tells us that the sun rose on Jacob for his
     benefit--to heal his limping.[72] The early sunset at
     Beersheba is balanced by the early sunrise here.
     Jacob was limping *when* the sun rose, not *because* it
     rose.

33   The nerve is called הנשה because it moved from its
     place, in the sense of coming up and out. Similar
     usages can be found in Jer 51:30, "Their strength
     went away," and Gen 41:51, "God has made my troubles
     go away from me."

4. Maimonides

     Maimonides mentions the Jabbok incident only once, in *Guide
to the Perplexed* 2.42. Angels "appear" in the OT in the sense of
prophetic visions or dreams. For example, the man who wrestled
with Jacob was a prophetic revelation because it eventually became
clear that he was an angel.

     In his *Mishne Torah*, Book 5 (קדושה), tractate מאכלות אסורות
chap. 8, Maimonides reviews the legislation and traditions concerning the sciatic nerve. Without presenting his opinions in
detail, I think it is safe to say that he rather closely followed
the stricter interpretations favored by the Rabbis; he seems to
ignore Rab. Judah's lenient tendencies.[73]

5. *Zohar*

     The *Zohar* brings many new interpretations to the Jabbok ac-
count.[74] The few elements in common with prior themes include
(a) that the opponent was Esau's angel;[75] (b) that the morning was
the time when angels had to sing praises;[76] (c) that the dust of
the match rose to God's throne (Nah 1:3);[77] (d) that Jacob was
seeking the right to his father's blessing;[78] and (e) that Jacob
was healed by the sun, since he is well in Gen 33:18.[79]

     The most striking exegetical item among the new *Zohar* exegeses
is the suggestion that Jacob was left alone at the river because he
had deliberately exposed himself to danger.[80]

Conclusions

     A comparison of the main interpretations found in the Targums
and translations with those found in later rabbinic materials shows
a good deal of continuity.

     The entire corpus of writings consistently holds that the
opponent of Jacob was an angel.[81] The identification of this angel
as Michael, made by *Ps.-Jonathan*, is one of the two traditional

identifications. The other, that he was Esau's guardian angel,
cannot be ruled out as a basis for Targum remarks, since Esau's
angel was not necessarily an evil force.

Later commentators also took steps to avoid any suggestion in
v. 29 that Jacob wrestled with God Himself. As in the Targums,
reference was usually made to his having wrestled with an angel.
One interesting later device was the Prince in Israel/Ruler in
Babylon interpretation.

All the items new with *Ps.-Jonathan* are later to be found
elsewhere--the matter of Levi and of tithing, the early sunrise,
and the development of Oral Torah with regard to Gen 32:33.

In the rabbinic traditions about the Mamre account we noticed
a good deal of variety in the identification of speakers in the
different verses. The Jabbok story, at first sight, does not have
such variety in interpretation. However, the rabbinic tendency
for elaboration is evident. The angel was a chief praiser, such
as Michael; or he was Esau's guardian, either neutral or partial
to Esau's intentions. The angel opponent is variously depicted as
a shepherd, robber, pagan, or scholar; he causes fire to erupt
from the ground, and Jacob boldly repels his magical maneuvers.
Other angels are employed, either to serve as a chorus to Michael's
doings, or to keep Esau occupied. The nature of Jacob's wound is
frequently mentioned, even though a miraculous sun will soon heal
his leg. The effect of many of these traditions, it seems to me,
is to heighten the sense of awe and mystery surrounding the actual
encounter.

We will now evaluate these Jewish materials in light of Patte's
hermeneutical norms which were mentioned at the beginning of this
investigation. His first guideline was that a biblical verse can
be interpreted by other biblical passages.

The first category of scriptural citations consists of those
which help us to view the story in its context.[82] Different Rabbis
reminded us of events in Genesis 28, when Jacob was first blessed
by his father, and where there was the early sunset, the dream of
the ladder, and his promise to tithe on his return. Genesis 33
also is often recalled, as Esau finally met with Jacob and Jacob
utters the fulsome praise of 33:10. Gen 35:10, the second mention
of Jacob receiving the new name, is also recalled.

Two other passages can help us understand details of the story.
Judg 13:18 shows us another angel refusing to give his name, in
that case to Manoah. Hos 12:5, a specific reference to the Jabbok
story, is used to demonstrate that the angel lost the struggle.[83]

Secondly, many citations serve as proof-texts for the Jabbok story. Perhaps the most frequently used are Mal 3:19-20 (Eng. 4:1-2); Nah 1:3; and Obad 1:18. If we reverse our viewpoint on the proof-texts, however, and ask what effect the Jabbok story may have had on their content, then passages such as Deut 32:10-12, Isa 44:24-28 and the book of Obadiah take on new riches for us.

We have two examples of everything being meaningful in Scripture. The first is the attempt to explain the force of ותקע in v. 26, by citing other verses in Scripture (five in all). Another fine detail, the definite article on הירך of v. 33, was used not only for the opinion that only right thighs should be cut, but also as a legal analogy in other Talmudic cases.

We have just a few examples of the telescoping of persons, places, and events in the rabbinic traditions. Perhaps the most surprising telescoping is the choosing of Levi by God for the priesthood during this same night. I assume that the *Ps.-Jonathan* and *Pirke Rab Eliezer* uses of this tradition are not the only cases where the origins of the Levitical priesthood were commented upon.[84]

At the end of grouping 7 we find a mention of Moses, who also "strove with God" during his lifetime. Since no other details are given, I suppose one could argue that we do not have a true case of telescoping here; but, since the tradition is that he too in some sense is named "Israel," I think it is an example of the idea that all sacred history is contained in the Scriptures.

Jacob is certainly presented as a moral example. He is self-reliant, solicitous for all his possessions, protective of his children, eager to receive a blessing from the angel, brave, courageous, and physically strong. We even have the concept of merit applied to him, although not on the scale with which it was applied to Abraham. Jacob's merit brings good fortune to his descendants in matters of holiness, business, war, and protection from persecution. God Himself will be "alone" on the Last Day, as Jacob was alone at the river Jabbok.

Patte's second norm was that Scripture is meant to be actualized. He found that such actualizations often dealt with current cultural changes rather than with salient events.

The bulk of actualizations which the Rabbis made about the Jabbok story concern themselves with cultural changes. Regulations concerning the sciatic nerve are primary among the applications to everyday life. In addition to these extensive regulations we have a few other pieces of practical advice such as to be careful about

being outdoors at night, and to be diligent in caring for
property.

There are some apparent references to salient events but
often these are quite general. For example, mention is made
several times of enemies of the Jewish people,[85] but only the
Emperor Hadrian and Rome are clearly singled out, and these
briefly.[86] Other specific elements mentioned are the Levitical
priesthood and the offices of Prince in Israel and Ruler in Babylon, but no further reflection on them occurs in our references.

Let us recall the hermeneutical modes and rules devised by
James Sanders which we examined at the start of our research. We
will first look for instances wherein the human faults and weaknesses of the biblical figures are mentioned. We find very little
of this "theologizing" hermeneutic in our Jewish sources.

For the Rabbis the primary reason why God sent the angel was
clearly to encourage Jacob to stand against Esau;[87] the implication *may be* that Jacob's fear was so great that, without special
encouragement, he might have fled. Rashi mentioned Jacob's past
deceptions and his superceding of Esau, but none of our other
sources brought these up (at least not within their analyses of
the Jabbok story).

The rest of the traditions moralize. They drew lessons,
mainly from Jacob's experiences. We are called upon to be like
him; we must be courageous, self-reliant, careful of our possessions and our promises.[88] Like Jacob, we should be eager for
divine blessings; we should be holy[89] and alone in righteousness.[90]

Granted that the actualizations of this passage by Jewish
writers were mainly cultural ones, and that a moralizing hermeneutic prevailed, we may reasonably classify ancient Jewish commentary
on the Jabbok story as supportive or constitutive rather than
challenging or prophetic, as Sanders uses these terms.

CHAPTER IV

EARLY CHRISTIAN AND ALEXANDRIAN JEWISH USE
OF GEN 32:23-33

Introductory Remarks

We will present Christian comments on the Jabbok passage in
the same manner as we did in Chapter II. For the reader who wishes
to choose from among them, I would recommend Justin Martyr, Philo,
Origen, Procopius, and Chrysostom in the East, and Ambrose, Jerome,
Augustine, and Gregory the Great in the West--with Philo, Chrysostom, and Augustine being the most important three of all.

We should recall at this point that some of the Christian
understanding that Jesus was at the Jabbok may have originated in
Jewish Christian readings of Christ into OT events involving
Michael. Daniélou has also postulated another Jewish Christian
concept, namely that there was a leading angel whose name was
Israel.[1] This angel, who gave his own name to Jacob, was seen by
Jewish Christians as a symbol for Christ. In his reconstruction
of this concept, Daniélou worked primarily with references in
Philo, Origen, and Justin. In this chapter we will touch on
Justin's statement on the matter.

A. Early Greek and Latin Apologists

1. Justin Martyr

In *Trypho* 58.10, Justin cites the Jabbok incident as one
wherein the Christ, in human form, wrestled with Jacob.[2] Justin
comments[3] elsewhere that Jesus changed Peter's name and also the
names of the sons of Zebedee; these actions on the part of Jesus
should be a clue to us that the same person had also changed
Jacob's name to Israel.[4]

In *Trypho* 125.3, Justin explains that in Hebrew the name
Israel means "a man conquering power" (ἴσρα = one conquers, and
ἤλ = power).[5] The mysterious event of Jacob wrestling with his
opponent is a sign of the Incarnate Christ's future battle with the
devil in the desert. There too the evil power would be defeated
and disgraced. Another sign[6] which was given at Jabbok was when
the opponent numbed Jacob's thigh. In this case Jacob's numbness
signifies the numbness of pain and suffering which Jesus would have
at His crucifixion.

Another relationship between Jesus and the Jewish people lies
in the name Israel. Israel was really an old name for Jesus; when
He gave this name to Jacob, He was signifying that Jacob and his
descendants are called to be a part of the true Israel--the
followers of Jesus.[7]

Justin is aware of the literal Hebrew meaning of the name
Israel, as well as of a tradition about Israel being another name
for Jesus. His attempts to find types at Jabbok for Jesus'
changing the names of some of His followers and for Jesus' tempta-
tion in the desert will not be followed by other Christians.

2. Irenaeus

In *The Apostolic Preaching* 5.1[8] Irenaeus implies that Jesus
is the subject of all OT theophanies; thus He would have been the
wrestler and the one who gave Jacob his new name.

3. *Ascension of Isaiah*

In 7.3-5 of this early anonymous work,[9] Isaiah is being
escorted by an angel; Isaia asks the angel what his name is, but
the angel refuses to tell him. It is possible that the author had
cases like Gen 32:30 and Judg 13:18 in mind.

4. Tertullian

Tertullian mentions the wrestling match once[10] as a case
wherein an angel took on human flesh and form. If angels can be
sent on missions like this, how much more could God have taken on
true humanity in Jesus.

On other occasions Tertullian advocates that the opponent was
Jesus.[11] In *Adv. Marc.* 4.39.7[12] Tertullian explains that the name
Israel means "one who prevails with God." This could certainly
have been based on the Jabbok story.

Tertullian's use of the fact of the temporary enfleshment of
an angel as an argument for Christ's Incarnation is a theological
interpretation more than an attempt at exegesis. Nevertheless it
is an attempt to take the story literally, as is his understanding
that the name Israel in Hebrew means one who prevails with God.

5. Hippolytus of Rome[13]

Hippolytus tells us that some people think that the name
Israel means "a man who sees God," while others think it means

"a man who will see God."[14] This is the first instance of a
Christian derivation of the name Israel based on the supposed
Hebrew אִישׁ רָאָה אֵל. Presumably Hippolytus knew this from Alexandrian circles, since the idea can easily be traced to Philo. This
derivation will dominate in both Eastern and Western hermeneutics.

6. Novatian

In *De Trin.* 19.6-14[15] Novatian comments on the Jabbok story.
I will briefly outline this commentary here, putting paragraph
numbers on the left.

6   Sometimes in Scripture Jesus is depicted as God and an
     angel, sometimes as God and a man. In the latter case
     the Scriptures speak of what Christ would be; they
     portray in an image what Christ would become in truth.

8   The struggle between the man and Jacob at the Jabbok
     makes no sense unless it prefigures that future conten-
     tion between Christ and the sons of Jacob, which is
     said to reach its fulness in the Gospels.[16]

9   The sons of Jacob strove against Jesus and prevailed,
     but they became lame and uncertain of their own faith
     and salvation. They still need His blessing.

10   The wrestler gave Jacob the name Israel, which means "a
     man who sees God." Jacob's opponent was not only a man
     but also God.

11   Jacob definitely knew that his opponent was divine since
     he was told "you have prevailed with God."

12   Jacob realized the importance of this event (*vim sacra-
     menti*), and so he called the place "Vision of God."

13   Jacob held onto the man as if he (Jacob) were the victor,
     but he asked for a blessing as a lesser.

14   God and man wrestled with Jacob; in Christ, God and man,
     this symbol is fulfilled.

Novatian takes the wrestling as a type of the future struggle
between Jesus and the Jews. This unfortunate "sermon illustration" typology, as well as the one about the spiritual lameness of
Jews, will often be echoed in our sources.

B. Alexandrian Hermeneutics

1. Philo

Philo frequently allegorized various elements of the Jabbok
account, although he does not have one major commentary on the
entire passage as such. Using the Loeb texts, we will collect

Philo's remarks under six categories which follow the general
sequence of the story.

(a) *Wrestling in the Soul*

   In *De Mut. Nom.* 12.81-82 Philo reflects on Jacob, the tripper
and supplantor. A supplantor is one who must disrupt the founda-
tions of passion; he must wrestle and fight hard, and know well
the exercises of the soul. In *De Sobr.* 13.65 we read that Jacob
represents the virtues of self-discipline since he was an athlete,
exercised in a contest with the passions. In *Leg. All.* 3.58.190
we see that pleasure lies in wait to overpower the good mind, but
pleasure shall be overthrown by "Jacob." He is an expert in
wrestling, the kind of wrestling in which the soul wrestles with
the ways which oppose her, fighting passions and evils.[17]

(b) *The Nature of Jacob's Opponent*

   Philo consistently regards the opponent as a good angel.[18]
In *De Mut. Nom.* 12.87 we note that Jacob was renamed by an angel
attendant on God, a word, and not by God Himself. In *De Somn.*
21.129 Philo identifies the opponent as a divine word.[19] This
angel first regards Jacob as a pupil,[20] and then at Jabbok as an
athletic trainee with himself as a coach. In *De Mut. Nom.* 2.14
the wrestler is called the "unseen" opponent; this could either
refer to the darkness of the night bout or perhaps to the angelic
nature of the wrestler.

(c) *Jacob is Graced*

   The principal effect of Jacob's encounter with this messenger
from God was to make him spiritually more perfect. In *De Ebr.*
20.82-83 Jacob is a symbol of good Jewish people.[21] Consider
Jacob at the river as he is raised to seeing God from a state of
only hearing of God; he is brought to deeds from mere words, and
to perfection from progress. It was God who helped him to understand all this. Thus Jacob's name is a sign of learning and progress, while Israel signifies perfection. The vision of God reminds
us of the meaning of the name Israel. In a sense Israel (seeing
God) is strong in God and Jacob (seeker of virtue) is strong among
men.[22]

(d) *Meaning of Jacob's Injury*

   Philo assigned spiritual values to Jacob's injury. Thus in
De Mut. Nom. 35.187 he discusses the limitations of human virtue.
Virtue sometimes seems to suffer some "numbness" or to be a bit
"lame," as when Jacob limped. In *De Praem.* 7.44 Philo speaks about

how truly blessed are those who receive a vision of God, tempered
to human limitations. Such was Israel, called a seer of God, who
saw that God exists. He also received "numbing" as a prize, a
numbing of false pretense and arrogance.[23]

(e) *Meaning of the Sunlight*

In *De Somn.* 14.79 Philo discusses figurative meanings for the
word *sun*. One meaning is sense perception, since the sun shows
all perceivable things to the understanding. For example, when
Israel left Penuel the fact that the sun was shining on him means
that Jacob reverted to a life of mere sense perception.

(f) *Other Aspects of Jacob*

In *De Mut. Nom.* 5.39 Philo praises those who are devout
toward God and, at the same time, are attentive to human matters.[24]
Jacob was such a person, strong with God and with men.[25]

In *De Sac. Abel* 36.120 Jacob is taken as a symbol of spiritual
work and progress, which derive from a natural goodness.[26] Israel
stands for the virtue of contemplating God.

These summaries show how completely wide of the literal was
Philo's treatment of the Jabbok story. He used it only as a basis
for spiritual allegories and did not relate it to its Genesis
contexts at all.

2. Clement

In *Pedagogus* 1.7.57[27] Clement says that it was Jesus who
wrestled with Jacob; it was Jesus who led and guided and wrestled
and anointed the athlete Jacob against evil. Jesus was at the same
time the trainer of Jacob and the teacher of all men, in that He
would not reveal His name to Jacob (because He had not yet been
born of the flesh). Jacob said that he had seen God face-to-face;
the face of God is the Word (Jesus). Jacob was renamed Israel,
which means that he had seen God the Lord.[28]

In the *Stromata* we have several explanations of the names
Jacob and Israel. We are told that Jacob means athlete because
Jacob exercised with many truths.[29] Israel means "he who sees
God."[30] The true gnostic, who has done much contemplation of
spiritual things, becomes a true Israelite, a true seer.[31]

3. Origen

The few citations which we have from Origen are almost all in
Latin translations by Rufinus. I will indicate those which are in
Greek.

Origen sometimes held for Christ having been at Jabbok. Thus
in *Homily 1 on Matthew*, 6[32] we learn that Jesus wrestled with
Jacob *per angelum*, and that He allowed Jacob to win so that He
might bless Jacob's purity of heart and that He might rename him
Israel. In his commentary on *Romans* Origen says[33] that Israel was
given that name when he saw God, and the new true Israelites
(Christians) will be those who have "seen" Christ.[34]

Another explanation is had in *De Princip*. 3.2.5[35] where the
topic is the waging of spiritual battles. The theme is that man
by himself needs divine aid to overcome the power of evil. In the
Jabbok story there were two angels: one who wrestled *with* Jacob,
and one who wrestled *against* him. The good angel (the one who
wrestled *with* him) also gave him the name Israel; the good angel
helped to keep the fight going. The Scriptures also say that
Jacob was strong with God. This means that Jacob finished the
fight and so was led to God.[36]

Origen noted the names given to the patriarch. In *Homily 11 on
Exodus*, 5[37] Jacob is described as an athlete in spiritual matters,
whose name means wrestler and supplantor. In *Homily 15 on Genesis*,
3[38] Origen remarks that both names, Israel and Jacob, continue to
be used after Jabbok. The sense of Origen's analysis of the two
names seems to be that the name Israel is somehow superior. For
example, Jacob asks the wrestler his name (an unwise move) while
the sons of Israel refrain from eating the thigh nerve (a devout
practice).

Most of Origen's allegorical remarks are spiritual in intent.
Presumably he came to the idea that there were *two* angels present
because he needed one to symbolize Jesus and one to symbolize evil.

C. Later Eastern Writers

Let us briefly consider here five Eastern writers later than
Origen. These Fathers generally concentrate on Christ's presence
at Jabbok, and on anti-Jewish lesser typologies and allegories.
Procopius' intention to preserve many traditions makes his Jabbok
commentary somewhat confusing.

1. Eusebius of Caesarea, in his *Church History* 1.2.7-9,[39]
holds that Christ was appointed as teacher of knowledge about the
Father to all men; therefore He is the subject of all scriptural
theophanies. He appeared to Jacob at the Jabbok in the form of a
man. Christ, and not an angel, was the wrestler.[40]

2. Didymus the Blind,[41] in commenting on Zech 2:2 (English
1:19)[42] notes that the name Israel means "he who mentally sees God."

3. Cyril of Alexandria identifies the wrestler as Jesus. In
Expositio Symboli Nicaeni 1.16[43] the wrestler is "the word of God
made man, in the form of the Father, according to a spiritual image
and according to all which is unchangeably His." In *De Incarna-
tione* 31[44] Jesus is described as the figure of the essence of the
Father.

In the former citation Jacob's lameness also symbolized later
Jewish lameness of unbelief in Jesus; in the latter the struggle
symbolized the Jewish struggle against Jesus.

4. John Maxentius, a Scythian monk of the sixth century,
wrote in *Contr. Nest.* 2.15 that Jacob wrestled with a man in a
vision; this man was Jesus.[45]

5. Procopius of Gaza has several insights on the Jabbok story
in his *Commentarii in Genesin* 32.[46] We will summarize them here,
by Migne columns.

455 The Jabbok is a river in Arabia, now called the
     Iambyces. The word Jabbok means "contest." Who was the
     man-God who fought with Jacob? It was Christ, the word
     of God. See that Jesus does not struggle with those who
     do not cross the river; they are precursors of those
     Jews who have refused the grace of Baptism.[47] They stay
     in the shadows of night and ignorance, etc.
     These unbelieving Jews are infirm and crippled.
     Jacob's lameness at Jabbok signified this because his
     thigh stands for his seed. Some of the Jews "recover"
     from their lameness through charity and faith in Christ.

457 Jacob grasps in order to seek salvation; his name
     is changed to Israel, which means "a mind which per-
     ceives God."[48]
     God does not reveal His name to Jacob since no
     creature can comprehend its essence. Any name could
     only tell of some aspect of God; for this reason Jacob
     called the place *figuram Dei*.
     Jacob then wrestled with a demon in the form of
     Esau. A helping angel stood by Jacob during the fight,
     whom no devil could overwhelm. In order to remind
     Jacob that he was the more powerful angel, the helping
     angel touched his thigh and made him limp.
     The phrase "he saw that he could not overwhelm him,"
     of v. 26, is ambiguous. If the subject were Christ,
     how could He not overwhelm Jacob? If the subject were
     Jacob, then the object could be Christ.

459 Procopius advances the suggestion that the subject
     was the demon. In any case, the helping angel also
     wrestled with Jacob in order to make him a stronger
     negotiator with Esau.
     The Jews do not abstain from the thigh nerve because
     it was numbed, but because God as a man wrestled with
     Jacob and touched his nerve. So in our own day it is
     easier to believe in the Incarnate Christ because of
     such lesser signs.[49]

Besides his reconstruction of the wrestling, Procopius does
bring in some positive explanations concerning the wounding of
Jacob's thigh. The wound was a reminder (perhaps not appreciated)
for Jacob as to who was sent from heaven. The Jewish custom of
abstaining from this nerve in animals is an attempt to honor God's
presence at Jabbok. As with Origen, Procopius' involved explanation of the wrestling is not at all in accord with the plain meaning of the text.

D. Antiochean Hermeneutics

1. John Chrysostom

Chrysostom's few literal comments on the Jabbok story are to
be found in *Homily 58 in Genesim* 2-3.[50]

(509) The wrestling match shows God's φιλανθρωπία;[51] He, in
the guise of a man, wrestled with the just one (Jacob) to teach
Jacob that nothing terrible was going to happen to him.

God touched and dislocated Jacob's thigh in order to drive
out cowardice from him, and to encourage him to meet with his
brother Esau.

God asked to be released in order to show Jacob his own
strength.

God asked Jacob his name to show His own condescension, and
to teach Jacob who the wrestler really was. He gave Jacob the new
name Israel, which means "one who sees God."[52]

Jacob asks his opponent's name but he is not told it. God's
refusal was as if He had said, "Remain within your own limitations."

Jacob's remark about having seen God face-to-face is another
indication of his new-found confidence.

(510) The sun rising on Jacob reminds Chrysostom of the sun
which had shone on Abraham at Mamre; general remarks follow on how
greatly God shines His blessings down on all of us.[53]

Chrysostom is concerned with the context of the Jabbok story.
He sees the wrestling as intended to help Jacob deal with Esau. As
simple as this interpretation may seem to us, many of his prede-
cessors preferred allegorical devices instead. Theodoret is close
to Chrysostom on this passage. Neither man spends time discussing
the mode of theophany or doctrinal points which could be made by
using verses in this passage.

2. Theodoret

In *Quaest. in Gen.* 36.92[54] it is asked why the angel had
wrestled with Jacob. It was to inspire courage in Jacob; it was

as if the angel had said, "If you can beat me, can you still fear
a man like Esau?" For further encouragement the angel again indicated the reason for Jacob's victory when he gave him his new
name, saying, "You have struggled with God, and with men you will
be strong."

E. Western Writers Through Augustine

1. *Commentarius in Symbolum Nicaenum*

The author notes[55] that the Father does not reveal His true
name (and hence His true self) to men. Jacob sought His name at
Jabbok and was simply told that "it is wonderful."[56]

2. Hilary of Poitiers

Hilary asserts that Jesus wrestled with Jacob at the river.[57]
He notes the incongruity of Jacob's prevailing and yet seeking a
blessing.

> Your mind and body are at cross purposes; your mind is
> elsewhere as you are acting.

Jacob seeks a blessing because he believes that the opponent is
truly God:

> You do not see with physical eyes that which your sight
> of faith perceives.

The wrestler is subject to Jacob, looking to the mystery of
His human suffering in the future.[58] Jacob's faith is not under-
mined by the appearance nor by the weakness of the wrestler.

3. Phoebadius

Phoebadius[59] points out that appearances of Christ to OT
figures such as Abraham or Jacob at the Jabbok do not imply that
at that time He was corporeal, visible, or mortal. Rather, these
appearances occur in image, mystery, dream, or vision.

4. Gregory of Illiberia

Gregory says that Christ appeared at the Jabbok as a man so
that He might present an image of the future struggle which would
take place with Israel when He would come according to the flesh.
Jacob believed his opponent to be Lord; and so he accepted the new
name Israel, which means "a man who sees God."[60]

5. Ambrose

Ambrose treats of the Jabbok story in his *De Jacob* 2.30-31.[61]
We will summarize that analysis here, adding in remarks from his
other writings.

(30) Jacob, who had a heart free of agitation and full of
peaceful feelings, cast away all his belongings and then wrestled
with God. This shows us that whoever keeps aloof from material
things becomes more spiritually perfect. "Wrestling with God"
means to take up the struggle for virtue.[62]

Jacob's faith and devotion were very strong. Christ touched
his thigh in order to signify that He would be born of Jacob's
line and would be coequal with God. Jacob's numbness foretells
the cross of Jesus--His own body would suffer numbness and uncon-
sciousness.[63]

The sun rose on Jacob to signify that the cross would beam
upon (*inluxit*) the sons of Jacob; also the Sun of Justice rises
over whoever perceives God.[64]

(31) Jacob limped, and the children of Israel do not eat
thigh nerves. This refusal to eat symbolizes a refusal to believe
in Jesus. Another interpretation of Jacob's limping is that his
two legs represent Jews and Christians; the one leg (Jews) will
have a numbness concerning the grace of faith.

Most of Ambrose's remarks are spiritual allegories or lesser
anti-Jewish observations of the sort we have seen before. His remarks that the touching of Jacob's thigh indicated Christ's equality with the Father is also simply an allegorical remark, even if
doctrinal in nature.

6. Hegesippus

This is a late fourth-century Christian free rendition of
Josephus' *The Jewish War* which mentions that Jacob wrestled with
and prevailed over the Lord, who is thought by men to be uncon-
querable.[65]

7. Jerome

Jerome's Vulgate translation of the Jabbok account differs in
some respects from the Vetus, LXX, and MT texts.[66]

In his commentary on Hosea[67] Jerome speaks of Jacob's
endurance against God, in wrestling with the angel (God's representative) all night long. Because he was so combative he received
the new name Israel, which means *directus Dei*.[68]

In *Contra Pelag*. 3.8[69] we read that Jacob wrestled with an angle in human form, who renamed him *rectissimus Dei*.[70] The Lord also encouraged Jacob to meet with his brother Esau.

In his commentary on Eph 6:12[71] Jerome discusses the role of evil powers in the spiritual life. They are very real, and they can often tempt us mightily to sin.

> Such a wrestling match we think Jacob had (not against
> flesh and blood) when he remained alone and a man
> wrestled with him. The man helped him and gave him
> strength against a third party who struggles in great
> sweat.

The third party was a devil, a very real devil who struggled all night long.[72]

Jerome discusses scriptural meanings of motions of the sun in his commentary on Eccl 1:5.[73] Sometimes the sun represents Jesus, the Sun of Justice; this sun "went down" when Jacob left the Holy Land,[74] and it "rose" upon Jacob when he returned.

In his commentary on Isa 6:1-10[75] Jerome remarks that men can "see" God, or wrestle with Him as Jacob did, only with the eyes of the mind, and that only when God wills it. No one can perceive (*cernere*) God with his physical eyes and still live.

Jerome focuses frequently on literal aspects of the Jabbok story. His interpretations of the name Israel, his interest in the match as related to Esau, and his disinclination to specify the exact nature of the wrestler testify to this. On the other hand, Jerome also comes up against the need to have a third party present when he allegorizes the story as a spiritual struggle. His allegory about the sun representing Jesus has little merit.

8. Augustine

Augustine has some new allegories in his treatment of the Jabbok story. The best example is found in *Sermon 5.6-8*.[76]

> 6   Jacob, signifying the Christian people, wrestled with
> the Lord; this opponent was actually an angel represent-
> ing God.[77] Jacob grasped for the kingdom of heaven; we
> should grasp for Christ by trying to love our enemies.
> Jacob asked for a blessing which resulted in the changing
> of his name. He was also lamed; thus he was one man,
> partly lamed and partly blessed.

> 7   The opponent's request to be released, in v. 27, is
> puzzling. The mystery is the same as when the risen
> Christ said to Mary Magdalene, "Do not touch me, for I
> have not yet gone to the Father." Mary Magdalene repre-
> sents the Church and Christ's prohibition means that we
> should not concentrate on His bodily person but rather

that we should realize that He is equal to the Father.
So Jacob attempted to hold on tightly to his opponent;
the request for release means that Christ was saying, "
"Do not consider me to be only a man."
        The morning is the light of truth and wisdom by
which we can learn of Christ's divinity; the night is
the evil of this age. At daybreak will come the Parousia.
        Jacob's refusal to release his opponent until he him-
self had been blessed signifies that Christ first blessed
us by His Incarnation.

8   Jacob's wounded thigh signifies bad Christians; indeed,
        in a way the Church is lamed by some of its own people.

The more well-known pattern of patristic commentary is reflected in the following selection from Augustine.

        In *City of God* 16.39[78] the angel who wrestled with Jacob is
clearly a type of Christ. The angel lost the bout voluntarily to
signify the passion of Christ wherein the Jews seemed to overpower
him.

        Jacob's new name means "one who sees God." Seeing God will
eventually be the reward for all holy people.

        Jacob was blessed in his offspring who later came to believe
in Jesus, and he was lamed in those who would be unbelievers. The
major part of Jacob's offspring are symbolized by the wide part of
the thigh muscle; i.e., most Jews do not believe in Jesus.[79]

        Many of the insights of Augustine mentioned in the above two
citations can be found elsewhere in his writings. We will group
them here in four categories.

(a) *The Presence of Jesus*
        In *Contra Maximinum* 2.26.9[80] Augustine tries to carefully
distinguish in what sense Christ can be said to have appeared at
Jabbok.[81] Christ is symbolized insofar as Jacob's offspring will
later seem to prevail over Him,[82] or insofar as some of Jacob's
offspring will see Him face-to-face, as believers. It would be
preferable to speak of the wrestler as *an angel and God*. God can
be *in* an angel (or *in* a man), especially when He speaks through
that angel or man. Thus Christ was there in *figura* but not in
proprietate; a *figura* is not a *res ipsa*.[83]

(b) *The Angel's Role*
        In commenting on Psalm 79, sect. 3,[84] Augustine notes that
the angel allowed Jacob to win. Jacob's request for a blessing
from the vanquished was a great mystery; the angel was physically
weak but great in majesty.

        Similarly, in Psalm 147, sect. 27,[85] we read that God made
Jacob wrestle with an angel, in whose person God Himself wrestled.
The angel allowed himself to be beaten out of mercy, not weakness.

(c) *The Meaning of the Names*
Augustine was particularly taken with the idea that the meaning of the name Israel prefigures the eventual condition of all
holy people. He notes[86] that the name Israel is not used exclusively after Jabbok. The name Israel refers to the later age
when we shall see God. We are Jacob *in re*, Israel *in spe*.[87]
In Psalm 83, sect. 12[88] Augustine prays to God, "Make me
Israel." He asks, "When shall I become Israel?" and replies,
"When God will appear...." In Psalm 146, sect. 4[89] we read that
the angels are like Israel in that they see God now; He is a wonderful vision for them.[90]

(d) *Other Remarks Concerning Jacob*
In *Sermon 4.15*[91] we learn that Jacob was tried and blessed at
Jabbok because he was without deceit. In his remarks on Psalm 147,
sect. 27[92] Augustine notes that Jacob fought so valiantly because,
as Matthew says,[93] the kingdom is taken by force. Further, a man
appreciates more something for which he has to make effort. In
Sermo Caillau-St. Yves 2.60.6,[94] Augustine notes that no one before
the Good Thief had ever been so clearly promised entrance into
heaven. When Jacob wrestled an angel in the form of a man and
claimed to have seen God, even he received no such promise.

Much of Augustine's treatment of the Jabbok passage is different from his handling of the Mamre theophany, yet the apologetic
basis is still there. While Augustine does not involve the Trinity
(as he could have), this opponent necessarily prefigures Christ as
must every OT event.[95] As in his Mamre commentary, he takes pains
to be precise in describing the exact relationships between God and
the angel.

The ecclesial allegories involving Jacob and the name Israel
are not found in other writers. Pontet claims that Augustine found
the Church more clearly prefigured in the OT than he did Jesus himself.[96] The allegory that the Church is "lame" (by having bad
members in it) could be a reaction against Donatist ideals. Augustine's anti-Jewish remarks are also part of a pattern.[97]

Among the allegories and sermon illustration types I want to
mention the one about Christ being equal to the Father. This
could have come to Augustine from his mentor Ambrose.

F. Western Writers After Augustine

To round out our survey, we shall include here fifteen Christian writers after Augustine. Many of these commentators deal with

Christ's presence at Jabbok, or with familiar allegories and
"sermon illustration" typologies, some of which are anti-Jewish.
Only Arnobius the younger seems to propose Jacob as a model for
us to imitate.

Africa

   1. Quodvultdeus (writing c. 440-450) has a short commentary
on our passage in *De Promissionibus* 1.24.33.[98] Jacob had a holy
struggle with an angel, who let himself be beaten. Jacob's lameness is a sign of Jewish unbelief; the name Israel means "one who
sees God."

Italy

   2. Arnobius the younger (d. c. 450) notes[99] that he who, like
Jacob, advances in long-suffering and in faith is worthy of seeing
God face-to-face; such a person would be a new Israel, a new
"seer of God."
   3. Epiphanius (c. 500) also mentions that Israel means "a man
who sees God." When Jesus later lived on earth, the Jews as a
people truly saw God.[100]
   4. Rusticus[101] (d. 565) observes that Jacob wrestled with a
man but called the place "face of God." The Holy Spirit had revealed to Jacob this mystery of embodiment (*humanationis sacramentum*). The two wrestled all night and separated at dawn; this
means that the enemies of Christ are in darkness of heart and
mind, while those who love Him are in the light.
   5. Cassiodorus' (d. 580) comments on Psalm 44:4[102] ("You are
my king and my God who ordains victories for Jacob") relate this
to our Lord and Savior Jesus who brought victory to Jacob when He
had him fight an angel in glorious combat. Jesus "ordained" the
victory by helping by means of the angel; we can see this in the
instance when Jacob was given a new name. Elsewhere Cassiodorius
briefly mentions Jacob's lameness and how it symbolizes Jewish
unbelief in Jesus.[103]
   6. Gregory the Great (writing 595-601) developed allegories
from the Jabbok account solely in regard to spiritual endeavor.
His main comment was in *Homily on Ezekiel* 2.2.12-13.[104]

12   The contemplative life involves much mental effort.
     Look at Jacob wrestling with the angel; now Jacob was
     on the aggressive, now on the defensive. The angel
     represents God: Jacob represents those perfect people
     who seek a life of contemplation. The "angel" is in
     a sense "conquered" when God is comprehended by an
     intimate contemplative (*intellectu intimo*).

13 Jacob was lamed when his thigh nerve was burned. So too
    our carnal desires wither when we seek to know God in
    desire and in mind. Jacob's two legs stand for seeking
    God and holding on to earthly things; whenever we
    succeed in seeking God our love of the world must be
    diminished, and so we limp.[105]

Later in the same book[106] the topic is the perseverance and
strength needed in the pursuit of virtue. Think of Jacob who was
exercised to such a level that he could not be overwhelmed by a
fighting angel!

In *Moralium Job* 23.12[107] we learn that the contact which we
may have with God in contemplation is not a firm and permanent
vision, but only a quasi-vision which we might call a "face" of
God. Jacob used this phrase to describe what he had experienced
at Jabbok. Elsewhere[108] it is said that patriarchs and others who
claim to have seen God do so only by means of forms; they do not
attain to the power of God's essence. Thus Jacob only saw God *in*
an angel.[109]

France

    7. Cyprian of Gaul (early 5th cent.)[110] writes that Jacob
struggled with a wrestling God; in fact, he had seen the lofty
features of God. The name Israel means "one perceiving the Lord."
Cyprian used no allegories in his poetry on this passage.[111]
    8. John Cassian (d. c. 435) in *De Incarnatione* 7.9[112] denies
that Jesus was or is in any way "hidden" in the Father. He was not
hidden even prior to His Incarnation. For example, Jacob wrestled
with Christ at the Jabbok; Jacob saw a man but he spoke of God,
whom he had seen with inner eyes. God was preparing men for the
Incarnation by events such as this wrestling match.
    9. Eucherius of Lyons (writing 428) explains that men such as
Moses and Jacob did not see God in the glory of His majesty but in
the lesser image of divine power which can be moderated to human
limitations.[113]
    10. Eusebius of Gaul (second half of 5th cent.) dwells on the
heavenly athlete who wrestled with Jacob.[114] He lost in order to
rise more glorious; He fell to elevate others. At this time He
battles with foes in the arena of the world.
    Jacob represents the Jews; the angel represents Jesus. The
angel being overpowered symbolizes Christ suffering at the hands of
the Jews. As the angel gave a blessing, so also Jesus prayed for
His executioners. Many Jews disbelieved; this was foretold by the
laming of the wide part of the thigh muscle. Another interpretation is that Jacob limped on his foot (that part of the Jewish

people who did not believe in Jesus after He rose from the
dead).[115]

11. Caesarius of Arle (d. 542) in *Sermon 88.5*[116] makes some
of the now familiar charges about Jacob's descendants. Assuming
that the opponent was an angel who symbolized Christ, then the
wrestling signifies Jewish persecution of Jesus; Jacob's lameness
represents Jewish unbelief, and so on. One new allegory is that
the dawn becomes a symbol of Christ's resurrection, which took
place very early in the morning.

Spain

12. Apringius (mid-6th cent.) in commenting on Rev 19:12,
"...he has a name inscribed which no one knows but himself," notes
that neither would Jacob's opponent reveal his name.[117]

13. Isadore of Seville (writing c. 624) notes[118] that the
terms *man* and *God* are both used in the Jabbok account. Similar
events in the lives of Joshua, Gideon, and others lead to the conclusion that the opponent of Jacob was actually God and Lord.

Elsewhere the visitor is more clearly identified as Jesus.
In *Liber de var. Quaest.* 17.2[119] we see that such appearances in-
volved Jesus as a man; later He would come into the world truly
Incarnate.[120]

The name Israel means "one who sees God" and is based on
Jacob's having seen God at Jabbok.[121] The wrestler's losing signifies Christ's crucifixion,[122] and the lameness of Jacob represents Jewish unbelief.[123]

14. Beatus of Liebana (writing 776-786) notes that the name
Israel means "a man who sees God."[124]

England

Bede (674-735) mentions the meaning of "a man seeing God" for
Israel,[125] and that Jacob's lameness signifies Jewish persecution
of Jesus, and that the blessing of Jacob represents the blessing
of those Jews who come to believe in Jesus.[126]

Excursus

The oldest Christian representation we have of a Jabbok scene
is a relief carving on a small ivory relic casket (lipsanotheca)
from Brescia, Italy. This dates from the fifth century.[127] The
whole panel displays different deliverance themes. In the section
of interest to us a robed man and Jacob have their arms crossed in
a wrestling posture. The man's right hand is touching the inside

of Jacob's thigh near the knee. There is no background scenery in
this carving. Unfortunately, Jacob's head has been broken off; it
was in high relief and must have been hit at some time.

Next we have two illuminations in the sixth century *Vienna
Genesis*, the oldest extant illuminated Christian manuscript.[128]
In the first picture the movement of the figures is clockwise from
the upper left. Jacob and his entourage cross a stone bridge over
the river. At the lower right, next to the stream, Jacob wrestles
a man who wears a long white garment. Both men are erect, with
arms clasped. Further to the left the man in white has his hand
on Jacob's bowed head in blessing, as both stand near each other.

In the second *Vienna Genesis* picture there are three scenes
clockwise from the upper left. In that area Jacob and a man in
white clothing converse. To the upper right Jacob is being blessed
much as in the first picture. Below these two scenes we see a
third in which a bright-rayed sun shines on Jacob as he walks.

There is an eighth-century fresco in Santa Maria Antiqua in
Rome which depicts an angel dealing with Jacob. Jacob is kneeling
and seeking a blessing from the angel, who has not yet moved his
arm and hand to the posture for blessing. To Jacob's left is the
inscription, "Ubi Jacob luctatur cum angelo ut benedicatur."[129]

From the ninth century we have a French illumination.[130] In
this representation an outsized, haloed, winged angel grasps for
Jacob's upper right thigh with his left arm. Jacob tries to fend
off the angel by pushing at both his shoulders.

Use of an angelic figure as the opponent persists. We have a
scene of Jacob and an angel, with arms clasped, in a thirteenth-
century illumination,[131] but we are going beyond the time scope of
our research.

Examination of the Christian artistic representations of Jacob
at the Jabbok leads one to compare them to the Mamre works. As at
Mamre, an angel eventually replaces the human figure of the biblical text. The only time the opponent is haloed is in the French
manuscript. Further, it seems that any of these human or angelic
figures could have been meant to symbolize Jesus. The artists were
able to be more vague and subtle about this than most patristic
writers.

Clearly the Jabbok incident received less attention in church
art than did Mamre. Our examples include a small lipsanotheca, one
mural, and three or four manuscript illuminations, whereas the Mamre
theme was prominently displayed in Ravenna and grew to be the major
Byzantine exemplar of the Trinity.

Except for the *Vienna Genesis* and the 1250 A.D. miniature
scenes, the artistic representations of the Jabbok story include
no people or objects which could help one to appreciate the context of the story. Nor do we find any attempts to weave in any of
the typological or allegorical motifs mentioned in the written
sources. Even the physical encounter of Jacob and his opponent is
portrayed in rather static forms. The most spirited wrestling
occurs in the French manuscript.

Conclusions to Chapter IV

Let us review the patristic commentary on Jabbok in light of
the eight guidelines which we established in the second chapter.

1. We proposed that OT events acquired significance for early
Christians in relation to, or as foretastes of, Christ's later
accomplishments. The great majority of our patristic sources considered Christ to have been the subject of the theophany at Jabbok
in some manner. A few, such as the Antiocheans and Jerome, were
less specific or favored speaking only of an angel.

2. We assumed that the literary contexts of an OT passage
need not be as important to the Fathers as typological considerations of it. Only a few Fathers showed interest in the immediate
literary context of the Jabbok story. Only Justin, Tertullian, and
Jerome derived the name Israel in ways consistent with the Hebrew
account. Only Chrysostom, Theodoret, and Jerome clearly brought
Jacob's fear of Esau into their considerations as to why God brought
about the wrestling at all.

3. In addition to looking for types and allegories which related OT passages to the life of Christ, we also planned to look
for ones which helped to explain the life of the Church. Some of
the patristic Jabbok commentary was Church oriented. The frequent
allegorical exhortations to spiritual asceticism were directed to
the faithful, as was the standard anti-Jewish thinking so frequent
in our sources. Only Augustine asked Christians to see themselves
in the lame patriarch, and that in just one passage.

4. We expected the early Fathers to mix together historical
types, sermon illustration types, and allegories. There were very
few historical types to be found in the patristic material on this
passage. Justin mentioned the fact that Jesus, in his earthly life,
changed the names of Peter and the sons of Zebedee. He also mentioned that Jesus struggled with the devil at the start of his public life. No Father after Justin mentioned either of these poten-
tial NT parallels again.

5. We held that Philo's allegories were frequently imitated
by Christian writers. Origen, Ambrose, and Gregory the Great were
obvious imitators. Origen, Procopius, and Jerome got so far afield
at times in using spiritual allegory that they had to have two or
three different opponents for Jacob to wrestle.

6. We anticipated differences in interpretation between the
Alexandrian and Antiochean schools. Chrysostom and Theodoret were
very much interested in the literal intent of the passage. Jerome
was so inclined most of the time. Their efforts were clearly in
the minority. Indeed, patristic commentary ignored almost all the
particularity of the story. There were almost no depictions of
the actual arrival and appearance of the stranger, no recountings
of the sweaty, dusty thrashing about in the dark, no appreciation
of the courageous determination of Jacob not to release his opponent. Christian commentators were satisfied with the idea that
Jacob in some way saw God; they were not interested in the fact
that wrestling is a very unusual way to see someone. Few Christians referred to the sciatic nerve prohibition at all, and none
showed interest in Jewish practice in this regard.

7. We mentioned that some events in the life of Jacob engen-
dered comment that he was a type of Christ. He was not seen as a
historical type of Jesus in our Jabbok sources. In fact only
rarely was he the subject of positive sermon illustration typology
or of positive allegory, aside from the general observation that
he had in some sense seen God.

8. We assumed that biblical passages served as proofs in discussions of other doctrines or aspects of theology as well as of
those directly involving Christ. The Jabbok passage was involved
in very few doctrinal proofs, aside from the frequent assertions
that the pre-Incarnate Christ was present. Tertullian used it in
one place to discuss the works of angels, and Ambrose and Augustine
briefly digressed on the divinity of Jesus.

Reflecting on the patristic and Alexandrian Jewish use of the
Jabbok story in light of the hermeneutical modes and rules suggested by Sanders, we again find that this material followed the same
general patterns as the rabbinic writings.

With the exception of the few literal commentators who assumed
that Jacob was very afraid of Esau, our other sources did not question Jacob's personal worthiness in the course of their remarks on
the Jabbok event. Most of the Christian writers focused so exclusively upon Jabbok as another Christophany that a theologizing
hermeneutic was impossible.

Most of our sources rather drew lessons for the faithful;
i.e., they employed a moralizing hermeneutic. These lessons,
whether involving doctrines about Jesus, angels, the Church, or
the like, were supportive or constitutive in intent.

CHAPTER V

CONCLUSIONS

At the beginning of this work, I proposed that a study of the
history of early hermeneutic of some biblical passages could be
helpful for our own practice of the art of hermeneutic. At this
point I want to explain some of the ways in which this historical
study can help us as we try to draw out authentic relationships
between the content and contexts of biblical passages and the life
situations and systems of thought of present-day congregations.

A sampling of ancient biblical commentary can help us to view
modern commentary from new perspectives and to evaluate it accord-
ingly. For example, many twentieth-century exegetes, with their
interest in pre-literary versions of the Mamre account, postulate
that originally Jahweh was not clearly identified in vv. 1 or 3.
The ancient Rabbis, who did not consider the question of pre-
literary traditions, reflected on the love manifested by Jahweh in
His appearance to Abraham. They accepted the identifications in
the early verses without hesitation. On this complex passage,
with its frequent changes of speakers, their explanations involving
the Shekinah and the three angels can be said to complement the
intent of the Jahwist's story as we have it in the MT. For that
matter, the patristic explanations that Christ or the entire Trinity was the subject of the Mamre theophany also represent their concern with the complete Genesis account.[132] Perhaps our own hermeneutical references to Mamre should likewise concentrate on the
story in its entirety.

To take another instance, modern exegesis of the Jabbok account is understandably divided as to whether it involves a genuine
theophany or an angelophany, since the account is ambiguous. This
division has its counterpart in ancient Christian and Jewish commentary; most of our Jewish sources spoke of an angel, while many
of our Christian sources considered the Jabbok encounter as a
theophany (or, more exactly, a Christophany). We do well to be
aware of the history behind the two current interpretations.

Another benefit which can be derived from researching a history of OT hermeneutics is that we may be better able to work with
an individual modern commentary. I found it helpful to know that
Benno Jacob's remarks on Mamre were *not* representative of ancient
rabbinic material. On the other hand, his comments on the

relationship of Jacob to Esau, and on Jacob as an ancestor upon
whom we should model our lives, do reflect earlier rabbinic lines
of thought.

We may certainly employ some of the ancient hermeneutical
remarks to supplement the principal achievements of modern exegesis. If one of the main thrusts of the Mamre story is to honor
the virtue of hospitality, then rabbinic developments of that virtue, such as their descriptions of the food served or of the
merits Abraham earned there, are truly in harmony with this thrust.
By the same token, God's initiative and loving power at Mamre are
also highlighted by some of the rabbinic commentary. The early
Christians, in their own way, also dwell on God's loving actions
at Mamre although they do not conceive of hospitality in the same
way as the Jewish commentators did.

So also, if the main theme of the Jabbok event is God's ini-
tiatives and the complex of Jacob's human traits, then the ancient
Jewish and Christian sources do center at times on God's initia-
tives and Jacob's virtues, although they do not at the same time
profile Jacob's shortcomings.

The hermeneutical categories of Daniel Patte for Jewish material, and of Jean Daniélou, R.P.C. Hanson et al., for patristic
material were adequate tools for this beginner.

The rabbinic materials did bear out the norms laid down by
Patte. In the Mamre and Jabbok commentary we found extensive use
of other biblical citations. Many of them helped us to be more
aware of the larger Genesis contexts into which these events in
the lives of Abraham, Sarah, and Jacob must be placed. Other citations may have been dependent upon the Genesis stories in some way,
while a third group of cross references were quite remotely related
by verbal or other formal characteristics.[133]

The two passages were also subject to a certain amount of
telescoping, and to a great extent the patriarchs were advanced as
moral examples for our imitation. The sciatic nerve prohibition
became the object of a considerable amount of legislation over the
years, some of which entailed further study of the Jabbok story.

The scope of rabbinic hermeneutic of these two passages was
mostly restricted to cultural changes, changes in everyday life,
laws, current ideas and ways of thinking, folklore, and so on. The
few brief references to Rome, Hadrian's persecution, the Princes in
Israel, and so on, only served to underscore the general absence of
references to salient events contemporary to the Rabbis.

Our eight guidelines to the Christian material were also
applicable in both passages. At Mamre and at Jabbok the presence
of the pre-Incarnate Christ (or the Trinity, in some Mamre commentary) invested the stories with relevance for early Christians.
Christian commentary was substantially less oriented toward considering Genesis contexts than was the Jewish. Ecclesial allegories were frequent, perhaps the most notable being Chrysostom's
consideration of Mamre as an example of Abraham's charity. Historical typologies between events in the lives of Abraham, Jacob,
and Jesus were not often drawn out, although we did have a good
amount of sermon illustration typology and spiritual allegory.
Philo's writings were much imitated and adapted by Christian
writers. In both cases, the Antiochean analyses were more often
concerned with literal understandings than was the Alexandrian.
Neither Abraham nor Jacob were seen as types of Jesus Himself in
these passages. Elements of both stories were used in the formu-
lation of Christian doctrines.

The categories of James Sanders assisted us to some extent in
gaining an overview of our hermeneutical materials. There was
relatively little Jewish or Christian consideration of the human
faults of the two patriarchs and Sarah. In most of the sources
they were depicted as quite worthy recipients of God's favors.
Much of the hermeneutic we have examined was constitutive; it was
used to encourage believers to greater interior devotion or to the
practice of virtues. Only rarely did we find challenging remarks
such as Chrysostom's ideas on almsgiving. Before using or imi-
tating points in any of these sources we should be aware of these
larger hermeneutical trends.

We should also admit that such rabbinic and patristic constitutive hermeneutic was authentic in itself. For Jewish audiences
hearing about the Mamre or Jabbok events, the way everything took
place and echoed throughout the Scriptures gave credit to God.
Comments on the Jabbok encounter encouraged them to reflect on the
their destiny as a Chosen People. The remarks of the early Christians revealed the various preconceptions with which they read the
OT. These remarks may not have represented as uniform a culture
as that of the Jews and they may not have been in close harmony
with the range of biblical Hebrew meanings at times, but they did
point to the initiative and power of God. An appreciation of the
sincerity behind such constitutive hermeneutic as we have come
across in this research can help us to see beyond Sanders' emphasis
on prophetic hermeneutic in the *IDB Supplement* article. This

caveat, that Sanders does not offer many examples of constitutive
hermeneutic, is my only criticism of his article on hermeneutics.

The fact that many of these ancient insights were of a constitutive sort need not in any way deter us from using them. I
have personally employed the Rabbis' remarks about the extent of
Abraham's large and fancy meal in homilies on hospitality, and
about God's white lie to cover over Sarah's remark about Abraham
in homilies on married life. Both applications have proved
effective.

I find it difficult to go beyond the basic patters of
Sanders in any attempt to find commonalities in the Jewish and
Christian sources. It is obvious that much of the Christian commentary did not include references to salient current events; the
Jewish material also exhibited this same tendency. The reasons
for such omissions may not have been the same in both cases. Jews
and Christians usually understood the nature of Jacob's opponent
in different ways (angelophany or Christophany) but, given the
difference in belief about the nature of God in the two systems,
one could say that in either case God was seen as truly inter-
vening in the life of Jacob in some mysterious way.

To put it another way, the belief systems of each faith weigh
heavily in the larger picture. Thus ancient Christian use of a
pre-Incarnate Christ or Jewish use of angels or of a food law such
as the sciatic nerve prohibition are such complex vehicles that
one would have to study other Genesis passages--ones not involving
mysterious appearances such as these--in order to gain more insights into how Scripture functioned for these two peoples. We
must be careful not to draw too many broad conclusions from our
study of the ancient Jewish and Christian use of these two passages.
We have looked at only two brief similar passages from the same
book, and those for a limited time period. We have not integrated
our findings into any larger analysis of Judaism or Christianity,
since to do so would be impractical in a study of this length.
Obviously skilled biblical, rabbinics, and patristics scholars
such as Childs, Vermes, and Daniélou are capable of such
integrations.

I must indicate my personal preference for some of the ancient
Jewish commentary on our passages. Credit should be given the
Rabbis for their careful scrutiny of the texts. Such attention to
the details of the personal generous hospitality and enthusiasm of
Abraham and Sarah, the initial reactions of Sarah, Jacob's intense

struggle with his powerful opponent, and his insistence on receiving a blessing, indicate a high degree of devotion to God's
word. The vividness and boldness of much of their hermeneutic
should encourage contemporary homilists to be more forceful in
their own presentations.

The ancient Christian commentators undervalue the literal
particularity of the stories. We find much less study of larger
Genesis contexts, of the full image of Abraham and Sarah formed
from all their acts of hospitality, of the wonder caused by the
startling message to a very elderly couple, of the extent of
Sarah's doubts, and so on. The Christians reflect less frequently
than the Rabbis on Jacob's courage and his trials, on his determination to receive a blessing, and so on.

The mention of scholars such as Vermes and Daniélou, and of
my own beginner's impression that the rabbinic materials are very
vigorous at times, leads me to perhaps the most important conclusion in this investigation.

Simply put, it is that each person called to do hermeneutics
should find what values he can in the history of the art. Few of
us will ever be able to do full-time work in this area, but any
research in the history of hermeneutics will inevitably be reflected in the quality of sermons or homilies. Any experience
gained in consulting such materials of the time period covered by
this study or later centuries will contribute to a deeper appreciation of the continuities of humanity over the years. One may
find insights in rabbinic materials; another perhaps in the insights of one of the Fathers; someone else may approach these materials from an interest in a particular doctrine or aspect of church
or synagogue life, Jewish or Christian art, or whatever. Over a
long period of time insights so gained will enhance hermeneutical
endeavors because they will sensitize the homilist to the life
situations and systems of thought of the people of God through the
centuries.[134]

APPENDIX I

JEWISH TRANSLATIONS AND TARGUMS OF GEN 18:1-16

In this appendix we will present observations on the ancient versions and Targums[1] in a more detailed fashion than was the case in the synopsis and chart of Chapter I.

We will begin with the Septuagint, which probably goes back to the third century B.C.[2] This Greek translation, as Bowker notes,[3] makes every effort to explain words and phrases which might be unclear, to avoid anthropomorphisms, to avoid leaving ambiguities in the larger context of the passage, and even occasionally to change a phrase for doctrinal purposes. The later more literal Greek versions of *Aquila* and *Symmachus* will receive some mention in the appropriate locations.

In v. 1, the time of the visit is more defined by μεσημβρίας.

With the MT, the LXX assumes that God (κύριε) is being addressed in v. 3.

In v. 4, the imperative "wash your feet" is modified to the jussive "let your feet be washed."

The MT phrase "a little water" becomes simply "water."[4]

By the same token, the MT "a bit of bread" in v. 5 becomes simply "bread."

"Refresh your hearts" finds its less ornate equivalent in φάγεσθε.

In v. 6 the סאים become the less specific μέτρα, and the two words designating the flour (קמח סלת) are rendered by the one word σεμιδάλεως. *Aquila* and *Symmachus*[5] speak of three σάτα. A few other texts specify that it is wheaten flour (ἀλεύρου) and locate the verb φύρασον exactly as the MT does, at the midpoint of the string of imperatives and without an object.

In v. 8, the LXX moves καὶ ἐφάγοσαν to an earlier position in the sentence than we have in the MT.[6]

In v. 9 the LXX has one person ask Abraham about Sarah. No other Targum or version will join LXX in this change, except for some copies of *Ps.-Jonathan*. In v. 10 (and 14) the difficult כעת חיה[7] is rendered εἰς ὥρας meaning "at this time a year from now" or "at this time in the proper season."

The LXX says that the door (where Sarah was) was behind the one speaking to Abraham.

In v. 12, *Aquila* renders בקרבה with the very literal ἐν ἐγκάτῳ αὐτῆς.

145

Aquila's translation of Sarah's remark, "After I am worn out, shall I have pleasure?" and *Symmachus*' "After I have become old, shall I have strength (ἀκμή)?" are much closer to the MT than the LXX paraphrase, "This has not happened to me up till now." We cannot, however, decide on the Hebrew Vorlag for the LXX in this case.

In v. 13, Sarah was said to laugh ἐν ἐαυτῇ, a detail appar-apparently repeated from v. 12.

In v. 16 Gomorrah is mentioned. We shall see that this city is mentioned earlier in the story in Targums *Neofiti*, *Fragmentary*, and *Ps.-Jonathan*.

Let us note some patterns of the LXX. There are attempts to clarify, such as μεσημβρίας in v. 1 and εἰς ὥρας in vv. 10 and 14, and the description of the location of the door behind the speaker of v. 10. More frequently we find simplifications: thus

    v. 4 water,
    v. 5 bread...eat,
    v. 6 measures...fine flour,
    v. 12 "This has not happened to me up till now" (perhaps
            a more modest remark, to the Greek mind).

Some changes may have been prompted by a desire to give the account a better flow: thus

    v. 4 "let your feet be washed" being in the same form
           as "let water be brought,"
    v. 8 the relocation of "and they ate," to immediately
           follow the description of his setting the food
           down,
    v. 9 the single speaker could be presumed to be the
           same as the speaker in following v. 10,
    v. 13 the ἐν ἐαυτῇ leaves no doubt that the visitor
           knows a lot about Sarah.

The Aramaic Targums, given from memory only, after each verse or couple of verses of the readings during synagogue services, became necessary as time went on due to the rise of Aramaic (and to some extent Greek) as the spoken language of a substantial part of the Jewish faithful. These recitations were not intended to be literal translations but rather translations which would bring clarity of understanding to the members of the congregations. This interest in having the Scriptures clearly understood was not con-fined to the words themselves but extended to making the spiritual message meaningful for the present. The Targums, then, attempt to do more than a translation such as the LXX, while not becoming radical retellings of Scripture, such as *Jubilees*, or *Genesis Apochryphon* or the like. They make an attempt to represent the text verse-by-verse but at the same time they introduce into it extensive and often far-ranging interpretations.[8]

There was no feeling that the text was being altered or
changed, since the text had already been read; the purpose of the
Targum was to make the text meaningful and to bring home its significance to the congregation.[9] The process of selecting proper
Targumic comments and of teaching new generations of מתורגמנים
shows the Jewish genius for unity in diversity. The Targum traditions[10] represent the middle of the stream of rabbinic interpretations; more eclectic commentary found its way into other writings.

What we have in the later written copies of the Targums would
then be "isolated moments"[11] from the continuous Targum process.
Another consequence of this, as Sperber notes,[12] should be a reali-
zation that variant readings from different manuscripts of a Targum
may be of almost equal value to the so-called critical text. A.
Diez-Macho takes a step in this direction in his edition of Targum
Neofiti by presenting the marginal and interlinear remarks found
on the manuscript in a more prominent format than is usual. I must
confess that, except for Targum *Neofiti* and LXX, I have not made
as extensive use of variant readings as would be the ideal.

Let us now examine Targum *Neofiti* as an example of the early
Palestinian Targum traditions.[13]

In v. 1 the three visitors are identified as angels, with
their specific duties also mentioned. Several cities are mentioned
in addition to Sodom. Twice mention is made of Abraham's circumcision, from which he was still recuperating by resting and being
warmed in the heat of the day. The "word" of Jahweh was revealed
to Abraham in the valley of the "vision." The "vision" probably
refers to this very theophany.[14]

In v. 2 we are told that the angels were in the form of men.
Abraham does not bow but asks after their health as was the custom
(כנימוס).[15] The word נימוס, borrowed from the Greek νομός, evidences an audience somewhat familiar with that language.

In v. 3 Abraham very politely addresses the Lord and refers
to the glory of the Shekinah.

In v. 4 *Neofiti* puts the first two actions of Abraham in the
first person singular.

In v. 5 we read that Abraham said that the visitors had come
exactly at meal time.

In v. 6 the bread is unleavened.

In v. 8 we are told that the (angelic) visitors *seemed* to be
eating and drinking.

In v. 10 (and 14) כעת חיה is simplified to "at this time."
The vague MT phrase about the door becomes "Ishmael was standing
near her (Sarah)."

In v. 12 we see that Sarah wondered (root חמה) in her heart.
The phrase "to have pleasure" is expanded to "...is it possible
for me to return to the days of my youth and for me to have pregnancies?" Abraham is then mentioned by name.

In v. 14 the question becomes "Is it possible to hide anything from before Jahweh?"[16]

Let us sum up some of the trends of Targum *Neofiti*. That the
visitors are angels is clearly mentioned in vv. 1 and 2 and, by
implication from v. 1, an angel seems to do the speaking in vv.
10, 14 and 15. Likewise the angels are not bowed to (v. 2) nor do
they eat earthly food (v. 8).

Possible anthropomorphisms are avoided in vv. 1, 3 and 14.
The Shekinah concept is clearly brought in in v. 3 as a separate
entity from the three angels. The matter of Abraham's circumcision
is brought up. Details are specified in vv. 5, 6 and 10, and
clarified in vv. 10 and 14 (at this time). Sarah's actions and
words in v. 12 are elaborated upon.

We will next examine the *Fragmentary Targum*.[17]

In v. 1 we see that the three visitors are angels; their specific duties are described. Several cities are mentioned in addition to Sodom. A "word (פתגם) of prophecy from before Jahweh" was
revealed to Abraham. The מימרא of Jahweh came to him in the valley
of the "vision"[18] as he was recuperating from his recent circumcision.

Verse 2 has a variant addition, "...according to the custom
of the land."[19]

In v. 10 כעת חיה is rendered "at that time when you (pl.)
shall revive." Ishmael is depicted as standing by Sarah as she
listens.

Verse 12 may be close to *Neofiti*.[20]

Obviously the few verses from the *Fragmentary Targum* are
similar to the Palestinian traditions which we have seen in *Neofiti*
and will see again in *Ps.-Jonathan*.

We should next examine Targum *Onkelos*. This Targum appears to
be closer to being an Aramaic *translation* than the Palestinian
Targums generally, although many haggadic traditions are alluded to
in it. Bowker[21] postulates that its production may have been a
part of the general attempt in Judaism from the second century A.D.
onward to provide authoritative translations as a safeguard against
Christian interpretations of Scripture based on the LXX. Sperber[22]
agrees that, in narrative portions, *Onkelos* will move away from a
literal translation only for the sake of clarity, or in order to
follow "explicit rabbinic interpretation."

In v. 1, the location is the valley of Mamre.

In v. 3, Jahweh is being addressed.

In v. 10 (and 14) כעת חיה becomes "at the time when you (pl.) shall revive."

In v. 12 (also 13 and 15), Sarah interiorly mocks (root חוך). She asks "...shall I have a child (עוליטן)?" rather than "...shall I have pleasure?"

In v. 14, we again have the question, "Is anything hidden from before Jahweh?"

Targum *Ps.-Jonathan* is in some ways the latest and most extensive of the Targums. It reflects much of the Palestinian and *Onkelos* Targum traditions and often adds comments unique to itself (sometimes from non-Targumic rabbinic traditions).[23]

First we will list the items which Targum *Ps.-Jonathan* has in common with one or more of the preceding Targums and versions.

In v. 1 the "glory of Jahweh" appears to Abraham, who was recuperating from his circumcision.

In v. 2 (and 16) the visitors are three angels in the form of men. Their specific duties are described. Gomorrah is mentioned.

In v. 3 Jahweh is addressed, if in a rather devout manner, and the Shekinah concept is employed.

In v. 5 Abraham notes that the visitors have come exactly at meal time.

In v. 8 Abraham serves food as humans do usually and the visitors seemed to him to be eating.

In v. 10 (and 14), the return time is specified as "in the coming year when you (pl.) shall be revived." Ishmael is with Sarah.

In vv. 12 and 15, Sarah wonders (root חמה) in her heart. She talks of whether she can have pregnancies. Abraham is mentioned by name.

In v. 14 the question is whether anything can be hidden from before Jahweh. Then there are several interpretative elements new with *Ps.-Jonathan*.

In v. 1, the place is called the חיזוי of Mamre, meaning a "look-out" position or perhaps, as Bowker would have it, a "crossroad."[24]

In v. 3, the Shekinah is implored not to depart "until I have received these travellers."

Then, in v. 4, Abraham speaks to these men, instead of to the Shekinah.

In v. 5 Abraham encourages the visitors to give thanks to God for the meal.

In v. 8 mention is made that the boy prepared תבשילין.

In v. 9 some manuscripts have *he* instead of *they* at the opening of the verse (as the LXX did).

In v. 10 the speaker is clearly identified as one of the three visitors. Later in the same verse, Ishmael takes note of what the angel said to Abraham.

In v. 11 the "way of women" is specified to be סובתא.

In v. 14 the speaker promises to return "at the time of the feast."

In v. 15 the phrase "for she was afraid" becomes part of Sarah's denial, "I did not wonder, for I was afraid." The *angel* reassures her in his reply.

In v. 16 we see that the angel who had spoken to Sarah went up to heaven while the other two went on to Sodom.

We can see that the tendency in *Ps.-Jonathan* is definitely to ascribe to the angels as much of the intercourse with Abraham and Sarah as is possible.

Let us review the Syriac *Peshitta*,[25] which has a few noteworthy items on our passage.

In v. 1 the place is called the *oak* of Mamre.

In vv. 1, 3, 13 and 14, the word for God is מריא.

In v. 4 the *Peshitta* puts the first two actions of Abraham in the first person singular, as *Neofiti* did.

In vv. 10 and 14, the time for returning is "while she lives."

We can conclude that the *Peshitta* is fairly close to the MT, and has less interpretative material than many of the Targums in regard to our passage.

In the Samaritan tradition we have a version of the Pentateuch and a Targum.[26]

In the *Samaritan Pentateuch* the principal difference from the MT is that in v. 3 אדני is taken as a plural (my lords) and all the other personal modifiers in the verse are also in the plural. A most striking change, and one which forces us to keep our attention on the "men."

In v. 10 we see that *Sarah* was behind it/him.

The *Samaritan Targum* is more interpretative.

In v. 1, the location is the valley of Mamre (so *Onkelos*).

In v. 3, consistent with the *Samaritan Pentateuch*, those addressed are called רבני, with the subsequent shift of the rest of the personal modifiers in the verse into the plural.

In v. 6 Abraham rushes to Sarah, who is at her mixing bowl.

In v. 10, we see that Sarah was behind it/him. כעת חיה becomes כזבן קיומה and כזבן קעים in vv. 10 and 14, respectively.

In v. 12, we see that Sarah doubted within herself (root קטרג from Greek κατηγορέω).[27] The word, according to Jastrow, means to denounce or bring charges against someone. The other Targum which had strong language here was *Onkelos*.

In vv. 13 and 15, Sarah wonders (root תמה).

APPENDIX II

JEWISH TRANSLATIONS AND TARGUMS OF GEN 32:23-33

In this appendix we will present observations on the ancient versions and Targums in a more detailed fashion than was the case in the synopsis and chart of Chapter III.

The LXX varies in minor ways from the MT and has an important change in v. 29. We will examine the more noteworthy cases here.

In v. 24 διέβη is not a causative form as is ויעברם.[1] In v. 25 *Aquila* and *Symmachus* use forms of κυλίνδω and κονέω, which convey the meaning of rolling in dust or raising dust. They are thus closer to the literal meaning of ויאבק than the LXX ἐπάλαιεν.

In v. 26 ἐνάρκησεν is not exactly like the MT ותקע.

In v. 29 the LXX has "...for you have prevailed with God, and you are strong with men." Further, Wevers notes several manuscripts which add εση, thus giving a future meaning to the second part, "you will be strong with men."[2]

In v. 31 פניאל is translated as Εἶδος Θεοῦ, which plays nicely with the following verb εἶδον.

In v. 32 פנואל is translated as τὸ Εἶδος τοῦ Θεοῦ, thus making it slightly different from its counterpart in the preceding verse, much as in the MT.

In v. 33 the LXX seems to ignore the noun הנשה, using instead the verbal phrases ὃ ἐωάρκησεν and καὶ ἐωάρκησεν.[3]

Turning to the Targums, let us look first at the interpretive remarks of *Neofiti*.

In v. 25 the opponent is identified as "the angel Sariel in the form of a man." Here and in v. 27 the dawn is referred to as the "column of dawn."

In v. 27 the angel asks to be released because "it is time for angels from on high to praise, and I am a chief of the praisers."

In v. 29 the angel renames Jacob Israel because "you have assumed superiority (אתרברבה) with angels from before God and with men, and you have prevailed against them."

In vv. 31 and 32 the place is called פניאל. Jacob (v. 31) called it this, saying "I have seen angels from before God face-to-face."

The changes in *Neofiti* clearly confine the encounter of Jacob to a wrestling bout with an angel.

153

The *Fragmentary Targum* has parts of vv. 26 and 27 of our
chapter. In v. 27 the opponent asks for release by Jacob because
"the hour comes for angels to praise." This is similar to *Neofiti*;
another similarity is the use of the phrase "column of dawn" in
this same verse.

Another Targum of the Palestinian family was edited by P.
Kahle in 1930.[4] We shall refer to it as the Cairo Genizah fragments (abbreviating as C.G.). The C.G. is rather close to *Neofiti*.

In v. 25 the opponent is identified as an angel in the form
of a man, although he is not named. The "column of dawn" phrase
occurs again here and in v. 27. In v. 27 the angel explains that
it is time for angels from on high to praise, and that he is a
chief of the praisers.

In v. 29 the angel explains why he is giving Jacob the new
name Israel, saying "...you have claimed superiority with holy
angels from before God in the form of men, and you have prevailed
over them." Here we lose not only "god" as a direct object, but
also the "men" of v. 29 of the MT as a direct object.[5]

Turning to Targum *Onkelos*, in v. 29 the wrestler's remark is
"...you are great (רב את) before God and with men, and you have
prevailed." In v. 31 Jacob says that he has seen the angel of God
face-to-face. This is the first explicit mention of an angel at
Jabbok in the *Onkelos* passage.

Targum *Ps.-Jonathan* has several new elements of interpretation
combined with the previous Targumic traditions.

In v. 25 Jacob's opponent is identified as an angel in the
form of a man. This angel then says to Jacob, "Did you not speak[6]
for a tenth of all your possessions?[7] Behold, you have twelve sons
and a daughter and you have not tithed them." Jacob then set aside
his daughter and his four first-born sons, which left him with
eight sons. He counted the eight, starting with Simeon and, on
recounting two to reach a total of ten, he came to Levi last. The
angel, now identified as Michael, accepted Levi and presented him
in prayer to God. These events kept Michael at the river until the
coming of the column of the dawn.

In v. 26 Michael, in wrestling with Jacob, noticed that he did
not have the power to seriously harm Jacob; so he dislocated
Jacob's thigh.

In v. 27 Michael points out that it is time for angels to
praise the Lord of the world, and that he is one of the praising
angels. He further notes that "from the day of the creation of the
world my time to praise has not occurred until now."

In v. 29 Michael says to Jacob, "...you have assumed superiority with angels of God and with men, and you have prevailed over
them." In v. 31 Jacob says that he saw angels of God face-to-face.

In v. 32 we find a strange remark; "The sun rose on him before
its time (which had set because of him before its time when he had
gone out from Beersheba)."

In v. 33 we are reminded that Jews do not eat the sinew which
moves up on the hollow of the thighs of cattle and of wild animals.
They do not eat this because the angel had touched and held the
hollow of Jacob's right thigh, in the place where the sinew moves
up.

The *Peshitta* has a few interesting variations. In v. 23
ואעבר is an Afel form, while the MT ויעבר is simply a Qal form.
Also the location is called a מדברא.[8] In v. 29 Jacob is told that
he had been strong with God and a man. In v. 31 Jacob says that
he had seen an angel. In vv. 31 and 32 פנואיל is used.

We should also look briefly at the *Samaritan Pentateuch* and
Targum. In the *Samaritan Pentateuch* the spelling פנואל occurs in
both vv. 31 and 32. In the *Samaritan Targum*, at v. 29, we have
immediately after the statement that Jacob had striven with God
the words אם אנשה.[9] The spelling פנואל occurs in both vv. 31 and
32.

NOTES

INTRODUCTION

[1]In recent years scholars have begun to stress the study of
early biblical commentary. Perhaps the most obvious foci for
scholars have been the areas of Intertestamental literature and
Comparative Midrash. These disciplines seek greater understanding
of extrabiblical thought which may have affected the NT milieu or
which may advance our knowledge of early Judaism and Christianity.
I would like to mention two writers in particular who have
called for a greater appreciation of the history of biblical study
and hermeneutics. Brevard Childs, in his recent commentary, *The
Book of Exodus* (Westminster, 1974), included historical outlines
of Jewish and Christian understandings of each section of the book.
These form an admirable example of the way to heal the "sharp
break" with the church's traditions which he speaks of in chap. 8
of his earlier *Biblical Theology in Crisis* (Westminster, 1970).
James Smart spoke convincingly of the need for the history of hermeneutics to be taught as a discipline of theology in *The Strange
Silence of the Bible in the Church* (Westminster, 1970).

[2]The reference systems available for biblical citations of
early Christian writers at the start of my research for this study
were the *Genesis* volume of the Bueron Abbey's *Vetus Latina* series
(Herder, 1954), edited by B. Fischer, microfiche lists from the
Centre d'Analyse et de Documentation Patristiques at the University
of Strasbourg, and the hit-and-miss method of searching in editions
of patristic works. The Bueron *Genesis* apparatus does not include
LXX or Vulgate citations, and the more complete Strasbourg citations only went up to a little after the time of Origen. It is
possible, therefore, that I have fewer LXX citations by Greek Fathers
than are extant. The Strasbourg citations are now available in book
form under the title *Biblia Patristica: Index des Citations et Allusions Bibliques dans la Littérature Patristique* (Centre National
de la Recherche Scientifique, Paris), and two volumes have been
issued so far.

[3]"Hermeneutics" in *Interpreter's Dictionary of the Bible
Supplement* (Abingdon, 1976) 402-407.

[4]Sanders offers some examples from Genesis traditions as used
by Ezekiel and 2 Isaiah. Several examples of biblical adaptations
of earlier traditions can be found in Renée Bloch, "Midrash" *Dictionnaire de la Bible, Supplement*, vol. 5 (Paris, 1957) cols. 1263-81;
Childs, *Biblical Theology in Crisis*, 151-200; James Sanders, "From
Isaia 61 to Luke 4," *Christianity, Judaism and Other Greco-Roman
Cults. Studies for Morton Smith at Sixty*, ed. Jacob Neusner (Brill,
1975) part 1, pp. 75-106; idem, "Hermeneutics in True and False
Prophecy," *Beiträge zur Alttestamentlichen Theologie: Festschrift
für Walter Zimmerli zum 70. Geburtstag*; ed. H. Donner, R. Hanhart
and R. Smend (Göttingen: Vandenhoeck & Ruprecht, 1977); also his
article "Hermeneutics," 404, 405 and 407; Geza Vermes, *Scripture
and Tradition in Judaism* (2nd ed.; Brill, 1973) 178-227; and M.
Gertner, "Midrashim in the New Testament," *Journal of Semitic
Studies* 7 (1962) 267-92.

[5]J. A. Sanders, "Hermeneutics," Rule 8g, pp. 406-407.

NOTES

CHAPTER I

[1]In his book, *Early Jewish Hermeneutic in Palestine* (SBLDS 22, 1975), Patte searched for hermeneutic patterns in the NT era (the period 100 B.C. to 100 A.D.). His study included an analysis of apocalyptic and Qumranian materials as well as the works of early Pharisees and Rabbis. Since there seems to be no apocalyptic or Qumranian commentary on our two texts, we shall not refer to his conclusions regarding these materials.

Since Patte had to make extensive use of writings from times well after the NT era, his findings may well be helpful to anyone using the same Jewish sources.

[2]These aspects include the choice of readings (i.e., Seder and Haftarah, as reconstructed by Jacob Mann in *The Bible as Read and Preached in the Old Synagogue* (Cincinnati, 1940), homily structures (discerned in Midrashim), the role of Targums, and prayers.

[3]Bloch, "Midrash," cols. 1278-79. Also Martin McNamara, *The New Testament and The Palestinian Targum to the Pentateuch* (Rome: PIB, 1966), and *Targum and Testament* (Grand Rapids: Eerdmans, 1972).

[4]Patte, *Early Jewish Hermeneutic*, chap. 4, esp. 55-76.

[5]Ibid., 66-67.

[6]Ibid., 67. The question of whether the synthetic view was the cause of the constant comparison or its effect is not resolved by Patte; see p. 72.

[7]We must also mention here the related custom of explaining discrepancies in the biblical texts by rearranging chronological sequences when necessary (cf. Patte, *Early Jewish Hermeneutic*, 69). Thus, in *Genesis Rabbah* 70.4 (on Gen 28:20), some Rabbis suggest that the vow should *precede* so that Jacob will not seem to have doubted God's assurance in that verse. We will use M. A. Mirkin (*Midrash Rabbah* [9 vols.; Tel Aviv: Yavneh, 1956-1964]) for most *Rabbah* texts; *Genesis Rabbah* texts will be taken from J. Theodor and C. Albeck (*Midrash Bereshit Rabbah* [3 vols.; Jerusalem: Wahrmann, 1965]). English translations can be found in H. Freedman and M. Simon (*Midrash Rabbah* [10 vols.; London: Soncino, 1951]).

[8]Patte, *Early Jewish Hermeneutic*, 72.

[9]Only one element is sometimes added--the eschatological event. For the Targumist, then, Scripture refers exclusively either to the sacred history contained therein or to the eschatological time, which is far in the future. Patte (*Early Jewish Hermeneutic*, 72) goes on to say that he cannot find reference in the Targums to present events (present to the Targumist) which could be considered as having this basic identity with the events of the sacred history.

[10]Patte, *Early Jewish Hermeneutic*, 74. Patte speaks of the figures being presented as moral types. They are types of the faithful Jew, the ideal believer.

[11]For examples, see ibid., 77-79.

[12]Ibid., 80.

[13]Ibid., 87-127.

[14]Patte speaks of the Rabbis' "utter inability to interpret the history of their own time" (ibid., 119).

[15]Ibid., 120.

[16]Most of our references will be in haggadic texts (we will take haggadah in its broadest sense--i.e., all ancient Jewish writings other than the halakah, which deals with religious law). It would extend the scope of this research too far were we to attempt to analyze how the various rules of evidence (e.g., the seven middoth of Hillel, the thirteen middoth of R. Ishmael, and the like) apply in each case.

[17]We should also allow for the possibility that the three "men" were the instruments of a theophany. If such a triple mode of appearance were a metamorphosis of Jahweh, it would be unique in the OT. See G. von Rad, *Genesis*, trans. John Marks (Westminster, 1961) 200; or Kenneth Kuntz, *The Self-Revelation of God* (Westminster, 1967) 122-23.

[18]The following works are listed in chronological order, beginning with H. Gunkel's 1910 research, except for Vawter's second book which is listed with his earlier *Path through Genesis* since their contents are very similar. Hermann Gunkel, *Genesis* (6th ed.; Göttingen: Vandenhoeck & Ruprecht, 1964) 193-201; John Skinner, *A Critical and Exegetical Commentary on Genesis* (Scribners, 1925) 298-304; Julian Morgenstern, *The Book of Genesis: A Jewish Interpretation* (Union of American Hebrew Congregations, 1919; repr. 1965) 115-21; Benno Jacob, *Das Erste Buch der Tora: Genesis* (Berlin: Schocken, 1934) 435-46 and 979-80; the abbreviated English rendition of the same: *The First Book of the Bible: Genesis*, trans. and ed. Ernest I. Jacob and Walter Jacob (Ktav, 1974) 116-23; Cuthbert A. Simpson, "Genesis," *The Interpreter's Bible*, vol. 1 (Abingdon, 1952) 616-21; von Rad, *Genesis*, 198-204; Bruce Vawter, *A Path through Genesis* (Sheed and Ward, 1956) 146-50; idem, *On Genesis: A New Reading* (Doubleday, 1977) 225-28; E. A. Speiser, *Genesis*, The Anchor Bible (New York: Doubleday, 1964) 128-35; and T. H. Gaster, *Myth, Legend, and Custom in the Old Testament* (New York: Harper & Row, 1969) 156-58.

[19]A close reading of the original German edition shows that Jacob's formal arguments are usually based on biblical parallels rather than on extra-biblical Jewish traditions.

[20]For Genesis 18 we will examine the Septuagint, Peshitta, and *Samaritan Pentateuch*, as well as Targums *Neofiti*, *Fragmentary*, *Onkelos*, *Ps.-Jonathan*, and *Samaritan*.

[21]The "oaks of Mamre" are also mentioned in Gen 13:18 and 14:13. The latter verse indicates that Mamre was an Amorite ally of Abraham. Text critical procedures (primarily LXX and *Peshitta*, also the oak of Moreh, Gen 12:6 and 35:4 becoming oaks of Moreh in Deut 11:30) could lead one to prefer the singular oak in Gen 13:18 14:13, 18:1, and Deut 11:30. In that case it would be possible to see the oak of Gen 18:1 as being identical with the tree of Gen 18:4 and 8. The United Bible Society's *Preliminary and Interim*

Report on the Hebrew Old Testament Text Project, Vol. 1: *Penta-teuch* (London, 1974) retains the plural form as a lectio diffici-lior against assimilation. In my research, the only ancient Jew-ish commentator to identify the oak with the tree of vv. 4 and 8 was Rashi. Simons points out that Gen 13:18, 23:19 and 35:27 seem to suggest that Mamre is an equivalent name for Hebron, while Gen 23:17, 25:9, 49:30 and 50:13 imply that the field and cave of Machpelah in Hebron were opposite Mamre. Therefore Machpelah and Mamre were distinct locations, although they could have been near each other. See J. Simons, *The Geographical and Topological Texts of the Old Testament* (Brill, 1959) 212-13.

[22]The Shekinah concept, often found in Targums and haggadic sources, refers to the cloud of bright light of God's glory. It is used to express the immanence of God, His special abiding among righteous men or among His chosen people. See *The Interpreter's Dictionary of the Bible* (4 vols.; Abingdon, 1962) 4.317-19 (here-after *IDB*).

[23]The principal source of information as to where such refer-ences occur is Aaron Hyman, *Sefer Torah Haketuvah Wehamesurah al Torah, Neviim, uKhetuvim* (3 vols.; Tel Aviv: Dvir, 1964-1965; orig. pub. 1936-1939). More recently published texts and translations frequently have helpful indices, but Hyman's work has not yet been improved upon in any systematic way.

[24]An excellent guide to ancient rabbinic materials and publi-cations is to be had in John Townsend's "Rabbinic Sources" in *The Study of Judaism: Bibliographical Essays* (A.D.L., 1972) 37-80.

[25]*Tanhuma B* is my designation for the text found in S. Buber, *Midrash Tanchuma* (Rome: Vilna, 1913). All other *Tanhuma* refer-ences are from E. Schrentzel, *Midrash Tanhuma* (Stettin, 1863).

[26]*Gen. Rab.* 42.8; the text in question is Gen 14:13.

[27]The connection between *oaks* and *palace* might be the synonym for oaks (בלוטין). Word plays of this sort were very common.

[28]The same sort of tradition is recounted in *Tanhuma* וירא §3, where it is mentioned that Mamre exhorted Abraham to accept cir-cumcision, and in *Yalkut*, Genesis 73. In this last citation we are again dealing with Gen 14:13; Mamre was the man who rebuked (מרי) Abraham on the question of delaying to circumcise. Much later, Rashi mentions the same tradition, calling the place Mamre's region. Our *Yalkut* references will be from *Yalkut Shimoni* (2 vols.; New York: Horeb, 1925; repr. Jerusalem: Lewin-Epstein, 1951).

[29]*Gen. Rab.* 47.10.

[30]Ibid., 52.1.

[31]In another section of *Gen. Rab.* (56.5), in a passage deal-ing with Abraham's near slaying of Isaac, we find a chain of verses from Isaiah 33 applied to Abraham. For v. 8a, "the high-ways are laid waste," the question is asked, "Does not Abraham receive travellers and dwellers?", thus reminding us that Abraham had invited travellers from the highways. Similarly, v. 8b of Isaiah 33, "the *way*farer ceases" calls to mind that Sarah no longer had the *way* of women. Also Isa 33:8c,""cities are despised," is interpreted to mean that Abraham sought to practice hospitality in the countryside.

[32]We will use M. Friedmann, *Pesikta Rabbati* (Vienna, 1880).
English references are from W. G. Braude, *Pesikta Rabbati* (2 vols.;
Yale Judaica Series, 1968).

[33]*Num. Rab.* 12.8.

[34]Abraham is praised for undergoing the ritual in *Tanhuma B*
וירא §4.

[35]*Gen. Rab.* 48.2ff.

[36]In *Gen. Rab.* 48.3, a further quotation of Job 31:13-14 is
mentioned to point out that Abraham felt obliged to circumcise all
his male kin. In §§4 and 5 there is further praise of circumcision as better than altars and sacrifices. The essentials are
repeated in *Yalkut*, Job 907.
   The theme that the Lord appeared to Abraham as a result of
or as a reward for his circumcision is found in *Zohar*, 97b; part
2, 36a; part 3, 13b and 187ab. We will normally use the English
translation by H. Sperling and M. Simon, *The Zohar* (5 vols.;
London: Soncino, 1933-1934). It is also in *Pirke Eliezer*, ch. 29.
We will use Abraham Broda, *Sefer Pirke de Rabbi Eliezer* (Antwerp,
1950).

[37]*Gen. Rab.* 48.8.

[38]This same tradition is recounted in *Yalkut*, Genesis 82.

[39]All modern editions of the Babylonian Talmud follow the
exact form of *Talmud Bavli* (Rome: Vilna, 1886). English translations may be found in *The Babylonian Talmud*, ed. Isadore Epstein
(London: Soncino, 1935-1952). There are now available some
volumes of a Hebrew-English set (Soncino, 1960-19--).

[40]This movement makes sense of the mutually exclusive phrases
עליו נצבים and וירץ לקראתם in v. 2. So in *Yalkut*, Genesis 82, we
read of the traditions that Abraham had to adjust the bandages,
that he was still weak on the third day, that the angels moved
back from near him. Rashi mentions that the Lord asked after his
health on the third day. *Zohar* 101a mentions the angels asking
after his health and about his resting from the circumcision.
Rashi also mentions the bandages and the angels moving.

[41]The same idea is repeated in *Tanhuma* וישלח §10; *Tanhuma* וירא
§2; *Tanhuma B* וירא §1; *Gen. Rab.* 8.13; *Qoh. Rab.* 7.2, where God's
visiting the sick is seen as one of a series of *firsts*, i.e.,
first wedding (Gen 2:22), first sick visit (Gen 18:1), first
funeral (Deut 34:6). A very similar list of divine ceremonies
prompted by Psa 25:10 ("all the paths of the Lord are love and
faithfulness") can be found in *Psa. Rab.* 25.11, and *Yalkut*,
Psalms 702 on the same verse. For *Psalms Rabbah* sources, see S.
Buber, *Midrash Tehillim* (Rome: Vilna, 1891). The Jerusalem 1965
reprint of this also contains *Midrash Mishle* on Proverbs. Another
Yalkut reference is *Yalkut*, Deuteronomy 886, which discusses false
signs and wonders (Deut 13:1-3). God performs true signs such as
visiting Abraham, burying Moses, etc. Further *Yalkut* passages
listing such works of mercy include *Yalkut*, Genesis 16 (on Gen
1:22) and *Yalkut*, Genesis 33 (on Gen 3:20). In *Yalkut*, Genesis 82,
God and the angels come to visit the sick man.

[42]*Pal. Talm. Rosh Hashanna*, ch. 1, hlch. 3. Palestinian
Talmud references will be from *Talmud Yerushalmi* (New York, 1958).

^{43}A similar instance is in *Pal. Talm. Biccurim*, ch. 3, hlch. 3; also in *Lev. Rab.* 35.3. Here the specific regulation in Lev 19:32 is cited: "You shall rise up before the hoary head." God, unlike earthly kings, is the first to carry out any one of His laws, as He does in standing before Abraham.

^{44}*Gen. Rab.* 48.7.

^{45}Thus *Tanhuma* וירא §2; *Tanhuma B* וירא §4; *Tanhuma B* וישלח §28; *Cant. Rab.* 2.9 (here the verse "My beloved is like a gazelle" is taken to refer to God, who skips from one synagogue to another. When He comes into such a place He stands as He did before Abraham, etc.). This is also the theme of *Pesikta Rabbati* 15.9; *Pesikta Rab Kahana* 5.8; *Num. Rab.* 11.2; and *Psa. Rab.* 22.19 (on Psa 22:4). Our *Kahana* references are from B. Mandelbaum, *Pesikta de Rab Kahana* (2 vols.; New York: JTSA, 1962).

^{46}*Gen. Rab.* 48.1.

^{47}Similarly, *Tanhuma* וירא §2; *Exod. Rab.* 41.4, which also mentions that Gen 18:22 is a Tiqqun Soferim related to our topic; *Psa. Rab.* 18.29; less closely related instances would include *Yalkut*, 2 Samuel 162 and *Yalkut*, Psalms 831. *Yalkut*, Genesis 82 and Rashi both mention the idea that Abraham wanted to stand but God told him to sit, as a sign.

^{48}*Gen. Rab.* 52.5.

^{49}On Lev 1:1, *Lev. Rab.* 1.13 offers a little more information. God appears to heathens at night, as He did to Abimilech (Gen 20:3), Laban (Gen 22:24), and Balaam (Num 22:20). He appears to His chosen ones in full day, as to Abraham (Gen 18:1), and Moses (Exod 6:28 and Num 3:1).

^{50}A similar comment on Gen 20:3 can be found in *Yalkut*, Genesis 88.

^{51}*Pal. Talm. Berakoth*, ch. 4, hlch. 1.

^{52}*Gen. Rab.* 48.8.

^{53}There follows the medical remark that "it follows that heat helps wounds." Similar notes are to be found in *Tanhuma* וירא §3; *Tanhuma B* וירא §4, which includes an excellent use of Mal 3:19-20 (English 4:1-2). *Mekilta Ishmael* ויסע 5, on the subject of manna and its melting when the sun gets hot (Exod 16:16-27), guesses that, like Gen 18:1, this occurs by noon. A very similar case is in *Mekilta Yohai* בשלח 16.21. *Mekilta Ishmael* references will be from J. Z. Lauterbach, *Mekilta de Rabbi Ishmael* (3 vols.; Philadelphia: Jewish Publication Society, 1933-1935). *Mekilta Yohai* references will be from J. Epstein and E. Melamed, *Mekilta d'Rabbi Simon b. Yochai* (Jerusalem: Mekitze Nirdamim, 1955).

Other citations include *Yalkut*, Exodus 261, on the time for gathering quails; *Yalkut*, Jeremiah 296, on the phrase in Jer 17:8, "the just man does not fear the heat"; *Yalkut*, Psalms 773, on Psa 55:21, "my companion stretched out his hand" in which we again have the depiction of Abraham guarding the entrance to Gehenna from entry by unworthy circumcised Israelites; and *Yalkut*, Song of Songs 986, on Cant 2:7, "until the day breathes." *Yalkut*, Genesis 82 describes the poking of the hole in Gehenna and the matter of the sixth hour and the healing of Abraham's wounds. In *Zohar* there are

new developments. This type of light or heat is of the kind that
can be withdrawn (temporary?). Another kind of light is used for
healing, as in Gen 32:30; so *Zohar* 21a.

[54] So also in *Yalkut*, Genesis 82 and Rashi. Rashi sees God
as repenting of this action due to Abraham's intense desire to
be hospitable.

[55] *Pirke Eliezer*, ch. 29.

[56] The Shekinah concept was already used in v. 3 of the Targums
Neofiti and *Ps.-Jonathan*. Maimonides in his *Guide to the Perplexed*
(part 1, sec. 4) says that every use of ראה when referring to seeing
God indicated an intellectual apprehension rather than a physical
one. For the English of Maimonides, see *The Guide to the Perplexed*,
trans. Shlomo Pines (University of Chicago, 1963). The Hebrew may
be found in *Doctor Perplexorum*, ed. Samuel Tibbon, rev. Yehuda
Shmuel (Jerusalem, 1946).

[57] *Gen. Rab.* 48.9.

[58] The same is retold in *Tanhuma* וירא §2; in *Tanhuma* תשא §15,
during a discussion about theophanies in general (such as Sinai),
it is said of the appearance at Mamre that God appeared to him and
afterward so did the three men; so also in *Tanhuma B* וירא §4.

[59] *Cant. Rab.* 1.13, on Cant 1:13, "my beloved lies between my
breasts."

[60] *Gen. Rab.* 48.10.

[61] Thus *Masseketh Soferim*, ch. 4, rule 6; *Sefer Torah*, ch. 4,
rule 6; *Yalkut*, Deuteronomy 856; and *Yalkut*, Genesis 82. The
first two references may be found in *The Minor Tractates of the
Talmud*, ed. A. Cohen (2 vols.; London: Soncino, 1965). For the
first we use M. Higger, *Masseketh Soferim* (New York: Debe Rabanan,
1937). Rashi says clearly that he thinks Abraham spoke only to
the chief of the three angels. If he had wished to speak to all
three he would have said *lords*. Besides, whatever the chief agreed
to, the others would also do. Rashi also admits that there is a
second opinion. In his commentary on *Yoma* 37a, Rashi seems to depict the precise arrangement of the three angels, i.e., next to
each other but with the leader just a bit forward. The gemara at
this point in the Talmud is talking about three men who are walking.
Proper manners would have the teacher in the middle of the trio,
with the senior student on his right. They should not be one behind the other but in one row, i.e., side-by-side. Rashi recalls
that the three angels who came to Abraham

> by implication, they were standing in one row, side-by-
> side; they were a bit behind the one--not the only one
> who came to Abraham--but the one who was their leader.

Zohar 101a (and 106b) says that Abraham had a separate vision of
the Shekinah. Maimonides (*Guide*, part 1, sec. 61 and part 2, sec.
42) holds for the side that Abraham was speaking only to the chief
angel. In *Guide* (part 2, sec. 45) the Mamre visit is listed as the
tenth highest of eleven grades of prophecy (I would use the word
"revelation" to express what Maimonides seems to mean by "prophecy").
However, in *Mishne Torah* הלכות יסודי התורה Perek 6, §9, Maimonides
says that all the names used by Abraham are holy, even the one in
Gen 18:3. He even repeats, "Behold, this is holy." For text, see
Mishne Torah, ed. David Arama (Jerusalem, 1965).

[62]*Exod. Rab.* 25.2.

[63]*Yalkut,* Judges 69 mentions that the angels who came to
Abraham were "as men." So also in *Yalkut,* Daniel 1063, and in
Maimonides, *Guide,* part 2, sec. 6.

[64]As found in *Exod. Rab.* 3.6.

[65]Note the new duty of healing Abraham. Michael and Gabriel,
at least, are heavenly princes, according to *Gen. Rab.* 78.1. In
Josephus' *Antiquities* 1.11.12, when Sarah objected that she and
Abraham were elderly and so could not have a son, the visitors
could no longer refrain from revealing their identities. They admitted that they were angels of God, one of whom had been sent to
deliver this message and the other two of whom had come to destroy
Sodom. For texts, see *Josephus,* ed. H. Thackery and R. Marcus
(8 vols.; Loeb Classical Library; London: Heinemann, 1926-1943).

[66]*Pirke Eliezer,* ch. 25.

[67]*Gen. Rab.* 48.9. The commentator says that we get the
names of the months of the year and also of the angels from
Babylon.

[68]In *Kiddushin* 32b a discussion about certain parental duties
evolves into a discussion on questions of public acts of respect
toward Rabbis. One of the examples used was a tale about several
Rabbis at table, being served by one of their most respected
Rabbis. Upon protesting that they were not worthy to be so served,
the ministering Rabbi said that Abraham had served others,

> and should you say that they appeared to him as minister-
> ing Angels, they appeared to him only as Arabs.

A similar invocation of Abraham's politeness is recorded in *Yalkut,*
Exodus 229.

[69]We have already mentioned the matter of how Targums *Neofiti*
and *Fragmentary* try to modify the bow of Abraham so as to avoid any
false impression along these lines.

[70]In *Tanhuma* תרומה §10, there is a discussion on the different
times when acacia wood is mentioned in the Bible. The tree under
which the angels reclined is thought to have been an acacia because
of the merits of Abraham. In *Zohar* 102b we are told that Abraham
had a special miraculous type of tree which he planted each time he
moved (same tree or seeds?), but which flourished especially in
Canaan. The tree would spread wide and healthy when believers were
around it but would droop when an unbeliever came near. Abraham's
invitation to the visitors to recline under the tree is therefore
seen as an additional precaution on his part.

[71]*Kallah Rabbati,* ch. 7, according to Higger's text and enumeration, in *Massekhtot Kallah.*

[72]This is the sequence of the verbs; i.e., there is no gram-
matical foundation for saying *and then.*

[73]Very similar traditions are recounted in *Derek Eretz Rabbah,*
ch. 4 (in Higger, this is *Pirke Ben Azzai,* ch. 2). See M. Higger,
The Treatises Derek Eretz (New York: Debe Rabanan, 1935). Here
Abraham speaks to the chief angel in v. 3, asking him to wait until
he can take leave of the Shekinah. The Shekinah had come at the

same time as the angels. Here one text (Soncino) cites Gen 18:3, while another (Higger) cites Gen 17:22, which describes God taking His leave *several days before*. Thus we really have two interpretations: that Abraham kept God waiting while he entertained (Higger); and that he kept his guests waiting for at least a short time while he listened to God (Soncino).

[74] *Zohar*, 101a.

[75] *Zohar*, 107a.

[76] *Zohar*, 102ab.

[77] *Sifre* ואתחנן §27, commenting on Deut 3:24, in which Moses calls himself a servant of God. *Sifre* references for Deuteronomy will be found in *Siphre d'be Rab*, ed. L. Finkelstein and H. S. Horovitz (Berlin, 1939).

[78] He also lists those who called themselves servants but were not additionally so designated by God, and vice versa.

[79] In *Psa. Rab.* 18.4, a reference to David as God's servant starts that author off on a similar list. *Yalkut*, Deuteronomy 814 repeats the item from *Sifre*, and another case is had in *Yalkut*, Joshua 4 (on Josh 1:2). *Yalkut*, Genesis 82 mentions a list as well as *Yalkut*, Isaiah 438 (on Isa 53:11-12).

[80] *Esth. Rab.* 7.9, on Esth 3:5, "Haman saw that Mordecai did not bow."

[81] This theme is repeated in *Yalkut*, Esther 1054; *Yalkut*, Numbers 765, on Balak seeing Israel's deeds (Num 22:2); and *Yalkut*, Job 908, inspired by Job 22:16.

[82] Almost all the Targums retain the exact measurement of three *seah*s of flour (approximately 20 liters volume); different words are used to describe the kind of bread product to be made, but they all seem to indicate kinds which would be made with little or no leaven and more heat contact. This is understandable since full-leavened loaves take a longer time to prepare.

[83] *Gen. Rab.* 42.8.

[84] Perhaps that Passover overtone is also conveyed by the same word עוגות in the MT. Another hint at this Passover theme is found in *Mekilta Yohai* בא ch. 12, §39 (on Exod 12:39); the Israelites baked the dough which they had brought from Egypt into עוגות מצות not cakes but scones אין עוגה אלא חררה כענין. Gen 18:6 is cited here to explain the exact kind of bread meant.

[85] *Gen. Rab.* 48.12.

[86] *Yalkut*, Genesis 82 mentions the 9 *seah*s and their use and the Passover time.

[87] There is a proverb which uses the words חמאה and חלב which we have in Gen 18:8; Prov 30:33, "If milk is pressed, curds result." *Midrash Mishle* 30.33 and *Yalkut*, Proverbs 964 note Abraham's use of these foods when serving his visitors.

[88] Similar mention of this "unclean breads" tradition is found in *Pirke Eliezer*, ch. 36, and *Yalkut*, Genesis 82.

[89]Gen. Rab. 48.14.

[90]Perhaps the פטירין of Targum Neofiti and Ps.-Jonathan's "time of the feast" are also indicators of this tradition.

[91]Sarah is a foil on this point.

[92]Even 3 seahs seems an excessive amount if one is in a hurry to prepare a meal.

[93]This is from Tanhuma B בשלח §23. It is also found in Gen. Rab. 48.12, and Yalkut, Genesis 82.

[94]Gen. Rab. 48.11.

[95]The same three biblical verses are mentioned in Psa. Rab. 104.12, on Psa 104:15; on the same Psalms verse in Yalkut, Psalms 862; on the Judges verse in Yalkut, Judges 75; Yalkut, Genesis 82, and Rashi.

[96]Gen. Rab. 48.11.

[97]In Yalkut, Psalms 757 (on Psa 48:14), we have a different case where לבכם has only one ב. Here we learn that there is no evil desire in the time to come, as can also be seen in Gen 18:5. Another instance would be Rashi on 1 Chr 28:9, "serve God with a whole heart." Rashi notes that the word is written with one ב and is in the singular. At Gen 18:5, the word לבכם has a plural suffix but has the one ב which proves that the angels who visited Abraham really had "one heart."

[98]Jacob Mann, The Bible as Read and Preached, 1.134.

[99]Gen. Rab. 48.6.

[100]So also in Exod. Rab. 25.8 (where Isa 33:17 is paralleled to Moses, not Abraham) and Yalkut, Genesis 82. In all these cases Abraham is the host and the bread is for him to give out. There is no implication that the "him" of Isa 33:16 is God.

[101]The Targums do not elaborate beyond the MT except that Ps.-Jonathan adds a term to describe the dish as "prepared meats (תבשילין)."

[102]Gen. Rab. 48.13.

[103]Some of the Targums had mentioned Ishmael with reference to v. 10.

[104]Yalkut, Genesis 82, mentions almost all these traditions; the three calves, the mustard sauce, Ishmael's duties, etc. Rashi mentions the three tongues in mustard and that Ishmael was the servant boy.

[105]Pirke Eliezer, ch. 36.

[106]There is also an allusion to this cave in Aggadath Bereshith, Perek 34, having to do with the flour used for the bread. I have not worked the translation out fully, but it seems that the flour was grown in a wheat field near or on top of the cave. See S. Buber, Aggadath Bereshith (Cracow: J. Fischer, 1902). Zohar 127b has the same story about the runaway calf, and Yalkut, Genesis 82 mentions it.

[107]*Tanhuma* וישלח §7.

[108]The author also leads up to a horrendous pun involving
Deut 22:10, "You shall not plow with an ox and ass (בשור ובחמר)
together."

[109]*Tanhuma B* חצוה §10.

[110]*Lev. Rab.* 21.11. This reference is also in *Pesikta Rab
Kahana* אחרי מות piska 26. Buber had placed it in the former
position in one of his editions. The same Aaronic sacrifice (Lev
16:3) is related to Gen 18:7 in *Pesikta Rabbati* 47.4, and *Yalkut*,
Leviticus 571.

[111]*Lev. Rab.* 27.9.

[112]*Pesikta Rab Kahana* 9.9.

[113]*Yalkut*, Leviticus 643. Other Leviticus allusions can be
found in *Tanhuma* אמור, part 3, §12, and *Tanhuma B* אמור §16.

[114]*Num. Rab.* 13.14.

[115]Rashi does the same at Num 7:21. On Num 7:51, we have
Num. Rab. 14.5. *Yalkut*, Numbers 714 is related to Numbers 7 and
Rashi has the same remark on Num 28:19. *Tanhuma* חצוה §13 is in a
similar vein.

[116]This is from *Cant. Rab.* 7.6. The same can be found in
Lev. Rab. 31.4.

[117]*Pesikta Rabbati* 27/28.1.

[118]*Tanhuma B* וירא §2.

[119]*Yalkut*, Isaiah 511.

[120]*Aggadath Bereshith*, ch. 19.

[121]Thus Isaac's and Abraham's pleas for their months not to
be associated with the destruction of the Temple and the analogy
involving Cant 7:6 (mentioned above, near the end of the last
grouping) are examples of the patriarchs' influence before God.

[122]*Psa. Rab.* 18.29, on Psa 18:36, "Your humility has made
me great."

[123]*Lev. Rab.* 1.9; the commentary is on Lev 1:1, "The Lord
called Moses."

[124]*Lev. Rab.* 11.5.

[125]In this verse there is a Tiqqun Soferim; God actually
waited for Abraham. Almost the exact same parallels are made in
Psa. Rab. 18.22. Rab Simon states clearly that the Shekinah
waited for Abraham until he left the angels.

[126]The merits so gained were applied to David (2 Sam 22:18).

[127]The act of *standing by* is commented on by Rashi. He cites
Gen 24:30, where Abraham's servant is described as standing by the
camels at the well. This standing by is the same as *caring for* the

animals. In the same way Abraham's standing by is caring. Maimonides, in *Guide* (part 1, sec. 13), discussing different levels
of meaning in the verb עמד, observes that its use in Gen 18:8 refers to the simplest sense of rising and standing.

[128]This last non-biblical tradition has to do with a miraculous well which followed (reappeard to?) the Chosen People during
the years in the desert.

[129]*Tosefta* סוטה perek 4. See S. Lieberman, *The Tosefta* (New
York: JTSA, 1955-19--).

[130]Non-biblical traditions expanded on the pillar of cloud
theme.

[131]Relatively similar lists of parallels may be found in
Tanhuma וירא §4; *Tanhuma B* וירא §5.
    In *Tanhuma* תצוה §6 and *Tanhuma B* תצוה §2, we again find com-
ments on Cant 7:6, "a king is held captive in the tresses." In
the former passage, God says to Israel, "I have bound myself forever to you by an oath, for whose merits? For the sake of Abraham,
who twice ran before me" (Gen 18:2 and 7). *Tanhuma B* וירא §5 also
has a very close examination of Gen 18:4, "let a little water be
brought" which may be too detailed to go into here. In *Pesikta
Rabbati* 14.3, on the matter of sacrificing a red heifer (Num
19:2), we have another account of the merits gained by Abraham
at Mamre. The only variations worth noting here are that for the
parallel to having the angels rest under the tree we think of the
booths of Lev 23:43, and, on the matter of the water and the calf
which were part of the hospitality, there are some references to
taking some of the ashes of the red heifer and making water pure
with them. Another list can be found in *Exod. Rab.* 25.5. Herē,
for the bringing of water by Abraham, we find cited Ezek 16:9.
Yalkut, Exodus 228 has a full set of parallels. *Yalkut*, Numbers
737 mentions only the quail parallel and *Yalkut*, Deuteronomy 850
speaks only of the well in the desert. Another traditional list
is in *Mekilta Ishmael* בשלח 1, §20.
    In *Lev. Rab.* 34.8, the passage under consideration is Lev
25:25. This leads to some technical remarks about the duty which
relatives have to make loans or other arrangements with a poor
man so that his property will not be alienated. The question
is asked, "Who showed kindness to persons not needing it?" The
answer is Abraham, who hosted the angels under the tree. In reward
for this kindness God gave his descendants the manna, quails, etc.
Therefore, since God has so rewarded an unneeded kindness, how much
the more will He reward a kindness shown to a needy relative.

[132]I am making no attempt here to date the growth of the
separate elements of these merit series. I am simply assuming that
the Exodus themes were chief among the earlier points of comparison,
based on their appearance in *Baba Mezia*.

[133]*Gen. Rab.* 48.10.

[134]*Qoh. Rab.* 11.1. A new citation here is Joel 4:18, "the
mountains shall drip sweet wine..." as the future parallel to
Abraham's action of bringing water (English enumeration is Joel
3:18). *Num. Rab.* 14.2 has a similar chart, except for parallels
involving the bringing of water (Exod 6:7 and Isa 14:2). *Yalkut*,
Leviticus 655 contains a list close to that in *Genesis Rabbah*.
Yalkut, Numbers 764 lists all the parallels for the water theme
only. *Yalkut*, Isaiah 401 has a nearly complete version. *Yalkut*,

Genesis 82 mentions that Abraham was very eager to host despite
his pain, that he ran or hastened three times; it has a very full
list of merit parallels for the desert, promised land, and
messianic future, and a more detailed analysis of the water parallels. *Mekilta Yohai* ואראֹ 6.2 mentions Abraham's hospitality to
the angels in commenting on Ezek 20:9.

[135] Patte, *Early Jewish Hermeneutic*, 72.

[136] So also Rashi on *Peshahim* 86b.

[137] *Aboth de Rabbi Nathan*, ch. 13. References will be from
S. Schecter, *Aboth de Rabbi Nathan* (Vienna, 1887; reprinted in
New York: Feldheim, 1945).

[138] This is the only case which I have found of an attempt to
count four calves. In context, the author was trying to stress
the great scale of what Abraham did. Most likely the tradition
which prevailed (three calves) did so because of the three visitors
and the three tongues in mustard sauce. In this account, Ishmael
is the servant boy.

[139] *Tanhuma* וירא §4.

[140] *Yalkut*, Genesis 82.

[141] On *Aboth de Rabbi Nathan* 6a, on mishnah 15.

[142] One other biblical event triggers this same opinion. That
is the contrast between Num 22:17, wherein Balak promised to do
great honors for Balaam, and the result in Num 22:40. In this
last verse, rabbinic tradition was that Balak's provisions of meats
were less than grand. Thus evil men like Balak promise to do a lot
but they deliver very little. The opposite is true of Abraham. We
find this account in *Tanhuma B* בלק §15; *Numbers Rabbah* 20.17 and
Yalkut, Numbers 765.

[143] *Yalkut*, 1 Kings 176. Also found in *Yalkut*, Genesis 82 and
Baba Mezia 86b.

[144] W. Eichrodt, *Theology of the Old Testament*, trans. J. Baker,
Vol. 1 (Westminster, 1961) 144.

[145] *Genesis Rabbah* 48.11.

[146] §14. I.e., they were disposed of in a miraculous way.

[147] *Qohelet Rabbah* 3.14. Text under study is Eccl 3:14.

[148] Basically the same idea is repeated in *Exodus Rabbah* 47.5
(on Exod 34:28). Another similar citation would be *Leviticus
Rabbah* 34.8. *Yalkut*, Genesis 82 repeats several of the above traditions. It mentions that the angels said, "we do not eat or
drink but...for yourself...do as you have said." It mentions that
the angels appeared to eat, and that the courses of food disappeared
one after the other. Rashi says that they seemed to eat. *Zohar*
102a says that the angels simulated eating in honor of Abraham.
This simulation was as when fire invisibly consumes fire. In
104a we read that the angels pretended to eat all the food so that
Abraham could gain as much merit as possible. Josephus (*Antiquities* 1.11.12) also says that the angels seemed to eat the food.

[149]*Pesikta Rabbati* 25.3.

[150]The implication is that they ate both foods at the same time. A similar account is in *Psalms Rabbah* 8.2.

[151]*Exodus Rabbah* 28.1.

[152]*Seder Eliyahu Rabbah*, ch. 12. See M. Friedmann, *Seder Eliahu Rabba and Seder Eliahu Zuta* (Jerusalem: Wahrmann, 1969). The discussion concerns the question of eating with Gentiles and gathering together with them. In *Yalkut*, Exodus 406 and *Yalkut*, Deuteronomy 852 we are told clearly that the angels ate when Abraham offered them food. *Yalkut*, Genesis 82 reports the tradition about God opening the mouths of the angels and making them eat. *Zohar* 144a flatly states that they ate, in contrast to Moses who did not eat when on high.

[153]In *Genesis Rabbah* 48.15, the Rabbis quote Judg 5:24 and compare Sarah with Jael, most blessed of tent-dwelling women. In *Psalms Rabbah* 128.3 (on Psa 128:3, "Your wife will be a fruitful vine within your house"), Sarah is mentioned as one who was modest in her tent. In *Yalkut*, Exodus 169 Moses' meeting with his future wife is recalled and it is said that he acquired a modest wife by the merits of Sarah. *Yalkut*, Psalms 881 repeats the essay on the fruitful vine of Psalm 128.

[154]*Yalkut*, Deuteronomy 933 repeats most of this in connection with Deuteronomy 23 and the original grievance against the Ammonites and Moabites.

[155]*Tanhuma* שרה §4.

[156]*Yalkut*, Numbers 722.

[157]My copy of *Yalkut* reads שהיו יודעין היכן הוא, but I assume this last is a scribal or printing error for היא. In *Tanhuma B* שרה §3, the many dialogues of Abraham and God are listed, among them this one in Gen 18:9. *Yalkut*, Genesis 82 mentions the exemption for Ammonite and Moabite women, and that the angels really knew Sarah's whereabouts but wanted to remind Abraham of her modesty. Rashi mentions her modesty and then goes on to detail some rules about how a guest should inquire after his host and hostess. *Zohar* 101b mentions Sarah's modesty but says that the angels did *not* know where she was. They wanted to be sure where she was because their instructions were to deliver the message to Abraham alone.

[158]*Masseketh Soferim*, ch. 6, rule 3.

[159]From all the rabbinic comments on this word it seems that in very early manuscripts the ל either did not have one of these points or that its point was ignored.

[160]*Aboth Rabbi Nathan*, ch. 34.

[161]In *Sifre* Num. בהעלתך §69, mention is made of a *punctum* on the final ה of רחקה from Num 9:10, about a person on a long journey observing Passover. *Sifre* references to Numbers are from H. S. Horovitz, *Siphre de'be Rab* (Leipzig, 1917). In noting this *punctum* the comments lead into a listing of other instances of *puncta* such as Gen 18:9. It is quite possible that this is the basis for the connection noted previously in *Yalkut*, Numbers 722 on Sarah's

devotion to home and Passover. A very similar list is occasioned
by another *punctum* in Num 3:39; this is recalled in *Numbers Rabbah*
3.13.

[162]This tradition could be at the base of Rashi's remarks
about how a guest should inquire after his host and hostess. The
business of taking the letters with *puncta* to have meaning by
themselves is spelled out a little more clearly in *Genesis Rabbah*
48.15. In any case where the dotted letters form the majority of
the letters in a word, one may interpret the dotted letters. Here,
just as they said to Abraham, "where is Sarah?" so they said to
Sarah, "where is Abraham?" *Yalkut*, Genesis 82, Rashi, and *Zohar*
101b all retell this איו tradition.

[163]*Yalkut*, Genesis 91 (on Gen 21:1) notes the promise made in
Gen 18:14.

[164]*Gen. Rab.* 53.4.

[165]Very similar applications are in *Pesikta Rabbati* 42.2.
Solomon's prayer is from 1 Kgs 8:24.

[166]*Psa. Rab.* 80.7.

[167]*Gen. Rab.* 78.2.

[168]*Seder Olam Rabbah*, start of ch. 5. See B. Ratner, *Seder
Olam Rabbah* (Rome: Vilna, 1894).

[169]*Tanhuma B* וירא §36.

[170]*Pesikta Rabbati* 6.5.

[171]Rabbinic tradition used Exod 40:2, interpolating this date
between the times mentioned in 1 Kgs 6:38 and 8:2. E.g., *Pesikta
Rabbati* 6.5.

[172]There is another view (*Pesikta Rabbati* 5.7, working on
Genesis Rabbah 53.7) that God chose first to appear in a tabernacle
on earth in honor of Isaac, in the same month as Isaac was born,
because of a play on Isaac's name (his birth ushers in a new law--
circumcision).

[173]Presumably the *mark* on the wall is a play on חיה of כעת חיה
and the Hebrew word מחיה, as used in Lev 13:10 and 13:24.

[174]*Yalkut*, Genesis 82 also says that the messengers came at
Passover time. *Yalkut*, 1 Kings 184 mentions the Passover bread,
Nisan, and the dedication of the Temple.

[175]*Gen. Rab.* 18.2.

[176]God instead fashions Eve from the rib, since this is the
most modest part of the body; even when a person is naked, the rib
is still covered.

[177]*Gen. Rab.* 45.5, in discussing the enmity between Sarah and
Hagar.

[178]In *Tanhuma* וישב §6 we have another long list of womanly
shortcomings, including Sarah's eavesdropping. Abraham by contrast
used his senses for good. He looked to see the mountain on which

to offer Isaac; he looked and found the substitute ram; lifting up
his eyes he saw the three visitors, and so on. All of this comparison was started by a reflection on Eccl 7:26, "And I found
more bitter than death the woman whose heart is snares and nets."
The fact that Dinah went out on a visit (Genesis 34) starts another
list in *Tanhuma B* וישלח §17. Miriam's transgressions are another
reason to consider what failings women have. In *Deut. Rab.* 6.11,
we consider Sarah's eavesdropping and her laziness (list started
by Miriam text, Deut 24:9); later in the same paragraph the creation of Eve is mentioned and Sarah's eavesdropping gets a second
notice. *Yalkut*, Genesis 24 repeats the basic charge of woman as
eavesdropper, based on Gen 2:22. Isa 3:16 is reviewed, with the
now expected results, in *Yalkut*, Isaiah 398. *Yalkut*, Genesis 82
repeats the charge of eavesdropping.

[179] *Gen. Rab.* 48.16.

[180] *Yalkut*, Genesis 82.

[181] *Gen. Rab.* 48.16.

[182] This and following citations help explain the Targumic
paraphrases of כעת חיה.

[183] *Pesikta Rabbati* 42.5.

[184] Another citation in the same text is that of Ezek 36:36,
"The nations shall know that I the Lord have restored the ruins
and replanted that which was desolate." Abraham and Sarah were
both "ruined" by age and Sarah was the desolate field. So also
Aggadath Bereshith, ch. 28. *Yalkut*, Isaiah 438 uses Isa 53:2, "he
grew...like a root out of dry ground" to furnish an image of Sarah
being as barren as "dry ground."

[185] *Pesikta Rabbati* 51.2.

[186] *Pesikta Rab Kahana* 27.9. A very similar development is to
be found in *Lev. Rab.* 30.10. So also in *Yalkut*, Leviticus 651.

[187] *Gen. Rab.* 53.1.

[188] *Yalkut*, Ezekiel 357.

[189] *Gen. Rab.* 48.19. The Soncino text must be quite different
here.

[190] Thus the Targumic paraphrases of Sarah's words in vv. 11
and 12.

[191] *Gen. Rab.* 48.17.

[192] The addition of the י and ו could originally have been a
mistaken vocalization.

[193] So also *Pal. Talm. Megillah*, ch. 1, hlch 9; *Gen. Rab.*
48.17; *Tanhuma* שמות §22; *Mekilta Ishmael* פסחא §14; *Yalkut*, Genesis
82; and *Masseketh Soferim*, ch. 1, rule 8. These all mention the
list of variants from the accepted Hebrew. The commentaries suggest that the reading "among her relatives" would be found in the
LXX. Neither the LXX editions which I consulted (Brooke-McLean
and Wevers) nor Field's *Origenis Hexapla* indicate any such extant
manuscripts. See Alan Brooke and Norman McLean, *The Old Testament*

in Greek, 3 vols. (Cambridge University, 1906), or John Wevers, *Septuaginta: Genesis* (Göttingen: Vandenhoeck & Ruprecht, 1974). Also F. Field, *Origenis Hexaplorum Quae Supersunt sive Veterum Interpretum Graecorum in Totum Vetus Testamentum Fragmenta* (Hildesheim: Olms, 1964).

[194] *Gen. Rab.* 48.16.

[195] *Lev. Rab.* 31.9.

[196] *Yalkut*, Psalms 673 repeats this analogy.

[197] *Yalkut*, Joel 538.

[198] *Yalkut*, Psalms 887.

[199] This can be seen in *Tanhuma B* בראשית §33 and *Yalkut*, Job 900.

[200] *Pal. Talm. Pea*, ch. 1, hlch 1 is similar to the preceding.

[201] *Gen. Rab.* 48.18.

[202] *Tanhuma* שופטים §18.

[203] The variant "with her relatives" is here taken pejoratively.

[204] *Tanhuma* צו §7.

[205] *Tanhuma B* צו §10. *Pesikta Rabbati* 50.2 gives a peace list in a discussion on days of atonement. In *Sifre*, Num. נשא §42 another peace list is suggested by the blessing in Num 6:26, "The Lord lift up his countenance upon you, and give you peace." Here it is said that the Holy One "changed the deed" of Sarah. *Num. Rab.* 11.7 repeats the remarks on Num 6:26. In *Kallah Rabbati*, ch. 10 the peace theme is again invoked. Note here that the question is whether one can tell a little white lie when congratulating a groom on the beauty of his new bride (when she is not so beautiful). It is allowable since it will help foster their marital union. *Perek Hashalom*, ch. 6 and *Lev. Rab.* 9.9, have peace lists. So also do *Yalkut*, Genesis 162, on Jacob's brothers; *Yalkut*, Numbers 711; and *Yalkut*, Psalms 711, inspired by Psa 29:11. *Yalkut*, Genesis 82 and Rashi record the theme. *Zohar* 103a holds that Sarah said her husband was old only after she felt herself menstruating. *Zohar* passes over the peace theme entirely.

[206] The only noteworthy Targum modification of the MT is in v. 15 of *Ps.-Jonathan* where an angel speaks and says "do not be afraid."

[207] *Gen. Rab.* 48.17.

[208] Using the variant reading.

[209] Thus *Pal. Talm.* סוטה, ch. 7, §1 and *Gen. Rab.* 20.6.

[210] *Gen. Rab.* 48.20.

[211] So also in *Gen. Rab.* 45.10 and 63.7; and *Psa. Rab.* 9.7. *Yalkut*, Genesis 80 and 82 record the same.

[212] All of these remarks were made in the context of applying
Deut 32:10-12 to Abraham. See J. D. Eisenstein, *Ozar Midrashim:
A Library of Two Hundred Minor Midrashim* (New York, 1915).

[213] *Yalkut*, 2 Kings 228.

[214] Rashi also mentions the different uses which the word כי
can have. In Gen 18:15, the כי of כי יראה means *because* and the
כי of כי צחקת means *but*. These observations are repeated in
Rashi's remarks on *Rosh Hashanna* 3a.

[215] *Gen. Rab.* 48.20.

[216] *Exod. Rab.* 20.3.

[217] This same contrast is spoken of in *Yalkut*, Exodus 226.
Here the opening line of *Mekilta Ishmael* בשלח is quoted, "the term
'letting go' has no other meaning than 'escorting.'"

[218] This paragraph ends with the following remark:
          Abraham says, "Let a little water be
          brought..." as it is written in the
          section *And the Lord appeared to him.*
This could be a reminder to the reader of the usual start to the
list of meritorious actions of Abraham, or the sense of the remark
might have been simply that the angels had enjoyed their rest and
had done their assignment and so it was time to go on.

[219] *Mishne Torah Sefer Shofetim* ה' אבל, ch. 14, §2.

[220] Rashi may possibly be an exception.

[221] E.g., that we should not be reluctant towards the wishes
of a great person; that a woman can size up travellers better than
a man; that we should do more than we promise to do; that a small
act is important, if it is a righteous one; and "I have had food
and drink, escort me."

NOTES

CHAPTER II

[1]R.P.C. Hanson, *Allegory and Event* (London: SCM, 1959) 7.
I consider Hanson's work on Origen and his review of ancient
Jewish, Christian, and pagan approaches to literature to be very
clear and stimulating. He is careful to supply many biblical
examples of each process which he defines. Patristics scholars
may prefer other working definitions or classifications, but I
will rely on Hanson here.

[2]Ibid.

[3]K. J. Woollcombe, "The Biblical Origins and Patristic
Development of Typology," *Essays in Biblical Typology* (London:
Allenson, 1957) 65.

[4]James Smart, in the fourth chapter of his book *The Interpretation of Scripture* (Westminster, 1961) 93-133, presents an ex-
extensive rebuke to proponents of biblical typology for our times.
Since the purpose of my own study here is to analyze Christian
sources within a definite period of history, I simply refer the
reader to Smart's work.

[5]G.W.H. Lampe, "The Reasonableness of Typology," p. 28 in
Essays in Biblical Typology.

[6]Ibid., 10.

[7]Ibid., 14.

[8]Ibid., 24-25. Yves Congar deals directly with the NT roots
of typology and its importance for the early Church in his *Tradition and Traditions*, trans. Michael Naseby and Thomas Rainborough
(Macmillan, 1967) 64-83. First he examines NT uses of OT wit-
nesses. For the NT writers, the OT reveals the economy of the
covenant as fulfilled in Christ. Christ included "in his death
and exaltation all the (new) People of God, to such an extent that
his destiny embraced their existence and destiny. The meaning of
Scripture is then relative to Christ and to the Church..." (68).
    In addition to finding strict *types* in the OT, the NT writers
make many allusions to details in the OT which they see as realized
in some action of Christ's or of his followers. In fact reference
is often made to a *zone* of texts which exemplify, perhaps by
analogy, constant factors in God's plan.
    Mutatis mutandis, the Fathers treat both testaments in the
same manner as the New Testament writers treated the Old. Their
main intention was to discover christological types. They also
develop other type patterns.
    Congar is particularly interested in two characteristics of
patristic exegesis. First is the fact that frequently the Fathers
refer to scriptural events as models for things still being realized in the present. The Fathers "do not base what they have to
say on Scripture after the manner of *Schriftbeweis*; if they quote
it, and they do indeed quote it, it is rather as an illustration of
what they are affirming than as a textual argument. Their real
foundation is the reality of the Church, that is to say, the
Church's tradition as a living transmission of lived realities" (79).

The second characteristic is a frequent ecclesial reference
to Scripture as the record of the wishes and plan of God. "The
Fathers are convinced that all Scripture refers not only to
Christ, but also the Church, and that it contains, under the form
of a type, all that is useful to its historical life" (80). As
examples of such ecclesial reference, Congar mentions the many
types concentrating on Christian priesthood and hierarchy, and on
sacraments such as penance and confirmation.

[9]Lampe, "The Reasonableness of Typology," 33.

[10]Ibid., 35.

[11]Woollcombe, "Biblical Origins and Patristic Development of
Typology," 53.

[12]So Woollcombe on pp. 69-70 of his article.

[13]So Lampe on p. 23 of his article.

[14]To be found in H. Strack and P. Billerbeck, *Kommentar zum
Neuen Testament*, 1.21-22.

[15]Jean Daniélou, *From Shadows to Reality*, trans. W. Hibberd
(London: Burns and Oates, 1960) 244.

[16]Ibid., 246-47. The French original of Daniélou's book,
entitled *Sacramentum Futuri*, was published in 1950. Lampe's
remarks, originally delivered as a lecture in 1955, were published
in 1957. Presumably, therefore, Lampe's dismissal of the sermon
illustration type of the scarlet cord is in response to Daniélou's
tolerance of it.

[17]Ibid., 115-18.

[18]Ibid., 117. No further explanation is given by Daniélou at
this point.

[19]Jean Daniélou, *The Theology of Jewish Christianity*, trans.
John Baker (Chicago: Regnery, 1964) esp. 117-46.

[20]Ibid., 118.

[21]Ibid., 121-27.

[22]Ibid., 127-31.

[23]J. Quasten deals with the life, writings, and theology of
Justin on pp. 196-219 of vol. 1 of his *Patrology*, 3 vols. (Newman,
1950-55). L. W. Barnard studies the persona and theologies of
Justin and Trypho in his article "The Old Testament and Judaism in
the Writings of Justin Martyr," *Vetus Testamentum* 14 (1964) 395-
406. Willis A. Shotwell examines Justin's relationship to other
Christian, Jewish, and Greek influences, and also his exegetical
principles, in *The Biblical Exegesis of Justin Martyr* (London,
1965). Hanson studies Justin's use of allegory on pp. 103-8 of
his *Allegory and Event*. I used vols. 8 and 11 of *Textes et Documents*, ed. H. Hemmer and P. Lejay (Paris, 1909) for G. Archam-
bault's Greek edition of the *Dialogue*.

[24]Quasten, *Patrology*, 1.202-203; Barnard, "The Old Testament
and Judaism," 395.

[25]Quasten, *Patrology*, 1.202-203; Barnard, "The Old Testament and Judaism," 396. Quasten (202) identifies Trypho as a Rabbi Tarpon who is mentioned in the Mishnah, but Barnard (396) argues against this, assuming Trypho to be an educated layman.

[26]Quasten, *Patrology*, 1.208.

[27]Quasten offers excerpts from chs. 60.2 and 127 of the *Dialogue* to prove his point.

[28]Quasten, *Patrology*, 1.209. Benedict Kominiak, pp. 27-47 in *The Theophanies of the Old Testament in the Writings of St. Justin* (Washington, DC: Catholic University, 1948), argues that Justin is not a thoroughgoing subordinationist.

[29]Shotwell (*Biblical Exegesis of Justin Martyr*, 103-15) presents a detailed comparison of the very different uses which Justin and Philo make of the Logos concept. Quasten (*Patrology*, 1.207-11) restricts himself to a brief overview of Justin's use of the concept.

[30]The use of this word reflects Justin's subordinationist Christology.

[31]Barnard ("The Old Testament and Judaism," 404) notes Justin's knowledge of this post-biblical Jewish exegesis. Shotwell (*Biblical Exegesis of Justin Martyr*, 74) reminds us that this explanation can be found in *Genesis Rabbah* and in Josephus. We found it in groupings 4a and 4b of Chapter I of this work, as well as in some Targums.

[32]Justin here cites Gen 21:12 as proof. Shotwell (*Biblical Exegesis of Justin Martyr*, 36-37) notes the technique of inferential analogy used here and in the latter half of ch. 56. Kominiak (*Theophanies of the Old Testament*, 32) points out that this citation is somewhat inappropriate as an arguing point.

[33]Justin again cites Gen 19:24.

[34]Trypho does not seem to know of Jewish traditions about the spiritualizing of the eating. Hanson (*Allegory and Event*, 104) points out that the pre-Incarnate Christ would not have eaten. Barnard ("The Old Testament and Judaism," 404) points out that at least Justin is acquainted with this post-biblical Jewish exegesis.

[35]Trypho allows this explanation to stand. Shotwell (*Biblical Exegesis of Justin Martyr*, 19) points out that this spiritualizing allows the text to be a clear prediction of Christ. R. M. Grant (p. 137 in *The Letter and the Spirit* [New York: Macmillan, 1957]) wants to translate τροπολογίας as "analogy" or "comparison," but does not explain why. Shotwell (13) explains that the "analogy" is the analogy of fire consuming something.
I would see Justin's explanation of the way to understand how the food was "eaten" as a logical consequence of his theology and as nothing less than a denial of the plain meaning of the text.

[36]Hanson (*Allegory and Event*, 105) sees this whole collection as "typology...trembling on the verge of allegory."

[37]Barnard, "The Old Testament and Judaism," 398.

[38]Ibid., 399-406.

[39]Shotwell ends his study of Paul's use of the Old Testament
with the remark that, in matters of exegesis, Justin was a "direct
descendant" of Paul, in that the Old Testament exegeses of both
are Christocentric (*Biblical Exegesis of Justin Martyr*, 50-55).

[40]Hanson, *Allegory and Event*, 108.

[41]Ibid.

[42]Ibid., 108; Barnard, "The Old Testament and Judaism," 399,
406; Shotwell, *Biblical Exegesis of Justin Martyr*, 46, 96-98 (a
close study of Philo and Justin on Gen 18:1-3 and 8).

[43]I consulted *St. Irenaeus: Proof of the Apostolic Preaching*,
trans. Joseph P. Smith (Ancient Christian Writers Series 16;
Newman, 1952), and *Irénée de Lyon: Démonstration de la Prédication
Apostolique*, trans. L. M. Froidevaux (Sources Chrétiennes Series;
Paris: Editions du Cerf, 1959). Smith provides an adequate overview of the history of the text (4-12), and several technical remarks with the translation itself. Froidevaux also discusses the
state of the text (7-25), and has technical notes, including many
patristic parallels. Quasten provides older bibliography (*Patrology*, 1.292-93).

[44]We also have an Arabic fragment of a commentary on Genesis
by Hippolytus of Rome, who claimed to be a disciple of Irenaeus
(Quasten, *Patrology*, 2.164; *New Catholic Encyclopedia* [McGraw
Hill, 1967] s.v. "Hippolytus of Rome, St.," by M. McGuire). The
German translation of the Arabic can be found in vol. 1.2 of *Die
Grieschischen Christlichen der Ersten Drei Jahrhunderte* series,
trans. H. Achelis (Berlin: Akademie Verlag, 1897-), p. 92, frag.
6. In this passage Hippolytus mentions that angels had come to
Abraham at Mamre and had eaten food with him. The NCE article
(1140) notes that Hippolytus' exegesis was usually literal, "with
little trace of Alexandrian elaboration."

[45]In §45 we find the same problem with the omnipresence of
God the Father which Justin exhibited in *Trypho* 60.2 and 127. The
Son is the mediator with men, since the Father can never be seen
by men or be limited to one location. Theophilus of Antioch, a
contemporary, also shows the same philosophical presupposition in
Ad Autolychum 2.22 (PG 6, col. 1088), although he does not cite the
Mamre story as an example. We will use the *Patrologia Graeca*
series (ed. J. P. Migne [168 vols.; Paris, 1857-1866]) only when
more recent editions and texts are not available.

[46]*Adversus Haereses* 4.7.4, 4.9.1, 4.10.1 (SC 100).

[47]On Tertullian, see Quasten, *Patrology*, 2.243-340. We do not
possess a firm critical text of the *Vetus Latina*; in this work I
will use the Bueron Abbey edition and will note significant variant
readings when necessary. Obviously, the *Vetus* is very close to the
LXX. Thus *ilicem* and *medio die* in v. 1; *super* and *super terram* in
v. 2; and the *ante te* of v. 3. In v. 4 *laventur*, as LXX, is not an
imperative; *panem* in v. 5 is not qualified. *Et postea* may have had
אחרי for a Vorlage or, more likely, simply the LXX. In v. 6,
consparge tres mensuras similaginis is quite close to the LXX and
ingriphios is a Greek loan word. At the start of v. 8, all our
Vetus texts seem to lack a main verb; *et ederunt* comes earlier than

in the MT. In v. 9 the opening *dixit* is singular as the LXX, unlike MT. In v. 10 the Vetus follows the LXX with the clumsy *ad
hoc tempus in futurum* and the final *post eum*. The Vetus goes
further than other versions in saying that Sarah was *post ostium*.
The *necdum mihi factum est usque nunc* of v. 12 is close to the
LXX; so are *verbum* and *in tempore hoc...in futurum* from v. 14.
למֹעֵד is ignored. In v. 16 *et Gomorrae* is added, with LXX.

[48]Quasten, *Patrology*, 2.243-46.

[49]Ibid., 247.

[50]*Corpus Christianorum, Series Latina* (Turnholt: Brepols,
1953-) vol. 2.

[51]Quasten specifies the Gnostic sects to be the followers of
Marcion, Appeles, Basilides, and Valentinus.

[52]Tertullian assumes that the flesh used by the angels is
not retained after the mission is over. He does not care to explain the process, noting that "if you had seen when it had been
brought forth from nothingness, you would also know when it was
sent back into nothingness" (3.7).

[53]We are reminded of Irenaeus' description in *Apostolic
Preaching* (44).

[54]In *Adversus Marcionem* (CC vol. 1), Tertullian battles the
theories of Marcion, who set up a dichotomy between the God of the
OT and that of the NT. In the third book he deals with Marcion's
assertion that the OT Messiah was not Jesus and had not yet in fact
come. In 3.9.1-5, Tertullian again reviews the idea that the
angels at Mamre had real flesh.
    The question is whether the angels in a vision, having
    merely putative flesh, dealt with Abraham and Lot, and
    yet truly met and ate and worked as was their commission.
He replies that they did have real flesh, made of real matter,
even though it had not been conceived and born in the usual way.
In his reply, Tertullian never refers to the eating or working
again. Context indicates that he believed that they truly ate.
    In 3.9.6, we read that Christ appeared with the angels,
    "and He appeared in the genuineness of the flesh with
    the angels to Abraham. The flesh was not yet born,
    since it was not yet going to die, but it was learning
    how to deal with men."
In 3.9.7, Tertullian again refers to the fact that the disposal
of the angelic flesh is of no concern to us and also that God can
transform us someday like unto angels, as in Luke 20:36.

[55]CC vol. 2. Quasten (*Patrology*, 2.285) considers Tertullian's writings opposing Praxeas to be "the most important
contribution to the doctrine of the Trinity in the ante-Nicene
period."

[56]Quasten, *Patrology*, 2.324-27. He also notes (319-20) that
Tertullian was never interested in drawing up consistent theological systems, nor in bringing harmony between faith and philosophy.

[57]See ibid., 212-33, esp. 217-18. Also NCE, "Novatian and
Novatianism," by P. H. Weyer.

[58]This was written some years before 250 A.D. Our text is
from *Novatian: De Trinitate*, ed. W. Y. Fausset (Cambridge Patristic Texts; Cambridge, England, 1909) 62-63. Weyer notes (535)
that *De Trinitate* was meant to bring the teaching on the Trinity
down to his time.

In it he defends the oneness of Almighty God, and God
the Creator, against the Gnostics; Christ as the Son
of God the Creator, against Marcion; Christ as true
man, against the Docetists; as true God, against the
Adoptionists, etc.
Our selections would presumably counter Marcion's errors.

[59]Ibid., 65.

[60]Ibid., 65-66.

[61]I am indebted to R.P.C. Hanson, *Allegory and Event*, ch. 2,
"Alexandrian and Hellenistic Allegory," 37-64; and to an article
by V. Nikiprowetzky, "L'exégèse de Philon d'Alexandrie," *Revue
d'Histoire et de Philosophie Religieuses* 53 (1973) 309-29. I used
Philo, ed. F. Colson, G. Whitaker, and R. Marcus (10 vols. and two
supplementary vols. on the Armenian commentaries on Genesis and
Exodus; Loeb Classical Library Series; Harvard, 1929-53). There
are other editions of the Greek text available such as Leopold Cohn
and Paul Wendland, *Philonis Alexandri Opera* (Berlin, 1896) and *Les
Oeuvres de Philon d'Alexandrie* (Paris), which is scheduled to be a
thirty-six volume work when completed.

[62]Hanson, *Allegory and Event*, 37-46.

[63]Ibid., 44.

[64]Ibid., 45.

[65]Ibid., 46-53.

[66]Ibid., 46-47.

[67]Loeb, vol. 1, p. xxiv. Vol. 6, pp. x-xi; Colson remarks on
p. xi that "it is difficult to see *how* Abraham pre-eminently
represents wisdom acquired by teaching."

[68]An example might help here. In *Deterius* (59-61) we are
told that when God asks questions of humans, it is for their benefit and not for His. When He asks Abraham, "Where is your virtue
(i.e., Sarah)?" the patriarch answers, "in the tent (i.e., in the
soul)." Possessing virtue is not a satisfactory state. God must
send down the joy of putting virtue into practice, just as He gave
Isaac to Sarah. Abraham learns then, from his own answer, that
without God's help, virtue is insufficient.

[69]Hanson, *Allegory and Event*, 41 and 49.

[70]Ibid., 49. Hanson then lists (49-52) samples of specific biblical events which Philo admits to be historical, but about which
he prefers to concentrate on the allegorical meanings almost exclusively. He then lists a middle group of examples where the
literal and allegorical treatments are about evenly handled; e.g.,
in treating of Abraham, Philo seems to be more ready to allow the
historicity of specific biblical events altogether. F. H. Colson
(Loeb, vol. 1, pp. xiii-xiv) draws the same conclusion that Philo
does not care for the mere historical content of OT events.

Hanson (*Allegory and Event*, 52-53) examines Philo's attitude toward observance of Jewish laws and customs and finds that he generally holds for their observance, even if he is not interested in the content of a law for anything other than its allegorical meanings. Colson (Loeb, vol. 1, p. xiv) agrees with this finding.

[71]Neither the MT nor the LXX identify the speaker of Gen 18:14.

[72]Presumably based on the phrase מִן מָרְאֶה.

[73]In §164, Abraham had given the land of Mamre to Eschol and Aunon, who were possessed of naturally good ways and were lovers of vision (φιλοθεάμονας).

[74]Hanson (*Allegory and Event*, 47) notes that this stress on the idea of burying or hiding, which is derived from ἐγκρυφίας, is one example of Philo's uncritical trust in the LXX as a faithful rendition of the Hebrew sense of the words.

[75]It is possible that Philo's allegorical equation of masculine gender to our better actions and inclinations, and of feminine gender to our lower ones, represents a development of rabbinic remarks such as we saw in grouping 12 of Chapter I of this study. Some Christian commentators will imitate him (Clement of Alexandria, Origen, Ambrose, and Gregory the Great).
There is another way of considering virtues and vices in mutual opposition which goes back at least to Tertullian's *De Spectaculis* 29.5 (CC 1, p. 252) and to Prudentius' *Psychomachia*. In these writings the virtues and vices are allegorized as feminine, insofar as human images are used. This tradition, as A.E.M. Katzenellenbogen has shown, is well represented in medieval iconography. See his *Allegories of the Virtues and Vices in Medieval Art* (London, 1939; reprinted New York: Norton, 1964). In the preface of the *Psychomachia* (lines 45-68), Prudentius does mention the theophany at Mamre, but his main interest is in the battle of Genesis 14. Text can be found in vol. 1 of *Prudentius*, ed. H. J. Thompson (Loeb Classical Library Series; Harvard Press, 1949) 276-79.
The Greek genders for the vocabulary which Philo normally used to describe virtue, good desires, passions, and emotions do not coincide with the genders in his allegorical system. On the other hand, the majority of the Latin nouns which depict the various virtues and vices are abstract and feminine, and so might provde some basis for the exclusively feminine Christian iconography.

[76]Similar categorizations of faults and vices as "female" can be found in *De Fuga* 128 and 167, where the "ways" are our human and rational customs, and vaguely in *De Somniis* 2.185.

[77]Here, and in *Leg. All.* 3.218, Philo is giving his own interpretation that Sarah's phrase, "my Lord is old," in Gen 18:12, applies to God and not to Abraham!

[78]So also in *Leg. All.* 3.218, we find Sarah joyful.
    She laughed in her mind and said, "There has not been
    happiness to me until now and my Lord, the divine word,
    is greater, to whom belongs this happiness by necessity,
    and He is to be believed when He promises good."
Similar remarks on human joy can be found in *De Spec. Leg.* 2.54-55. There God reassures Sarah that creatures are not entirely denied joy.

[79]*Questions and Answers on Genesis*, trans. Ralph Marcus (Loeb,
Philo Supplement, vol. 1 [1953]). Our selection is from book 4,
1-20, pp. 265-93. The manuscript ultimately depends upon a 5th
century Armenian text, presumably translated from the Greek. I
will use Marcus' English translation exclusively. The style of
this work is more elaborate than other writings of Philo, but I
think that the content of these twenty paragraphs is certainly
very similar to what we already have found in Philo. In restrict-
ing myself to noting the few items which seem to filter into later
Christian traditions, I do not mean to cast judgment on the
genuineness of the rest of the text.

[80]I am not implying direct borrowing.

[81]Colson (Loeb, vol. 6, pp. xi, xii, and xv n.) points out
that elsewhere Philo does cite many OT texts in his exegeses.

[82]Nikiprowetzky's article concerning Philo's exegetical work
can be very helpful here. He is interested in reviewing Philo's
Jewish concepts rather than his Greek background ("L'exégèse de
Philon d'Alexandrie," 320). This study leads Nikiprowetzky to an
appreciation, based on the Synagogue services in Alexandria and on
the format of *Questions and Answers on Genesis*, and *on Exodus*, that
Philo almost always subordinates allegory to the prior duty of ex-
plicating any problems in the text (323, 325). The other commentaries of Philo are studied literary adaptations of the *Questions*
format. Further, Nikiprowetzky postulates that the Platonic theme
of a "spiritual migration" underlies all of Philo's thought (326-
327).
    The problem of how to control the use of allegory was not a
real one for Philo. He relied on a "general understanding of the
biblical text, a certain linguistic approach, or philosophical inspiration," in each case to guide him in his exegesis (328). The
only principle more basic for Philo than the "general understanding" just mentioned was his determination to avoid any *systematic
denial* of the literal sense of the text (328; Hanson is offended
by any denials; Nikiprowetzky is looking for patterns among them).
    Since Philo saw allegory as an aid to exegesis, even though a
rich and many-faceted one, we should not look on his literal and
allegorical comments as mutually exclusive. Nikiprowetzky sees
the different commentaries of Philo as forming one system, applied
to different sections of the Bible. This system is an imitation of
the very structure of the Pentateuch itself, perhaps best expressed
by the terms Cosmopoietica, Historica, and Nomothetica. Thus Philo
does have an overall view of the Pentateuch and the importance it
plays in the life of the Jewish people. This view is what unites
his work, even as the varied allegories often distract us from
seeing that unity.

[83]Hanson, *Allegory and Event*, 55-62.

[84]Ibid., 62.

[85]Ibid., 63.

[86]Ibid., 53.

[87]See Quasten, *Patrology*, 2.1-36; Hanson, *Allegory and Event*,
117-20; and Grant, *Letter and Spirit*, 85-89. The *Pedagogus* text
can be found in GCS 12 (reprinted in 1972); *Stromata* is in GCS 52.
See also J. E. Oulten and H. Chadwick, *Alexandrian Christianity*
(London: SCM, 1954) 15-39. Chadwick notes Clement's use of other
sources such as Philo (21).

[88]Hanson, *Allegory and Event*, 118.

[89]Ibid., 120.

[90]The subject of this chapter is the benefits of physical exercise! Quasten (*Patrology*, 2.10) calls books 2 and 3 "a kind of casuistry for all spheres of life."

[91]The *Stromata* deal with "moral perfection, consisting of chastity and love of God," and are anti-Gnostic writings (Quasten, *Patrology*, 2.14). The *Stromata* 6.12 reference is as follows:
And is not thus a woman changed into a man, when she becomes equally unfeminine and manly and perfect. Such then was the laughter of Sarah when she had been informed of the birth of a son; not, I think, that she disbelieved the angel but that she felt ashamed of the renewed intercourse by which she was destined to become the mother of a son.

[92]There is a very brief reference to Abraham's faith in Jesus at Mamre in *Stromata* 5.1, but the Scripture citation is actually from Gen 17:8. A reference in Pseudo-Clement *Homily* 20.7 (GCS 42) mentions the angels who took on real flesh for their visit at Mamre; such spiritual beings who can undergo change cannot be immortal.

[93]See Quasten, *Patrology*, 2.37-101; Hanson, *Allegory and Event*, and also a smaller, earlier work, *Origen's Doctrine of Tradition* (London, 1954). Hanson citations will be from *Allegory and Event* unless otherwise noted. See also J. Daniélou, *Origen*, trans. W. Mitchell (Sheed and Ward, 1955) 131-99. Daniélou recalls Origen's linguistic and textual studies, his work on the canon of biblical books, and his use of typology. Daniélou, of course, regards Origen's use of types favorably (esp. 148-49), although he allows that Origen usually preferred types which spoke of the inner spiritual life of individuals (163-64). Finally, Origen's use of non-Christian allegorical devices is studied. Philo and Origen were too eager to find spiritual meanings in *every* scriptural passage (181-82), which led them to very uneven evaluations of certain specific biblical events.

[94]Quasten, *Patrology*, 2.37-40.

[95]Hanson (*Allegory and Event*, 133-61) depicts the spectrum: Marcionites (135), Predestinarians (142), literalists (149), "Judaising" Christians (152), polemical Rabbis (154), Ebionites (157), and pagans, especially Celsus (159).

[96]Hanson, *Origen's Doctrine*, 40-47.

[97]Quasten, *Patrology*, 2.47: "These works thus belong to the history of Christian spirituality and mysticism rather than to biblical science."

[98]Hanson, 184.

[99]Our concern here is with pp. 187-374, esp. 235-88.

[100]Hanson, 177.

[101]Ibid., 179.

[102]We are reminded of Philo's exegetical format (Hanson, 50).

[103]Hanson, 186. Quasten also notes the division Origen makes between ordinary men and the elite (*Patrology*, 2.91-92 and 94-95).

[104]Hanson, 188.

[105]Ibid., 198-99.

[106]Ibid., 204.

[107]Ibid., 367.

[108]Ibid., 208-9.

[109]Ibid., 219.

[110]See ibid., 224-31. Hanson wonders if one of the precursors of this theory of accommodation, which can also be found in Philo and Clement, was rabbinic exegesis. He offers as an example the rabbinic exegesis of the "peace" theme, wherein divine "white lies for peace" are recorded. We had such a case in Chapter I about God not repeating Sarah's jibe to Abraham. I would think that one way to test this speculation would be to see if Philo used any such rabbinic themes. Philo did not do so with the Mamre "peace" theme, as far as I can see.

[111]Ibid., 231.

[112]Ibid., 235. In *Exégèse Médiévale* (4 vols.; Paris: Aubier, 1959-64) 1.1.198-207, H. De Lubac discerns two different exegetical systems in Origen's writings. One is the well known progression of literal, moral, and allegorical meanings (supposedly analogous to man's body, soul, and spirit). In this system the moral meanings are frequently not developed, or are not specifically Christian in content if they are developed.

The second pattern is a progression of literal, allegorical, and moral meanings. In this pattern the literal meanings are more often shown to have ecclesial or sacramental import, the allegorical derivations are more deeply christological, and the moral senses developed upon these other meanings bring more asceticism and more specifically Christian aspects to bear on the individual. The comments of Origen on the Mamre passage seem to conform to the characteristics of the former system.

[113]Hanson, 243.

[114]Ibid.

[115]Ibid., 245. Quasten (*Patrology*, 2.42) calls it "dangerously subjective."

[116]Hanson, 248.

[117]Ibid., 242.

[118]Ibid., 252.

[119]Hanson lists some of these cases on pp. 238-41 and 265-66. Two other interesting OT examples would be his denial of David's complicity in the death of Uriah (262) and his spiritualizing of Abraham's dealings with Abimilech and Sarah (279).

[120]Hanson, 264. Origen likened such passages to condiments, stumbling blocks, obstacles, etc. (265).

[121]Note that throughout the writings collected here Origen refers to the visitors as angels or as men. He feels free to use either term, since Scripture often does the same (so *Comm. in Joannem* 2.23, citing Genesis 18 and 19; see GCS 10, p. 79).

[122]Latin by Rufinus; see GCS 33, p. 139.

[123]All the Genesis homilies are in Latin, by Rufinus; see GCS 29, pp. 50-54 for this *Homily 4*.

[124]In *Genesis Homily 6*.1, Origen briefly mentions the Mamre visit of the three men, and that Lot was spared destruction either by merit of his own hospitality or of his relationship to Abraham. In *Selecta in Genesim*, on Gen 19:1 (PG 12), Origen notes that perhaps Lot sat at the city gates of Sodom to watch for travellers, as Abraham also did. Lot could have been alert for strangers since he knew how badly his fellow citizens treated such people. Origen also notes that, in Gen 19:3, Lot had to persuade the visitors to enter his house, whereas Abraham had not needed such persuasiveness.

[125]*Sic*; some manuscripts have *subcinericios*.

[126]*Comm. in Matt*. 15.33 (GCS 40, p. 448) also mentions the serving of the bread and meat, but there the context is a five-ages-of-man theme.

[127]In *Leviticus Homily 13*.3 (GCS 29, p. 472), Latin by Rufinus, Origen notes that Abraham's ἐγκρυφίας were made of fine flour and signify hidden and deep revelations. Lot made his ordinary bread from ordinary flour, even though he was not a poor man. This difference between Abraham and Lot signifies Abraham's greater virtue and greater rewards.

[128]In *Cant. Cantic*. 2 (GCS 33, p. 158), Latin by Rufinus, Origen says that at Mamre the angels represented something greater than themselves, in their service. There the mystery (*mysterium*) of the Trinity was brought to the surface.

[129]It is remotely possible that Origen also intended to allude to the *Mandatum* here, in that he refers to the *Dominica sacramenta*; in *Comm. in Joannem* 32.4 (GCS 10, pp. 431-32),when noting that Jesus did the actual washing at the *Mandatum*, Origen briefly mentions that at Mamre Abraham had had this chore done by servants.

[130]Origen elsewhere notes the presence of Christ at Mamre. In *Hom. Matt*. 1.6 (GCS 41, p. 245), on Matt 1:18-25, the theme is "They shall call Him Emmanuel." Christ has dealt with men before, not only in figures and images, but also in face-to-face encounters.
By Abraham, the father of believers, He was seen at the third hour of the day although not in the ineffable substance of His divinity, but rather in an angelic image (*per angelicum speciem*) at midday.

[131]Hanson (220) notes Origen's impatience with (or lack of interest in) the literal sense of this verse.
It is not to be believed that it was the Holy Spirit's highest purpose to mention, in the Pentateuch, where Abraham stood. I have come to hear what the Holy Spirit wants to teach mankind; how does it help me when I hear that Abraham stood under a tree?

132 Origen usually allegorizes the eating of the meal.   In his
Treatise on Prayer 27.11 (GCS 3, p. 370) he explains:
   For sometimes the saints are able to share mental and
   logical food not only with men but also with more
   heavenly powers, either as to help the powers or to show
   them that they have been able to procure nutrients for
   themselves; rejoicing and feeding on such a proof the
   angels have also become more ready to cooperate in every
   way, and for the future to co-understand the fuller
   truths and to co-grasp the better truths with him who
   earlier had enjoyed nourishing lessons and who has made
   the angels rejoice and, if I may say so, has nourished
   them.
Oulton (in *Alexandrian Christianity*, 198) notes this passage as
one of the relatively few allegories in the Treatise. He also
points out (368, notes to his translation) that this allegory, in
context, praises human good will; men can truly please God, according to their abilities.
   Jay's translation (Eric G. Jay, *Origen's Treatise on Prayer*
[London, 1954]) of this difficult passage has better explanatory
notes than O'Meara's translation (John J. O'Meara, *Origen: Prayer*,
vol. 19 [ACW Series; Newman, 1954]).
   In *Comm. in Joannem* 13.33 (on John 4:32, "I have food to eat
of which you do not know"), Origen allegorizes food to mean virtue.
Angels who "feed" on virtue can never get enough of it. That is
why Abraham was able to feed his visitors at Mamre, because they
can never have fullness in this regard.

133 A legitimate Vetus variant reading.

134 In *Genesis Homily* 6.1 (GCS 29, p. 66), Abraham represents
sapientia, and Sarah represents *animi virtus*. In *Genesis Homily*
8.10 (GCS 29, p. 85) we are told that we too might spiritually gen-
erate an Isaac. We would have to cast out all effeminate inclinations from our souls and so bear a "son" (joy, gladness) by the
husband (virtue and wisdom).

135 Despite the first impression, this remark does not seem to
be like a rabbinic "merit" parallel.

136 In *Selecta in Genesim*, on Gen 18:11 (PG 12), Origen speculates that the phrase "advanced in days" is used only of the just;
if this is so then no evil person truly "advances."
   In *Comm. on Romans* 4.6 (Rufinus, PG 14, cols. 983-84, on
Rom 4:1ff.), it is said of Abraham that luxury did not excite him,
nor was he disturbed by passion; the passions of women were not in
Sarah, nor the frenzy of incontinence. Sarah and Abraham were not
being drawn unwillingly into the old marital habits.
   In his *Treatise on Prayer* 2.1 (GCS 3, p. 298) Origen praises
Tatiana as being like Sarah in that her "way" had ceased. Context
does not indicate whether Tatiana is past child-bearing age or has
taken a vow of virginity. Oulton (*Alexandrian Christianity*, 331)
opts for agedness as the explanation.

137 *Genesis Homily* 3.3 (GCS 29, p. 42) has a brief reference to
this same matter of the title *presbyter* not being used for anyone
before Abraham and Sarah.

138 *De Abraham* 118.

139 *Genesis Homily* 4.3.

[140]GCS 9.1, p. 14.

[141]GCS 9.1, p. 40.

[142]GCS 7, p. 101.

[143]Thus he records the appropriate Council of Sirmium decree in *De Synodis* 27.15 (PG 26, col. 737); he argues against an adoptionist Christology by seeing Christ in the OT in *Contra Arianos* 1.38, 2.13, and 3.14 (PG 26, cols. 92, 173, and 352 respectively).

[144]*Catechesis* 12.16 (PG 33, col. 744).

[145]*De Theol.* 28.2.18 (PG 36, col. 49). Quasten (*Patrology*, 3.242) outlines the content of the five Theological Orations. It would seem that in *Oration* 28 he is speaking of God without specifying that the Second Person is the focus.
Gregory compares his sister Gorgonia's devotion to her husband to that of Sarah in *Discourse* 8 (PG 35, col. 793).

[146]PG 76, cols. 532-533.

[147]*Confutatio* 13 (PG 28, cols. 1377-80).

[148]*Commentary on Leviticus* 1.2 (PG 93, col. 805).

[149]This is found in *Letter 21* from Baradotus, an Eastern ascetic, to Emperor Leo at Constantinople; *Acta Conciliorum Oecumenicorum* 2.5, ed. E. Schwartz (Berlin: De Gruyter, 1927-71) 37.

[150]*Genesis*, PG 87A, cols. 363-68.

[151]In his commentary on Isaiah 6:1-5 (PG 87.2, col. 1929), Procopius implies that Jesus alone was seen at Mamre.

[152]PG 90, cols. 360-61.

[153]PG 91, col. 400.

[154]The life and writings of Chrysostom are treated by P. W. Harkins in NCE, "St. John Chrysostom," and more extensively in Quasten, *Patrology* 3.424-82. Walter J. Burghardt's article "On Early Christian Exegesis" (*Theological Studies* 11 [1950] 78-116) contains an analysis of J. Guillet's article "Les Exégèses d'Alexandrie et d'Antioch. Conflit ou Malentendue?" (pp. 257-302 of vol. 34 [1947] *Recherches de Science Religieuse*). Both Burghardt and Guillet are concerned with specifying the sound insights of both schools and with revealing the elements which they actually had in common.
A most helpful book for someone who wishes to set Chrysostom's handling of a specific passage in proper perspective is Frederick H. Chase's *Chrysostom, A Study in the History of Biblical Interpretation* (London, 1887). A recent article which echoes some of Chase's conclusions is "Relativité et Transcendance du Texte Biblique d'après Jean Chrysostome" by Jean-M. Leroux (*La Bible et les Peres: Colloque de Strasbourg* [Paris: Presses Universitaires, 1971] 67-78).
Another helpful work is C. Baur's *John Chrysostom and His Time* (2 vols.; Newman, 1959). In vol. 1, Baur has a chapter on Chrysostom

as a pulpit orator (206-30) and another on his exegetical skills
(315-29). In this latter section some study is made of his dis-
tribution of OT citations (316); Genesis is second only to the
Psalms as a source for quotation. Most interesting are Chrysostom's views on the need for the frequent *private* reading of Scripture (322-26).

[155]Chase, *Chrysostom*, 3-4. The first chapter of his book
(1-27) gives a brief history of the development of the Antiochean
school, including Syrian influences.

[156]Ibid., 14.

[157]Ibid., 18.

[156]Ibid., 23-27.

[159]The first two of these writers fall within our time frame
but I was not able to investigate their work due to lack of scriptural indices. In the future, perhaps the *Biblia Patristica* or
other patristic reference services will give us more Greek Christian scriptural indices to work with.

[160]Chase examines his use of the OT on pp. 28-78 of *Chrysostom*.

[161]Ibid., 40-41.

[162]Leroux notes several passages from Chrysostom's works
which clearly imply that he considered the Scriptures to be not
only the result of a gradual revelation, but even more the *imperfect* result. Leroux develops an image used by Chrysostom and
refers to the Scriptures as a set of correspondence from God to
men ("Relativité et Transcendance," 75-76). This correspondence
is a tangible support (77) for the average Christian. Leroux then
concludes:

> L'Ecriture n'est donc pas parfaite en soi. Elle n'est
> même pas le moyen idéal de communication entre Dieu et
> l'homme. D'une certaine manière, et Chrysostome l'af-
> firme explicitement, elle est un pis-aller, le moyen
> imaginé par Dieu pour rééduquer l'humanité. Comme
> tout moyen pédagogique, elle dépend de son objet autant
> que de ses origines. Elle ne transmet donc pas une
> image parfaite de la vérité et de la sagesse, mais
> simplement la meilleure expression possible de cette
> vérité et de cette sagesse, selon le degré de maturité
> réalisée par la communauté humaine. Nous touchons là
> un aspect fondamental de l'exégèse de Chrysostome:
> s'il admet en effet que l'Ecriture considérée en son
> ensemble, représente la somme de vérité et de sagesse
> susceptible d'être assimilée par la raison humaine,
> il affirme avec autant de netteté que l'un quelconque
> des textes de l'Ecriture, pris isolément, ne contient,
> même en ce qui concerne la thème qu'il développe, que
> la seule partie de vérité ou de sagesse nécessaire
> dans le contexte pédagogique de la révélation. Ce
> principe d'une extrême importance se résume dans la
> notion de *sugkatabasis* qui constitue la clef de voûte
> du système exégétique de Chrysostome, car elle exprime
> la disponibilité bienveillante de Dieu, qui soumet
> sans aucune restriction la révélation aux contingences
> de l'histoire humaine; en effet, cette soumission ne se
> révèle pas seulement par le caractère progressif de la

révélation, mais encore par l'acception des impréci-
sions et des imperfections imputables aux vicissitudes
de la transmission des textes révélés ou plus simple-
ment aux limites des auteurs sacrés. (77-78)
This confident attitude on the part of Chrysostom contrasts with
Origen's conviction that every verbal detail was directly inspired
by God. Consequently, we should find Chrysostom treating passages
in a less "oracular" manner.

[163]Chase, *Chrysostom*, 42.

[164]Ibid., 46.

[165]Ibid., 48.

[166]Ibid., 50-51. Given this profile of the Antiochean
appreciation of biblical history and Chrysostom's own principles,
we might expect literal exegetical results from Chrysostom as he
comments on the Pentateuch and the historical books. However, in
the actual examples given by Chase (51-61) we find that Chrysostom's desire to find moral applications can just as easily limit
some of his literal interpretations as did the Alexandrians' use
of allegory limit theirs. Also, the Antiocheans allowed for types
of Christ in the OT, even if they had stricter norms for using
them. In this matter of finding types of Jesus, Chrysostom's
methods of interpreting prophetic and wisdom materials (62-78)
could not be considered literal either.

[167]Chrysostom died in 407 A.D.

[168]PG 53, cols. 374ff.

[169]This is a rare positive reference to circumcision and the
context of Genesis 17 by a Christian Father.

[170]Chrysostom digresses to criticize the wearing of too much
jewelry by women.

[171]PG 63, cols. 715-18.

[172]There is also a clear mention of Abraham and Isaac's hos-
pitality in *Homily 21 on Ephesians* (PG 62, cols. 153-54). Offhand,
I do not know what biblical or non-biblical tradition about Isaac
Chrysostom had in mind.

[173]PG 60, cols. 318-20.

[174]Quasten (*Patrology*, 3.454) notes:
Chrysostom's keen sense of social justice was shocked by
the violent contrasts of wealth and poverty in both
Antioch and Constantinople. He estimates the number of
poor in Constantinople at about 50,000 and the Christian
population at 100,000. While he constantly upbraids the
rich for their selfish indifference to the fate of their
less fortunate brethren, he never forgets to insist on
the duty of almsgiving. This topic returns so often in
his sermons that he has been called "St. John the Alms-
giver."
Baur's biography is helpful here. In vol. 1 (29-44) he sketches a
brief picture of social conditions in Antioch in Chrysostom's day.
In vol. 2 (21-28 and 56-71) we learn of contemporary life in

Constantinople and of Chrysostom's initial social reforms after
becoming bishop. In vol. 1 (217), Baur reminds us of the extensive number of Chrysostom's extant homilies on almsgiving, poverty,
avarice, and the improper use of wealth.

For an extensive survey of Byzantine public assistance up the
twelfth century, see Demetrios Constantelos' *Byzantine Philanthropy and Social Welfare* (New Brunswick: Rutgers University, 1968).
The author traces the use of the word "philanthropia" from ancient
Greek sources. The twofold content of the term has to do with
divine love for men and also with human love for mankind. This
second aspect was invoked by Philo in *De Abraham* 107, mentioned
earlier in this chapter.

Greek Christians inherited the concept but were more energetic
in their practical philanthropy to the poor, the elderly, the
blind, and the sick. At several points (24, 68, 71, 155f., 186,
208, 257-59), the author mentions Chrysostom's writings and personal involvement with hospitals, hospices, poorhouses, and the
like. The last reference goes into greater detail on how the
figure of 50,000 poor in Constantinople is derived from his
sermons.

[175]PG 61, cols. 294-95.

[176]PG 49, cols. 40-41.

[177]Abraham's commendable attitude toward material riches is
mentioned briefly in *Homily 10 on First Thess.* (PG 62, col. 459),
and *In Propheticum Dictum Illud (Isaia 45:7)* 4 (PG 56, col. 147).

In a few places Chrysostom compares Abraham's generosity with
that of the widow who fed Elijah. In *Homily 19 on Second Corinth.*
(PG 61, col. 535), we are reminded that the widow did not have a
herd of cattle, but she took from the handful which was all she
had. In *On Sts. Peter and Helia* (PG 50, col. 732), we recall that
Abraham was wealthy, while the widow gave from her hunger. In
Pseudo-Chrys. *Homily 50* on 1 Kgs 17:13 (PG 59, cols. 489-90; same
sermon also appears in PL 95, col. 1514, attributed to Paul the
Deacon, an 8th century writer), the request of Elijah that the
widow hasten to make the bread is compared to the hastening of
Abraham and Sarah.

[178]PG 60, col. 606.

[179]PG 61, cols. 302-3.

[180]PG 62, cols. 573-74.

[181]PG 57, col. 412.

[182]PG 48, cols. 988-90.

[183]Lazarus and Abraham are linked also in *De Lazaro*, concio
6.5 (PG 48, col. 1039) and *Second Letter to Olympias* 17 (SC 13,
p. 210).

[184]PG 55, cols. 505-10.

[185]Sarah's service is also mentioned in some detail in
Homily 30 on Romans (PG 60, col. 666).

[186]PG 63, cols. 379-80. Latin by Mutianus.

[187]PG 57, col. 69.

[188]PG 62, col. 141.

[189]PG 62, col. 143.

[190]PG 61, cols. 661-64.

[191]PG 60, cols. 553-54.

[192]Quasten's remarks about Chrysostom's "lack of inclination for systematic presentation" and about his Christology would fit with our findings here (*Patrology*, 3.474-76). The presence of a pre-Incarnate Christ in OT events need not imply that one has a subordinationist Christology, even if that is often the case.

[193]PG 56, cols. 545-46.

[194]Quite brief allusions in *Homily 33 on John* (PG 59, col. 190), regarding the Samaritan woman at the well, and in *Homily 9 on Ephesians* (PG 62, col. 71) regarding Paul, also indicate that Chrysostom thought that it was Jesus who had appeared at Mamre.

[195]PG 54, cols. 385-89.

[196]PG 54, col. 387.

[197]Chrysostom for the moment ignores the *escorting* by Abraham.

[198]Chase, *Chrysostom*, 192.

[199]See Quasten, *Patrology*, 3.536-54.

[200]PG 81, col. 1500.

[201]PG 80, col. 117.

[202]Both Quasten (*Patrology*, 3.539) and Chase (*Chrysostom*, 21) point out that Theodoret did allow for a certain amount of allegorizing in his scriptural commentaries. Thus it is not surprising to see him spiritualizing the eating of the meal.

[203]PG 82, col. 780.

[204]*De Trinitate*, 4.25-28. Text in PL 10, cols. 115-18. We will use the *Patrologia Latina* series, ed. J. P. Migne (222 vols.; Paris, 1844-64), only when more recent editions and texts are not available.

[205]In his refutations of the Arians, Hilary used the Mamre and Jabbok theophanies, showing the activity of Jesus prior to his Incarnation, as part of his exposition of Christ's consubstantiality with the Father. For Greek and Latin Fathers, the use of the term "angel" with regard to Jesus referred to Christ's mission rather than to his nature. A careful examination of Hilary's use of the term "angel" for Christ shows that it does not take on any subordinationist senses. See W. G. Rusch, "Some Observations on Hilary of Poitier's Christological Language in *De Trinitate*," *Studia Patristica*, vol. 12 (Berlin: Akademie Verlag, 1975) 261-64.

For a brief but clear analysis of how Hilary employed all the Genesis theophanies in *De Trinitate*, see G. T. Armstrong, "The Genesis Theophanies of Hilary of Poitiers," *Studia Patristica*, vol. 10 (Berlin: Akademie Verlag, 1970) 203-7.

[206]This seems to be the first patristic use of this text from John, in connection with Genesis 18.

[207]*Commentary on Psalm 118*, Đ, §§6-7 (CSEL 22, p. 510). This is from the *Corpus Scriptorum Ecclesiasticorum Latinorum* series (Vienna: Akademie der Wissenschaften, 1866).

[208]Hilary reads here *respexit Dominus super Sodomam*, a Vetus variant in Gen 18:16.

[209]This seems to be the first patristic use of Psa 119:132 in connection with Genesis 18.

[210]Tractates 1.62.1-2 (CC 22, p. 141).

[211]CC 69, pp. 12-19.

[212]This is a minor Vetus variant. In §3 this highway exit is called a crossroads (*quadruvium*).

[213]CC 69, p. 22. §10 repeats the contents of *Tractatus 2*, §30.

[214]There is a minor allusion to the presence of Christ at the Mamre event in his *De Fide* 80 (CC 69, p. 242); "God was also seen by Abraham, but in the form of a human being, in order to show exactly that in a later time He would come as a man."

[215]CSEL 32.IB, pp. 526-34.

[216]Abraham's hospitality impressed Ambrose. He mentions it in *On Luke* 5.63 (SC 45, p. 206) and urges clergy to imitate it in *De Officiis* 2.21.104 and 107 (PL 16, cols. 139-40. Lot is also considered to be hospitable in this excerpt, 105 and 107).

Abraham's hospitality at the footwashing is contrasted with the humility of Jesus at the *Mandatum* in *De Sanct. Spir.* 1, Prologue, 15 (CSEL 79, p. 21).

In *De Helia et Jejunio* 5.13 (CSEL 32.2, p. 420) Ambrose approvingly notes the absence of wine from Abraham's table at Mamre.

[217]God's appearance at noon indicates His splendor and love. So *De Joseph* 10.52 (CSEL 32.2, p. 108) and *On Psalm 118*.8.50 (our Psa 119:62) (CSEL 62, p. 181).

[218]In *De Sanct. Spir.* 1, Prologue, 4 (CSEL 79, p. 17), the calves used by Gideon and Abraham were types of Christ. The reference to Abraham can be called an allusion to Mamre only, in that John 8:56 is cited.

[219]Sarah's lack of monthly periods is allegorized in *De Fuga* 47 (CSEL 32.2, pp. 200-201). "Womanly ways" are our evil inclinations. Sarah had to cease from these before being deemed worthy to have Isaac. The lessening of desires and vanity is at the same time a building up of virtue. "Isaac" means joy and gladness before God.

[220]In *On Luke* 2.17 (SC 45, p. 80), Sarah's laughter at the news is mentioned; in contrast the Virgin Mary (Luke 1:38) asks not about the fact of her conceiving, but about *how* her pregnancy is to be initiated.

[221]In *On Psalm 118*.17.12 (CSEL 62, p. 383) (our Psa 119:132),
Ambrose notes that *respicere* (Gen 18:16 Vetus variant) often indicates God's anger.

[222]CSEL 73, p. 302.

[223]Similar opinions can be found in *De Cain* 1.30 (CSEL
32.IA, p. 365) and *De Sanct. Spir.* 2, Prologue, 4 (CSEL 79, pp.
87-88).

[224]*De Fide* 1.13.80 and 2.8.72 (CSEL 78, pp. 35 and 82); *On
Luke* 5.97 (SC 45, p. 218).

[225]SC 45, p. 59.

[226]In detail, Chrysostom is much the master preacher on the
matter of aiding the poor. I do not mean to imply that Ambrose
borrowed directly from Chrysostom.

[227]There are some usages in the Vulgate which should be mentioned. We will use *Biblia Sacra Juxta Vulgata Versionem*, ed. R.
Weber (Stuttgart, 1969). In vv. 1, 3, 12 and 13, Jerome uses
Dominus (*dominus* in 13) whereas the MT uses two different words.
Further, Jerome uses *Deus* in v. 14, while the MT does not use a
new word. In v. 15, Jerome identifies the rebuker as *Dominus*; the
MT does not identify the rebuker at all. Other striking changes
include the first person *adferam* in v. 4, the superlatives *tener-
rimum* and *optimum* in v. 7, and the phrase *timore perterrita* in v.
15. It is difficult to say how many of these expressions are peculiar to Jerome, since the MT we use is from a later date, but we
must at least admit the possibility that Jerome was capable of
making his own modifications of the Hebraic sense. The Roman
Catholic Douay version faithfully keeps all of Jerome's nuances,
except for the *timore perterrita* phrase in v. 15.

The use of *convalle* in v. 1 might point to Jerome's awareness
of the rabbinic use of מִישׁוֹר. Many phrases indicate how similar
Jerome's Hebrew text must have been to our MT. Thus *propter* (v. 2),
in oculis tuis (v. 3), *pauxillum aquae* and *lavate* (v. 4), *buccelam*
(v. 5), *sata* (v. 6), and *dixerunt* (v. 9) are all close renditions
of our MT. In v. 10 (and similarly in 14), *tempore isto vita
comite* is a very serious effort to render כעת חיה היה. *Consenui* and
voluptate operam dabo in v. 12, and the *juxta condictum* of v. 14
are also close to the MT. In v. 16 the Vulgate, like the MT, does
not mention Gomorrah.

As an example of his attention to style, let us look at
Jerome's sensitivity to the frequency of the conjunction *waw* in
Hebrew. Jerome uses an alternative for the Vetus *et*, or drops it
altogether, in twelve instances where the MT has a *waw*. These are
וחנה and the second וירא of v. 2; ואקחה and ויאמרו of v. 5; וימהר
and ויאמר of v. 6; ואל and ויתן of v. 7; ואכלו of v. 8 and ויאמר in
vv. 9, 10 and 13. The Vetus retained all twelve of these and the
LXX kept ten, dropping the cases in vv. 9 and 10. In addition, the
LXX and Vetus may have read ואחר in v. 5 and ומהרי in v. 6, but
Jerome adopts neither reading. In fact, Jerome has only two new
uses of *et* in the entire passage: the *et coxit* of v. 7 and the *et
desierant* of v. 11. The effect of using these alternate construc-
tions or of simply dropping the *waw* in the translation is to produce a more flowing, less wooden Latin reading.

In Jerome's *Quaestiones Hebraicae in Genesim* (CC 72, p. 22),
we find a few examples of the kind of scholarship which was behind
his translation. Concerning v. 6, he notes that the *mensuras* of

the Vetus is a vague unit. He understands it to mean three *sata*,
or *amphorae*; he also notes that three *sata* are spoken of in Matt
13:33. On v. 10, Jerome's Vetus text read *in tempore hoc et in
futura* (a Vetus variant). He observes that the Hebrew means *vitam*
instead of *hora*. Thus the sense should be:
    I will return to you in the time of life. It is as if
    he had said "If I live, if there is life accompanying..."

    Revertar ad te in temporae vitae: quasi dixerit Si
    vixero, si fuerit vita comitata...."
On v. 12, Jerome notes that the Hebrew means "Postquam attrita sum,
facta est mihi voluptas"? rather than the milder statements of the
LXX and Vetus. He acknowledges that *Symmachus'* Greek is close to
his own tastes. Indeed, in the Vulgate, *consenui* might be due to
the influence of *Symmachus*. In v. 12 the Vulgate *operam dabo* seems
to be a little stronger than any *factum/a est mihi* construction.

[228] CSEL 54, pp. 661-62.

[229] In his *Letter 108*.11 to Eustocium (CSEL 55), Jerome mentions the Holy Land travels of a certain Paula, who reportedly was
shown "the remains of Abraham's oak." It is conceivable that
Jerome's phrase in *Letter 66* does refer to a real twig. One or
both of these references might have been made in regard to Constantine's basilica at Mamre, where a tree and a well were fea-
tured in the courtyard.

[230] This from the *adferam* in the Vulgate of Gen 18:4.

[231] His commentary on *Habbakuk* 2.3.3 (CC 76A, pp. 622-23).

[232] Jerome was an admirer of Origen and the Alexandrian school
of allegory, in spite of his own concern for the literal meaning
of biblical texts. His teachers included representatives of both
major schools, Alexandria and Antioch, as well as Palestinian Jews
and proselytes. Louis Hartmann, in his article on Jerome's background, works, and worth as an exegete, shows that Jerome's eclectic borrowing from all three systems was a consistent and deliberate procedure (72). Cf. L. Hartman, "St. Jerome as an Exegete,"
A Monument to St. Jerome, ed. F. X. Murphy (Sheed and Ward, 1952)
37-81.

[233] *Letter 122*, to Rusticus, 1 (CSEL 56, p. 57).

[234] So in *Against Helvidius*, 20 (PL 23, col. 214); *On Zephaniah*
1.2-3 (CC 76A, p. 660); *Letter 65*, to Principia, 1 (CSEL 54, p.
617); and *On Micah* 2.4.8-9 (CC 76, p. 476).

[235] PL 23, col. 551.

[236] CC 75A, p. 857

[237] For a brief overview of Augustine's treatment of Scripture,
see G. L. Keyes, *Christian Faith and the Interpretation of History*
(University of Nebraska, 1966) 83-123 (esp. 111-23). Keyes shows
that Augustine approached history, philosophy, theology, and the
Scriptures primarily as an apologist. As such, he uses these disciplines in an uneven, a priori fashion. Keyes' observation that
Augustine frequently takes an OT use of the number three as a
symbol for the Trinity should not keep us from appreciating Augustine's precision in analyzing the Mamre theophany as a *mediate*
vision granted to Abraham and Sarah. M. Pontet (288) also notes

Augustine's frequent discovery of Trinitarian symbols in the OT, in *L'Exégèse de Saint Augustine Prédicateur* (Paris: Aubier, 1947). J. B. Payne offers the suggestion that much of Augustine's allegorizing of difficult scriptural passages may stem from the problems such passages cause for one who adheres to the concept that the Scriptures were verbally inspired. Augustine will use allegory with the Jabbok story. Cf. J. B. Payne, "Biblical Problems and Augustine's Allegorizing," *Westminster Theological Journal* 14 (1951) 46-53.

[238]See NCE, "St. Augustine," by O. DuRoy, esp. pp. 1051-53.

[239]Most of our citations will be from *Sancti Aureli Augustini Hipponensis Episcopi Opera Omnia* (Benedictine monks of St. Maur, Paris, 1835-39). This reference can be found in OA 8, cols. 1127-1131.

[240]This singular is the Vetus reading (also the Vulgate); the MT has a plural.

[241]In *Sermon 7*.3-6 (OA 5, cols. 56-59), Augustine again stresses the full Trinitarian nature of the Mamre theophany. The triune God has come as a single figure in the burning bush, as two people at Sodom, and as three at Mamre. The best way to express it is to say that God can appear when and where He wishes, and in whatever form He wishes. Brief similar analyses can be found in *City of God* 16.29 (OA 7, cols. 702-4); *De Trinitate* 2.10.19/2.11. 20-22/2.18.34 (OA 8, cols. 1204/1205-6/1216).

In *De Trinitate* 3.11.25 (OA 8, col. 1237) we are again reminded that there were three real angels at Mamre, in whom God was seen. In *De Genesi ad Litteram* 11.34 (46) on Gen 3:10 (BA 49, p. 306), we read that God dealt with Abraham at Mamre "as men who speak with a man." BA references are from *Oeuvres de Saint Augustine* (Bibliothèque Augustinienne Series; Paris: Desclée, 1947-52).

One NT observation of Augustine's should be mentioned here. Several commentators have previously applied John 8:56 to the Mamre story as a proof that Abraham had dealt with the pre-Incarnate Christ. Augustine instead, in *Contra Max*. 2.26.8 (OA 8, cols. 1131-32) prefers to understand "my day" as meaning "my years on earth." Thus Abraham, and other prophets, were gifted with the knowledge that at some time in the future God the Son would live on earth. This interpretation leaves the Mamre story free to be explained by Augustine as a theophany of the full Trinity.

[242]OA 2, col. 389.

[243]OA 5.2, col. 1640.

[244]Brief references to angelic bodies at Mamre may also be found in *Letter 158*.6 (OA 2, col. 839) and *Enchiridion* 59 (OA 6, col. 376).

[245]So *On Psalm 78*.29 (OA 4.1, cols. 1190-91).

[246]OA 10.1, cols. 1007-9.

[247]Similar remarks can be found in *City of God* 10.8 (OA 7, col. 391) and *De Genesi ad Litteram* 9.17 (32) (BA 49, p. 140). The miracle of Sarah's rejuvenation is compared with the greater miracle of Mary's virginal conception of Jesus in Pseudo-Augustine *Christmas Sermon 19*.2 (Caillau-St. Yves series 2.27. PL Supp. 2, col. 1042). In *De Mendacio* 5 (OA 6, col. 715), Augustine mentions that Sarah's

198   Mysterious Encounters

denial of her laughter seems to have had a good result. Even so,
Augustine is not satisfied that, on that account, we too may sometimes bend the truth. He does not return to the Mamre account
when explaining his dissatisfaction.

[248]OA 3.1, cols. 615-18.

[249]In *Locutiones de Genesi* (OA 3.1, col. 525), Augustine
notes that, literally translated, the LXX would read *accucurrit in
boves* in v. 7, and *progressi dierum* in v. 11.
In Pseudo-Augustine *Speculum* 141 (CSEL 12, pp. 693-695),
there are collected together the texts of Gen 18:1-5, Gen 43:23-24,
John 13:2-17, and 1 Tim 5:9-10. In these four passages Abraham,
Joseph, Jesus, and approved widows respectively are involved in
the service of footwashing. There is no additional commentary.

[250]For a brief perspective of this period, see R. E. McNally,
"Exegesis, Medieval," NCE 5.707-12, esp. 707-10.

[251]*Monumenta Germaniae Historica, Auctores Antiquissimi*, vol.
9 (Berlin, 1892), "Liber Genealogus," 160-96. This passage is
from section 226, pp. 172-73.

[252]*De Promissionibus* 1.15.22 (PL 51, col. 745).

[253]DuRoy, "St. Augustine," 1056.

[254]So *Contra Arianos* 2.43 (PL 62, col. 225), and also Pseudo-
Vigilius *Contra Varimadum* 1.1 (PL 62, col. 353).

[255]*Adversus Pintam* 8 (PL 65, col. 715).

[256]In *Contra Judaeos* 2 and 11 (*JTS* 20 [1919] 295 and 309),
Maximinus uses the Gen 19:24 proof that Christ sent the fire upon
Sodom at His Father's command. In *Contra Ambrosium* 106 (PL Supp.
1, col. 718), he also asserts that Christ was at Mamre.

[257]PL 75, cols. 917-18.

[258]*Heptateuch, Genesis* lines 596 to 622 (CSEL 23, pp. 23-24).

[259]Cyprian is also credited with a biblical image essay entitled *Coena* (PL 4, cols. 1007-14). In this work important biblical figures attend a mysterious banquet and say or do things which
remind us of biblical stories. While the literary merit of this
essay is rather small, we can point out the actions of Abraham and
Sarah. Abraham sits under a tree; he has his own servants with
him. He donates a calf for the banquet and later is depicted as
eating veal. He also donates milk. Later he thanks God for His
favor (the gesture of Abraham towards his thigh indicates that he
is grateful for having been father to Isaac). Sarah donates fire-
wood for the banquet and later she kneads some dough. She too is
grateful for her motherhood, pointing to her abdomen. In one ar-
cane allusion, Abraham buys a field in which to bury Achar, son of
Charmi, and Sarah laughs when Judas takes the money. This could be
a reminder of her laughter in Genesis 18, if an indirect one.
Cyprian does not use allegory in this theme in *Coena*.

[260]*Formulae Spirituale* 7 (CSEL 31, p. 40).

[261]CSEL 45, p. 4.

[262]Commentary on 1 Pet 3:6 (CC 1088, p. 87). This is the
first instance I have found of someone apparently citing the Vulgate translation of Genesis 18.

[263]*De Spir. Sanct.* 1.6 (CSEL 21, p. 109).

[264]OA 5.2, cols. 2301-03, identified as Pseudo-Augustine
Sermon 5; also in CC 103, pp. 340-43, attributed to Caesarius.

[265]This is similar to Ambrose, *De Abraham* 38, mentioned
earlier.

[266]Pseudo-Augustine *Sermon 3*.2-3 (PL 39, cols. 1743-44). In
the Bueron index volume (56), it is pointed out that the same
pseudonymous author who wrote this *Sermon 3* also wrote *Sermons 7*,
23, 27, 46-50, 59, 60, 99, and *135*; Caesarius made use of *Sermon
135*. We will therefore include this *Sermon 3* here with the writings of Caesarius, since its author was probably influenced by
Augustine in much the same way as Caesarius was.

[267]Note the Augustinian formula concerning the mode of
theophany. In *Sermon 121*.2 (CC 103, p. 505; also known as Pseudo-
Augustine *Sermon 37*), we again see that Abraham saw the Trinity *in*
his visitors.

[268]*Monumenta Germaniae Historica, Auctores Antiquissimi*,
vol. 6.2 (Berlin, 1883), "Dialogi cum Gundobadi Rege," 1-15. This
passage is from section 18, p. 8.

[269]PL 83, cols. 243-44. Isadore seems to use the Vulgate.

[270]English translation by C. Albertson, *Anglo-Saxon Saints
and Sinners* (Fordham University, 1967) 42-43. The Latin text and
a translation can be found in B. Colgrave's book, *Two Lives of St.
Cuthbert* (Cambridge University, 1940) 76-79; notes on 317).
    Bede's prose *Life of St. Cuthbert*, ch. 7, in which he used
the anonymous *Life* extensively, tells the same story, but fails to
explicitly mention the Mamre parallel. Bede's metrical *Life of
St. Cuthbert*, ch. 8, also does not explicitly mention Mamre. The
Latin text and a translation of the prose *Life* can be found in
Colgrave's book (174-79). The Latin text of the metrical *Life* can
be found in PL 94, col. 580.
    Colgrave's article ("Bede's Miracle Stories," in *Bede, His
Life, Time, and Writings*, ed. A. H. Thompson [London, 1932; reprinted New York: Russell and Russell, 1966]), introduces one to
the world of patristic hagiography, a world with which our research
only makes contact in this one event from Cuthbert's life. As to
why Bede failed to mention explicitly the Mamre connection discussed above, Colgrave postulates several other scriptural stories
which Bede could have considered to be equally well involved (210).

[271]*In Genesim* 4 (CC 118A, pp. 209-19), arranged by biblical
chapters and verses. The CC 118A apparatus identifies borrowed
material. Bede uses the Vulgate.

[272]Claude Jenkins, in his article "Bede as Exegete and Historian," in the same book, *Bede, His Life, Time, and Writings*,
points out that Bede was often reluctant to include his own personal exegesis of a verse (153). Sometimes he even repeats the
explanation of another writer while using the first person singular.
Nevertheless, Jenkins affirms that Bede's editorial work alone
entitles him to be considered as an original author (170).

[273]Bede notes Tob 12:19 here.

[274]This synagogue is very famous in the history of Jewish art. A good color plate of the three men can be found in E. R. Goodenough, *Jewish Symbols in the Greco-Roman Period* (13 vols.; Pantheon, 1952) 11. plate 13. His commentary is in 10.91-97.
Cf. Michael Avi-Yonah, "Goodenough's Evaluation of the Dura Paintings: A Critique," *The Dura-Europos Synagogue: A Re-evaluation*, ed. Joseph Gutmann (AAR/SBL, 1973) 117-35. This study of Goodenough's artistic interpretations is helpful for putting Goodenough's remarks about Philo in perspective. Gutmann's article ("Programmatic Painting in the Dura Synagogue," 137-54 of the same book), relates the paintings to the liturgies held in the same room. See esp. 146-49.

[275]See color plate 24.2 in A. Ferrua, *Le Pitture della Nuova Catacomba di Via Latina* (Rome, 1960). There is also a color plate in A. Grabar, *The Beginnings of Christian Art* (Thames and Hudson, 1967) pl. 254.

[276]Text in GCS 7, pp. 99-101.

[277]GCS 6, pp. 231-32.

[278]E. Mader published a two-volume condensed version of the 1926-28 expedition; cf. Evaristus Mader, *Mambre* (Freiburg: Wewel Verlag, 1957). Vol. 2, figs. 40a and 47a are diagrams of the floor plan. Fig. 38 of the same volume shows an artist's conception of the original shrine. The basilica was 66 x 54 feet set within a 160 x 214 foot courtyard, and was built around 333 A.D. The Madaba mosaic map of the late 7th century depicts schematically a church and tree at Mamre.

[279]G. Armstrong, "Imperial Church Building in the Holy Land in the Fourth Century," *Biblical Archaeologist* 30 (1967) 90-102.

[280]W. Telfer, "Constantine's Holy Land Plan," *Studia Patristica*, vol. 1 (Berlin: Academie Verlag, 1957) 696-700.

[281]Massey H. Shepherd, "Liturgical Expressions of the Constantinian Triumph," *Dunbarton Oaks Papers* 21 (Washington, DC, 1967) 59-78.

[282]The most complete list of ancient Christian art work by theme which I used is Louis Reau's *Iconographie de l'Art Chrétienne* (6 vols.; Paris, 1955). Vol. 2.1 concerns OT themes and deals with Mamre on pp. 19-20 and 131-32. Unfortunately Reau does not provide research information for the art works he lists. His first entry for Mamre is the Maria Maggiore mosaic.
Color plates of this can be found in *Die Römischen Mosaiken der Kirchlichen Bauten vom IV-XIII Jahrhundert*, ed. Walter N. Schumacher (Herder, 1976). This is a revision of Joseph Wilpert, *Die Römischen Mosaiken und Malereien der Kirchlichen Bauten* (4 vols., 1916); see pl. 29. Or, see A. Grabar, *Early Medieval Painting from the Fourth to the Eleventh Century* (Skira, 1957) 37. There is a black and white print in Goodenough, *Jewish Symbols*, 3. fig. 1.
I am told that the best source of information on early Christian art in this country is the Index of Christian Art, housed at Princeton University. The Index, which I have not been able to consult, is a card catalogue, with multiple cross-referencing, of published reproductions of individual works of art.

[283]J. J. Tikkanen in *Die Genesismosaiken von S. Marco in Venedig* (Helsinki, 1889) argues for a relationship between a thirteenth century mosaic in the atrium of St. Mark's and fragments of the Cotton Bible. The bible, described by Reau as a Byzantine work of the fifth century, has been severely damaged by fire. The fragment relating to the Mamre story shows three winged haloed angels seated at a round table with two items on it. In the background is a tent. Sarah watches from the tent doorway, which can be seen above the halo of the central figure (Pls. 11.79 and 13.96).
     The later Venetian mosaic has two scenes. On the left three winged haloed angels carrying staves stand before Abraham. He is on his knees near the central angel. In the scene on the right the three angels are seated in front of a tent at a squarish table which supports two loaves, two knives, and a chalice. Sarah watches from the tent doorway, which can be seen above the halo of the central figure (Pl. 6.40).

[284]There are color detail plates in G. Bovini's *Ravenna* (New York: Abrams, 1972) pls. 78-79. A floor plan of the church can be found on p. 111. There is a black and white print in Goodenough (*Jewish Symbols*, vol. 11, fig. 100). An excellent black and white photographic treatment of the entire church can be had in Bovini's *San Vitale, Ravenna*, trans. Basil Taylor (3rd ed.; Milan: Silvano, 1957).

[285]So Gutmann, 146-47. The depictions of Abraham, Abel, and Melchisedech naturally call to mind the commemorative paragraph of the old Roman eucharistic canon.
     The nearby mosaics of Emperor Justinian and Empress Theodora, in which they are leading offertory processions, can be understood to set up the royal couple as types of the Church.

[286]Some of Reau's remarks about later Western art works lead one to believe that several of these are full of details from the story. On the other hand, it is fairly clear that in the East artists preferred to concentrate upon the three angels as a symbol of the Trinity. Goodenough has black and white reproductions (*Jewish Symbols*, vol. 11, figs. 264-66) of later manuscript illuminations. Number 264, from Codex Vat. Gr. 747 (p. 39a), depicts Abraham kissing the foot of one of three haloed men. Number 266, from the same page of the same eleventh century manuscript, depicts three haloed men, of whom the middle figure has a cruciform halo. Sarah watches from a window as he serves them food at a round table. Number 265, from the Constantinople Octateuch, shows three winged, haloed angels at a table set with three chalices. Sarah watches Abraham from a window as he serves the guests. This is only the second example of the guests having wings in our sampling (the other was the Cotton Bible fragment).
     Perhaps the most famous Byzantine representation of the Mamre angels as a symbol of the Trinity is the icon by Andrew Rublev (Tretiatov Gallery, Moscow) done in the early fifteenth century. Here we have three winged, haloed angels seated at a table on which is one chalice. Abraham and Sarah are not included in this scene. As described by Leon Ouspensky and Vladimir Lossky (*The Meaning of Icons* [Graf, Olten-Switzerland, 1952] 201-6; color plate p. 200), the three angels symbolize, from left to right, the Father, Son and Holy Spirit. Later imitations of Rublev's Trinity sometimes depict three chalices and some token food items (e.g., three fist-sized radishes) in what is otherwise substantially the same scenario.
     In the West the baptism of Jesus by John eventually became the usual biblical scene for Trinitarian iconography, while the theophany at Mamre remained the locus for Byzantine Trinitarian iconography.

[287]L. Thunberg has reviewed a great many patristic sources on Mamre in his article "Early Christian Interpretations of the Three Angels in Gen. 18," *Texte und Untersuchungen*, 92.560-70. He concludes that we should always assume Christ to be the central figure, if any of the visitors are to be taken symbolically. He also points out that Western iconographic material on Mamre with a "clear Trinitarian arrangement" comes much later than clear Trinitarian written material on the same passage.

[288]Reau has a list of patristic Old Testament types (*Iconographie de l'Art Chrétien*, 1.201-7). If his list is an accurate approximation of patristic *written* traditions, then clearly only some of the many possible Old Testament types were fostered.

[289]I am assuming that any use of the Mamre material as proof texts for doctrinal statements about Jesus, the Trinity, angels and the like was a *constitutive* use in the sense that the usual audience for such "proofs" is the faithful, and not the heretics, schismatics, Jews, or pagans to whom it was often technically addressed.

NOTES

CHAPTER III

[1]The Revised Standard Version verse numbers in chapter 32 of Genesis are one lower than those in the Hebrew. We will use the Hebrew verse numbers throughout, as is done in many editions of the LXX, and in many English translations.

[2]The English v. 1 of Hosea 12 combines vv. 1 and 2 of the Hebrew. Therefore the English verse numbers are one less than the Hebrew for the verses we are considering.
As an etymology for the name Israel, the saying "you have striven with God" is not in the expected form; God is normally the subject of such a verb.

[3]Speiser and the NAB render the former as "divine beings," instead of "God." The NAB translates the same word as "God" in Hos 12:4.

[4]The *Preliminary Report on the Pentateuch* retains וחוכל as a *lectio difficilior*.

[5]The following studies on the Jabbok story are listed in chronological order, except for the later work of Vawter which is placed with his first entry. Those commentaries already mentioned in the introduction to the first chapter are cited here only by the name of the author, when that is sufficient.
Gunkel, *Genesis*, 359-65; Skinner, *A Critical and Exegetical Commentary*, 407-12; Morgenstern, *The Book of Genesis*, 252-57; Jacob, *The First Book of the Bible*, 221-25; *IDB* commentary by Simpson, 722-29; Karl Elliger, "Der Jakobskampf am Jabbok," *Zeitschrift für Theologie und Kirche* 48 (1951) 1-31; J. Schildenberger, "Jakobs Nächtlicher Kampf mit dem Elohim am Jabok," *Miscellanea Biblica B. Ubach* (Barcelona, 1953) 69-96; von Rad, *Genesis*, 314-21; Vawter, *A Path through Genesis*, 223-24, and his *On Genesis: A New Reading*, 347-51; F. Van Triqt, "La Signification de la Lutte de Jacob pres du Yabboq," *Oudtestamentische Studien* 12 (1958) 280-309; Speiser, *Genesis*, 253-57; Nahum Sarna, *Understanding Genesis* (Schocken, 1966) 203-6; Gaster, *Myth, Legend, and Custom*, 205-12; and R. Barthes, R. Martin-Achard, et al., *Analyse Structurale et Exégèse Biblique* (Neuchâtel: Delachaux et Niestlé, 1971) 21-56.

[6]For example, G. von Rad argues that the Jahwist consciously wrote about a theophany in this passage (319 of his *Genesis*). He holds for this interpretation consistently (*Genesis*, 319-20; *Old Testament Theology*, trans. D. Stalker [Harper and Row, 1962-65] 1.110, 171-72, 182, 2.325-26, 378). K. Kuntz (*The Self-Revelation of God*, 105, 109, and esp. 128-32) also concludes that the mysterious opponent is most likely Jahweh.

[7]Speiser's translation of אלהים as "divine beings" assists him in avoiding a discussion of whether or not the Jabbok account was intended to be a theophany. Similarly, at the end of v. 30, it is mentioned that the opponent finally blessed Jacob. Speiser, citing Gen 44:7 (a greeting) and Gen 47:10 (a farewell), prefers to translate that the opponent "bade him goodbye." Speiser argues that the blessing which Jacob sought had already been given in the change of his name, and that greeting and farewell formulae would normally

include an invocation of the good will of the deity. Speiser's suggestion, not noted by any of the ancient Rabbis, also supports the interpretation that the opponent was an angel.

[8] In addition to the Targums cited in Chapter I of this study, we have a section on part of the Jabbok story in the Cairo Genizah Targum fragments.

[9] *Massorah Gedolah* (ed. Gerard Weil [Rome: PIB, 1971]) indicates three other biblical cases where an expected definite article is lacking (217).

[10] The UBS *Preliminary Report* retains the MT as a *lectio difficilior*. The committee sees the addition of כל as a device which merely facilitates the setting of the scene. The passage thus concentrates on the two wrestlers to the exclusion of any relative or possession of Jacob.

[11] *Gen. Rab.* 76.9.

[12] Ibid.

[13] *Ozar Midrashim*, p. 244, right col., §23.

[14] Num 23:9.

[15] Here are cited Isa 2:11 (mentioned in the preceding paragraph of this work) and Deut 32:12, "The Lord alone did lead him."

[16] *Yalkut*, Isaiah 447 mentions this.

[17] In succeeding formulae credit is given to the merit of the dust of Jaoob for Israel's success in trade, wars, and Torah.

[18] While none of these allusions in *Cant. Rab.* may seem to be directly connected to the Jabbok incident, we assume that the dust of the wrestling match is the connecting link in these traditions because of the mention of wars, the citation of Nah 1:3 (which will be more clearly used later in this paper, in *Hullin* 91a), and because of the immediately subsequent remarks in *Cant. Rab.*
The same verse from Canticles and citations of Gen 32:25ff. can be found in *Yalkut*, Deuteronomy 890 and *Yalkut*, Canticles 986.

[19] *Gen. Rab.* 77.2.

[20] Such "double-checking" is praiseworthy; an example is given of a Rabbi-trader who checked his supplies on a journey and found that he had left a bolt of silk behind at an inn.

[21] Much the same tradition is found in *Cant. Rab.* 3.6.

[22] *Gen. Rab.* 77.2.

[23] L. Ginzberg (*The Legends of the Jews* [6 vols.; Philadelphia: Jewish Publication Society of America, 1909-38] 5.305 n. 247) notes that magic usually does prevail at night; the words of Jacob attest to his courage.

[24] Jacob Mann (*The Bible as Read and Preached*, 260-69) reconstructs the Seder containing the Jabbok account as including Gen 32:4-33:17. There were three different Haftaroth. One older one was Joel 3:13-21 and Amos 1:11-12; a local selection which held

for some time in Palestine was Isa 21:11-17 and 22:21-23. The
third Haftarah, which eventually became dominant, consisted of ch.
1 of Obadiah, perhaps vv. 1-9 and 21. With the exception of the
Obad 1:18 citation, I have found no other citations from Mann's
Haftaroth in the materials for this investigation.
    A very similar account can be found in *Cant. Rab.* 3.6. There
Jacob takes a woolen rope and winds it around the angel's neck;
later the angel causes fire to shoot forth from a rock.

[25]*Gen. Rab.* 77.3.

[26]וישלח §§7-8.

[27]*Yalkut*, Ruth 604.

[28]In *Lamentations Rabbah* (on Lam 5:1, "Oh, Lord, look and see
[הביט וראה]") there are remarks on semantic differences between
נבט and ראה. One nuance mentioned is that ראה means to look from
nearby, as we have it used in Gen 32:26.

[29]In the same way, when other nations in the future move
against Israel, God will say to them, "Your angel was not able to
prevail over Israel, and you all the less."
    A similar tradition can be found in *Cant. Rab.* 3.6. God says
to Esau's angel, "Jacob comes at you with five amulets in his
hand. Compare yourself with him; you cannot stand up to his merit
alone."
    In *Antiquities* 1.20.2 Josephus treats the Jabbok incident;
we will summarize his work here.
        Jacob wrestled with a ghost (φαντάσματι) who had
        started the fight. When he won the match, Jacob
        realized that his opponent was an angel; Jacob asked
        the angel what his lot in life would be. The angel
        told him to rejoice for having conquered an angel of
        God, and that his victory was an omen of good things
        to come. His people would never be abandoned or
        become extinct; he himself would never meet a
        stronger man. The angel named him Israel, meaning
        an opponent of an angel of God.

[30]This is the sole reference to the Shekinah being at Jabbok
which I have found in the rabbinic material.

[31]*Cant. Rab.* has the same tradition. Rabbinic usage normally
equated the generation of persecution with the victims of Hadrian's
violences.

[32]*Cant. Rab.* 3.6 offers the first two meanings and cites Ezek
23:17, "she removed (ותקע) her soul from them," to advance the
meaning that the angel could have pulled the muscle out from its
place.

[33]So also in *Psalms Rabbah* 91.6 (on Psa 91:11) the question
is "who is greater: the dismisser or the one dismissed?" The dismisser is greater, as was Jacob in Gen 32:27. A similar brief remark on Psa 91:11 can be found in *Yalkut*, Psalms 843. There the
question is who is greater: the sender or the one sent.

[34]Angels who depart go back to their source, which is the
river of fire. This river comes from the sweat produced by the
living beings who carry God's throne. A parallel development initiated by Lam 3:23 can be found in *Lam. Rab.* 3.8.

[35]This was also mentioned in grouping 11 of Chapter I above.

[36]This is in reference to a rabbinic tradition (*Gen. Rab.* 50.9 and 68.12) that the angels should not have revealed in Gen 19:13 that they were "about to destroy this place." They were not sent on another mission until Jacob's ladder dream, calculated as taking place 138 years later.

[37]The basis for the angel's promise to be present at Bethel can be found in the MT of Hos 12:5, "and there God spoke with *us* (עמנו)." This analysis of Hos 12:5 can also be found in *Yalkut,* Hosea 528.

[38]Both of these opinions are mentioned in *Yalkut,* Genesis 81. In *Mekilta de Rab. Ishmael* 16, and *Yalkut,* Exodus 217 the second opinion is favored. In *Gen. Rab.* 63.3 and *Yalkut,* Genesis 110 the name change is mentioned without further comment.

[39]This theme can be found in *Pesikta Rabbati* 17.2; *Pesikta Rab. Kahana* 7.3; *Tanhuma B* בא §17; some editions of *Gen. Rab.* 78.3; and *Gen. Rab.* 82.2. *Gen. Rab.* 82.2 notes that the angel will be present at Bethel (Hos 12:5 עמנו exegesis). Almost all of these sources note the latter part of Isa 44:26, "...The Lord says of Jerusalem, 'she shall be inhabited.'" As God confirmed the angel's word to Jacob, how much the more will He confirm all the messages of hope about Jerusalem.

[40]Note the change to a single angel in this exegesis.

[41]When Jacob spoke to Esau in Gen 33:10 he was referring to Esau's angel (אלהים), as we already saw in grouping 4 (*Gen. Rab.* 77.3). Another way to understand Jacob's statement in Gen 33:10 is that he was saying to Esau, "As the face of God stands for judgment, so does your face stand for judgment." In the context of Genesis 33, this paraphrase speaks of God's (and Esau's) merciful judgment.

[42]These terms, Prince and Ruler in exile, refer to the Jewish religious leaders in these two lands. The translation of אלהים as "princes" can be grounded on Gen 23:6.

[43]The *Gen. Rab.* text explains this to mean, "you are he whose features are engraved in heaven above." This is based on a tradition, recorded in *Gen. Rab.* 68.12, that the angels who went up and down the ladder had an image of Jacob's features at the top of the ladder, in heaven.

[44]In *Tanhuma B* וישלח §22 the Judges citation is repeated. We are also told that sometimes angels are made of wind (e.g., Psa 104:4) and sometimes they are made of lightning (e.g., Job 38:35). Thus their names must be changed often.

[45]So *Pesikta Rab. Kahana,* on וזאת הברכה (Deut 33:1); *Tanhuma* and *Tanhuma B* ברכה §1; and *Yalkut,* Deuteronomy 950.

[46]English, Mal 4:1-2.

[47]*Gen. Rab.* 79.5 notes that, in Gen 33:18, Jacob is described as being sound of body (שלם), whereas he had been lamed previously at Jabbok. The implication is that the healing effects of the sun had cured Jacob.

[48]This tradition depends on one appreciating the force of the perfect בָּא as a *completed* action. In *Gen. Rab.* 68.10 God causes the early sunset because He wishes to speak to Jacob in private. Later, in *Gen. Rab.* 69, further traditions are given that this place where Jacob rested for the night and had his dream was the site of the future Temple.

[49]E.g., Jer 15:9, "...her sun went down while it was yet day."

[50]E.g., Mal 3:20 (English 4:2), "For you who fear My name the sun of righteousness shall rise, with healing in its wings." Brief versions of this tradition can be found in *Sanhedrin* 95b; *Yalkut*, Genesis 107 and 118; *Yalkut*, Jeremiah 293; and *Yalkut*, Malachi 593. It was also in Targum *Ps.-Jonathan*.

[51]We must remember that Rome was symbolized by Esau in rabbinic lore.

[52]Commentators conjecture that "bringing wood" must be a reference to stocks or scourging or some such affliction involving wooden implements.

[53]S. Levin and E. Boyden, *The Kosher Code of the Orthodox Jew* (1940) 184.

[54]In Jewish tradition there are two positive commands in the earlier portions of Genesis, namely Gen 1:22, "Be fruitful and multiply," and Gen 17:9-10, "Every male shall be circumcised." The first negative command in the Bible is Gen 32:33, "They do not eat the nerve." We will use *Mishnayoth*, ed. P. Blackman (7 vols.; New York: Judaica, 1965).

[55]It is not clear if both thighs need be from the same animal.

[56]The Soncino Talmud edition postulates that these are probably the great sciatic nerve and the common peroneal nerve respectively.

[57]It is not clear in the Talmud exactly why Rab. Judah keeps calling for the minimum of observance (and of penalties) in regard to the sciatic nerve. Patte mentions *takkanoth*, which were mitigations or even abrogations of Pentateuchal laws (pp. 106-7). These *takkanoth* were employed when a law was too often transgressed. Perhaps Rab. Judah was aware of public disinterest in this matter, perhaps brought about by the difficulty in removing the nerve or in deciding where to stop with it as it descends the leg and subdivides.

[58]A similar consideration can be found in *Jerus. Talm.* פסחים 2.1, concerning the disposal of leftover portions of leaven. In *Babba Batra* 74b, two Rabbis speak of a meal they once had which included a flank of meat. They say that they opened it and cut at it--a possible allusion to the removal of the nerve.

[59]In *Keritoth* 21a there is question of rules concerning the koy (כוי), which is a cross between a goat and an antelope. Since the thigh is shaped like that of most other animals (i.e., with the bulge), the sciatic nerve prohibition does apply.

[60]In this passage the preference seems to be for leaving the nerve in place.

[61]In *Peshahim* 83b there is a discussion on the destruction of edible remains of Paschal lambs in which many of Rab. Judah's lenient legal opinions on the sciatic nerve question are reviewed, including the specification of the right thigh.

[62]Chap. 9 in Higger; chap. 10 in Soncino.

[63]This fivefold case is mentioned in *Peshahim* 47b, *Bezah* 12a, and *Makkoth* 21b.

[64]*Yalkut*, Genesis 133 contains a digest of *Gen. Rab.* 78.6 and abbreviated summaries of certain Bab. Talm. *Hullin* passages. These start with the end of 90b, the matter of whether we are speaking only of the right thigh. Almost all of 91a is mentioned; the reference to the angel appearing as a pagan becomes a reference to an angel appearing as a Gentile (כנוי). From 91b we have the fact that the angel wished to go to praise God, and a digression on the duties of praising angels. From 92a we have mention of the Ruler in exile in Babylon and the Prince in Israel. Related to Mishnah 2 are comments from 96a and 96b and a review of the question of uses of the sciatic nerve other than nutritional. There is a brief review of the application of the custom to unclean animals (probably from *Hullin*) and material very similar to 101b on Mishnah 6. The author of *Yalkut* also included the *Keritoth* 21a question on the sciatic nerve of the koy.

[65]The chapter then goes on to speak of a violent encounter between Jacob and Esau, based on a severe interpretation of Gen 33:4.

[66]*Yalkut*, Genesis, end of 132, start of 133.

[67]The author skips the violent encounter between Jacob and Esau, but goes on for a bit about other dealings between the two.

[68]Tradition presumes that the match took place in heaven.

[69]Mal 3:20 (English 4:2) is cited here.

[70]Here are cited Dan 10:21, "Michael, your prince, contends by my side," and Dan 12:1, "Michael shall arise, the great prince."

[71]This is the first instance we have come across of conjecture on the exact nature of the blessing which Jacob sought.

[72]Mal 3:20 (English 4:2) is cited here.

[73]If one were to judge by Maimonides alone, one could conclude that, up to his time, the prohibition against eating the sciatic nerve had been faithfully followed by devout Jews.

[74]Most of these interpretations are so involved with the movement toward mystical spirituality current in the author's time as to be effectively outside the scope of our work. I will just mention them here in a very schematic outline.

1.21b   Symbolic meanings of "sunlight" and "limping"
1.26b   More on "limping" and the *left* leg
1.35b   Jacob, as the new Adam, opposes Samael
1.144ab Questions about the corporeal aspects of a
         wrestling angel, the sense in which Jacob
         encountered God, and the work of good and
         evil spirits

1.146a	Wrestling match with evil spirit on unlucky night; other patriarchs help Jacob
1.169ab	Evil spirits rule the night, especially certain unlucky nights
1.171ab	Symbolic meanings of Israel's "night" and "day." Jacob represents the Torah. The sciatic nerve represents Israel's strength.
1.203a	Allusions to 2 Sam 23:4
2.163b	Relationship of Samael to Esau

[75] Here identified as Samael, an evil figure.

[76] *Zohar* 1.146a.

[77] *Zohar* 1.170a.

[78] This is clear in *Zohar* 1.144b and implied in *Zohar* 1.146a and 2.163b. Rashi also has this interpretation.

[79] *Zohar* 1.203b.

[80] *Zohar* 1.166a. Admittedly, this statement is not elaborated upon in *Zohar*; Rosenberg's edition reads "...because he brought himself to danger (לפי שהכניס עצמו לסכנה) and he saw that danger with his own eyes." It is possible that the author meant that Jacob should not have gone out at night, as was mentioned in *Hullin* 91a and *Yalkut*, Ruth 604. See Yodel Rosenberg, *Sefer Zohar Torah* (Montreal: Rothchild, 1924).
    T. H. Gaster suggests that Jacob *actively sought* the encounter (*Myth, Legend, and Custom*, 206-7). I have not found any rabbinic suggestion dating prior to this *Zohar* instance which could support Gaster's interpretation.

[81] The only mention of the Shekinah being at Jabbok was in *Cant. Rab.* 3.6.

[82] Even the Mamre story was recalled in one place as an example of angels giving a blessing.

[83] Note that Hos 12:4b has the same ambiguity with the word אלהים as does Gen 32:29. In v. 5b, "he wept and sought his favor," the Rabbis always assume that the subject is the angel.

[84] Another case of telescoping is the miraculous early sunset of Gen 28:11, which led Jacob to sleep on the site of the future Temple; the only connection with our story is, of course, the early sunrise of Gen 32:32.

[85] Thus the references to hostile nations and wars in groupings 3A, 4, 5 and 9; and the references to God's fulfilling of His many promises about Jerusalem, in grouping 7.

[86] In groupings 5 and 9 respectively.

[87] Thus *Tanhuma B* in grouping 4, and the opening section of *Midrash Abkir*.

[88] E.g., Jacob promised to tithe upon his safe return to the Holy Land.

[89] Cf. end of *Midrash Abkir*.

[90] Cf. grouping 3.

[1]Daniélou, *Theology of Jewish Christianity*, 132-34.

[2]The context places more emphasis on the Mamre account and the burning bush of Exodus 3; the need for a "second God" is postulated in all these cases because God the Father cannot be confined within limits of time and space.

Justin's use of the term "second God" for Christ may be an unfamiliar one to our ears. Eusebius of Caesarea (*Church History* 1.2) variously refers to Jesus as the second cause of the universe, the divine Word who holds the second place to the Father, and the second Lord after the Father. Later Arian controversies will force the abandonment of such terms.

B. Kominiak, on p. 74 of his unpublished dissertation, points out that Justin considered the wrestler at Jabbok as a real divine person distinct from God the Father, rather than as an angel who represented the Father.

[3]*Trypho* 106. Here the themes of Psalm 22 are related to Jesus. Verse 24 (English v. 23) mentions Jacob and Israel.

[4]In *Trypho* 126.3 Justin again cites Jacob's words of vv. 31 and 32, about seeing God face-to-face and calling the place Εἶδος θεοῦ, in order to show that Jacob's adversary was truly divine.

[5]Presumably Justin is referring to the verb שָׂרָה and to the noun אֵל.

[6]*Trypho* 125.5.

[7]So *Trypho* 125.5. The name Israel for Jesus is mentioned in *Trypho* 75.2. One of the bases for saying that it is an old name for Jesus is the LXX reading of Isa 42:1, taken together with the whole of Isa 42:1-4; this can be found in *Trypho* 123.1.

[8]The text is in Armenian. I am relying on Froidevaux's French translation (SC 62).

[9]The principal text is Ethiopic; I used pp. 652-53 of vol. 2 of *New Testament Apochrypha* by E. Hennecke (Westminster, 1965). Wilhelm Schneemelcher edited the original German work, and R. Wilson edited this English translation. The *Ascension of Isaiah* was translated by H. Duensing, who includes a technical introduction on pp. 642-44. E. Tisserant edited Latin manuscripts of parts of this work in his *Ascension d'Isaie* (Paris, 1909); pp. 144-45 contain our passage.

[10]*De Carne Christi* 3.6 (CC 2, p. 877). As before, we will use the Bueron Abbey edition of the *Vetus Latina*. The *Vetus* is a rather literal Latin translation from the LXX. Thus in v. 24 *transi(i)t*, like διέβη, is not causative; in v. 25 *luctatus est* renders ἐπάλαιεν; and, in v. 26, *obstipuit* is also not too close to וַיֵּקַע. In v. 29 the *Vetus* divides the phrase exactly as the LXX, "for you have prevailed with God, and you are strong with men," and many manuscripts add a future sense to the second part, as was the case with LXX manuscripts. In v. 31, פְּנִיאֵל is translated as *faciem*

Dei or *visio Dei* or the like.   In v. 33 the *Vetus* also seems to
ignore חַנֻבָּה and to use verbal phrases instead.

[11]Thus in *Adv. Praxean* 14.5 and 8 (CC 2, pp. 1177-78) mention
is made of Gen 32:31 as part of a proof to show that Christ
appeared to men before His Incarnation.

[12]CC 1, p. 652.

[13]See Quasten (*Patrology*, 2.163-207 for a biography and
digest of Hippolytus' works.

[14]*Pentateuch Fragment* 16, on Gen 49:7 (GCS 2, p. 58; Hans
Achelis, ed.).

[15]CC 4, pp. 48-50.

[16]*De Trin.* 9.4 also says that the book of Genesis makes
Christ known when it speaks of a man wrestling with Jacob (CC 4,
p. 25).

[17]A somewhat similar development can be found in *De Sac. Abel*
4.17.   In *De Mut. Nom.* 12.83-86 Philo notes that Abram is always
called Abraham after his name change, but Israel is often referred
to by his former name of Jacob.   This is because Abraham's virtue
came about by teaching by God, while Jacob's virtue came from
self-discipline and so is subject to human weakness at times.

[18]In Ps. Philo *Biblical Antiquities* 18.6 the angel is described as "the one who takes charge of the praises" (*qui stabat
super ymnos*).   Cf. John Bowker, *The Targums and Rabbinic Literature*
(Cambridge University, 1969) 312.

[19]Context indicates that this "divine word" is an angel and
not God.

[20]When Jacob had the ladder dream.

[21]Good Jewish people have education for a "mother," which
leads to good customs; they have right reason for a "father," which
leads to good laws.

[22]A similar analysis, of Jacob as a seeker and Israel as one
who has become worthy of "seeing" God, can be found in *De Migr.
Abr.* 36.200-201; the term "principle of seventy" is explained in
§199.

[23]In *De Somn.* 21.130-32 "numbness" signifies Jacob's humility
in the presence of the angel opponent.

[24]In §44 "human matters" are further specified as life and
the sense world.

[25]§44.

[26]The mention of natural goodness as a meaning for Jacob is
somewhat different from Philo's normal interpretation, which tends
to stress Jacob's self-discipline.

[27]GCS 12, pp. 123-24.

Notes: Chapter IV

213

[28] In Ps. Clement *Homilies* 18.13 (GCS 42, p. 247) there is a brief assertion that it was truly Jesus with whom Jacob wrestled.

[29] *Stromata* 1.5.31 (GCS 52, p. 20).

[30] *Stromata* 1.5.31 and 2.5.20 (GCS 52, pp. 20 and 123).

[31] *Stromata* 4.26.169 (GCS 52, p. 323). In some Ps. Clementine writings the wrestler is depicted as an angel, and not as Jesus. Thus in *Homilies* 20.7 (GCS 42, p. 272) we read that on this occasion God gave an angel a human body for his task; after wrestling, the angel was allowed to return to his proper state (that of fire). The fiery angel lamed Jacob by causing a minor burn on his leg, but he did not burn him severely. In *Homilies* 16.14 (GCS 42, p. 224) we learn that sometimes Scripture calls an angel by the term God, as in the Jabbok account.

[32] GCS 41, p. 245.

[33] Origen, commentary on *Romans*, Bk. 7, §14 (PG 14, col. 1141).

[34] The same explanation that Israel means "a man who sees God," can be found in *On John* 2.31 (25) (GCS 10, p. 88).

[35] GCS 22, p. 254.

[36] This idea of a good angel and a bad angel both being involved at Jabbok appears again in *Homily 1 on Exodus*, 5 (GCS 29, p. 152). In two locations Origen mentions an *Apochrypha of Joseph*, in which Jacob's angelic opponent is identified as Uriel, who sought to take Jacob's place on earth. So *On John* 2.31 (25) (GCS 10, pp. 88-89) and *Philocalia* 23.19 (J. Robinson, *The Philocalia of Origen* [Cambridge University, 1893] 208). Both these citations are in Greek.

[37] GCS 29, p. 257.

[38] GCS 29, p. 131.

[39] GCS 9.1, pp. 14-16.

[40] In 1.4.8 (p. 40) a remark is made about Jesus speaking with Israel in the past; Jacob/Israel is clearly meant rather than the people as a whole. Christ is also the opponent in *Demonstratio Evangelicae* 5.11 (GCS 6, pp. 233-35).

[41] Cf. Quasten, *Patrology* 3.85-100. Quasten points out that Didymus (d. 398) was the last important teacher in the catechetical school at Alexandria.

[42] Book 1.88 (SC 83, p. 238).

[43] *Acta Conciliorum Oecumenicorum* 1.5, ed. E. Schwartz, et al. (Berlin, 1924) 348.

[44] Ibid., 208.

[45] *Acta Conciliorum Oecumenicorum* 4.2 (Berlin, 1914) 36.

[46] PG 87A, cols. 455-60. For the final verse we have Greek fragments; for all the verses we have a Latin translation.

[47]Allegories about sacraments are rather rare in the exegeses of our two passages.

[48]Later he uses the phrase "one who contemplates God."

[49]The Greek is ἀληθείας ὕστερον ἴχνος, "lesser footsteps of truth." The Latin translation speaks of *certissima veritatis... vestigia*, which is not very close to the Greek.

[50]PG 53, cols. 509-11.

[51]Note the use of the same word for divine love for men as was used to explain the human motive for hospitality by Philo, Chrysostom, and others in Chapter I.

[52]There is a series of homilies on Matthew, now assumed to be by an anonymous author dating from the middle of the sixth century, which were formerly attributed to Chrysostom. In *Homily 15* (PG 56, col. 717) the author comments on the "face" spoken of in Matt 6:16. It refers to one's "spiritual" face--one's conscience or heart. This is what Jacob was talking about at Jabbok when he said that he had seen God face-to-face. He could not have seen God's face, since He appeared in human form; this bodily form was a veil and not the essence of God. Rather, Jacob saw God mentally. So he was renamed Israel, which means "a mind which sees God." In turn, God looked at Jacob's conscience at Jabbok.

[53]See also 510-11. Jewish avoidance of the thigh nerve in meats prompts some criticism by Chrysostom as to their lack of appreciation of the deeper meanings which lie behind such customs.

[54]PG 80, cols. 200-201.

[55]This is an anonymous work from northern Italy, c. 350. I am using the edition of C. H. Turner, *Ecclesiae Occidentalis Monumenta Juris Antiquissima* 1.2 (Oxford, 1913) Ch. 8, p. 339.

[56]This phrase is a frequent Vetus variant, borrowed from Judg 13:18.

[57]*De Trin.* 5.19 (PL 10, cols. 141-42).

[58]In *De Trin.* 4.31 (PL 10, col. 119) it is Christ who appeared as a man to Jacob, wrestled with him, and lost.

[59]Phoebadius was an early bishop of Agen, France, in the latter half of the fourth century. The material cited here is from *Liber Contra Arianos* 17 (PL 20, cols. 25-26).

[60]*De Fide* 80-81 (CC 69, p. 242).

[61]CSEL 32.2, pp. 49-50.

[62]In *Liber de Institutione Virginis* 16.101 (PL 16, col. 344) the context is that virgins should wear the "garment of virtue"; Jacob was wearing this garment when he saw a man at the Jabbok and requested a blessing from him as if from the Lord God.

[63]In his comments in *On Psalm 43*, §17 (CSEL 64, p. 275) Ambrose notes that Jacob's numbness is a sign that his descendants would have Jesus wounded in His passion. The Jews would not eat

of the thigh nerve because they continue not to understand the
mystery of Christ. They cheat only themselves in this.

[64] In §6 of this same commentary on Psalm 43 (pp. 263-64) the
sun which rose immediately upon Jacob was the Sun of Justice,
Christ born of a virgin. Jacob saw *in specie* and believed; his
descendants saw Christ in truth and did not believe. Their days
are few; we are shone upon. The day fails them; it comes upon us.

[65] *Hegesippus* 5.16.1 (CSEL 66, p. 325).

[66] Jerome's v. 24 is somewhat abbreviated and simplified; v.
25 adds an *ecce* but has a simple *mane*. In v. 26 the *statim* could
be interpreting the initial ב on בהאבקו; Jerome's use here of
emarcuit seems to be closer to the LXX than to the MT. In vv. 25
and 27 MT has שׁחר; the Vulgate, like the LXX, uses a different
word in v. 27. In v. 29 Jerome has the opponent explain the name
Israel as meaning that "if you have been strong against God, how
much the more shall you prevail against men?" In vv. 31 and 32
Jerome uses *Phanuhel* and does not translate. In v. 32 the *statim*
might reflect the כ in כאשׁר. Verse 33 seems to be closer to the
LXX than to the MT. The Roman Catholic Douay version faithfully
retained all these nuances of Jerome's.
      In *Hebr. Quaest. in Genesim* (CC 72, pp. 40-41) Jerome dis-
cusses the meaning of the word Israel. He prefers a meaning such
as *princeps cum Deo* or *princeps Dei* (based on שׂר), and he criti-
cizes Josephus, LXX, *Aquila, Symmachus*, and Theodotion for their
renditions. He then explains his translation of v. 29 by the
following hypothetical words of the opponent:
            As indeed I am a ruler (*princeps*) so also you, who
            have been able to wrestle with me, shall be called a
            ruler. If you have been able to fight with me, who
            am God or an angel (since many people understand this
            in different ways), how much the more shall you be able
            to fight with men--that is, with Esau, whom you need
            not dread.
Another possible derivation of the word Israel could be *directus
Dei*, based on the verb ישׁר. In any case the frequently used
אישׁ ראה אל אל etymology is not valid, and Jacob's opponent did not
use it in v. 29.
      Jerome also defends his use of *Phanuhel* as a place name (i.e.,
his not translating the word), since it is found elsewhere in the
OT.
      In this passage Jerome's abilities as a Latin stylist are
fairly evident. We have eleven uses of the conjunction *waw* in the
MT which are retained by the Vetus. These are ויעבד and ויעברם
and ויקחם of v. 24; וירא and ויגע of v. 26; both uses of ויאמר in
v. 27; the second ויאמר in v. 29; both uses of ויאמר in v. 30;
and ויקרא in v. 31. The LXX retains a καί in eight of these cases,
dropping the conjunction in its translation of the וירא from v. 26
and of ויאמר in its second occurrences in vv. 27 and 28. Jerome,
on the other hand, uses other methods of expression in all eleven
cases.
      When comparing the Vulgate with the Vetus, we are struck by
the repetitions in the Vetus. The Vetus, for example, has the
chain of *suas, et...suas, et...suos* in v. 23; Jerome uses the
possessive adjective just once. The Vetus has the chain *dixit,
dic*, and *dixit* in v. 30; Jerome uses *dic*, but avoids both uses of
dixit. The Latin of the Vulgate translation is thus more polished
than that of the Vetus.

[67] Book 3.2/6 (CC 76, pp. 132-34).

[68] This is another instance of the use of the verb יִשַׂר, which Jerome transliterates as *isar* (p. 133). In the same place, Jerome interprets Hos 12:5b, "he wept and sought his favor," to mean that Jacob did the weeping and beseeching.

[69] PL 23, col. 604.

[70] Presumably based on יִשַׂר. In *Liber Interp. Hebr. Nom.* (CC 72, pp. 67-68) we have entries for Jacob (supplantor) and Jabbok (battleground or contest), but no entry for Israel.

[71] *Commentary on Epistle to Ephesians* 2.6 (PL 26, col. 579).

[72] Something of the same idea can be found in Jerome's comments on Psa 11:2 (CC 78, p. 358). This text is entitled *Tractatus de Psalmo X*, and is part of a second series of fourteen Psalm commentaries edited by G. Morin. Here a devil admits to having wounded Jacob's thigh hollow.

[73] CC 72, p. 254.

[74] It is certainly possible that Jerome is in some sense adapting rabbinic traditions about the early sunset in Gen 28:11.

[75] CC 73, *In Esaiam* 3.6.1, p. 85.

[76] CC 41, pp. 57-59.

[77] *Angelus gestans personam Dei*. Later the phrase *angelus in persona Domini* is used.

[78] CC 48, p. 545.

[79] Remarks similar to this passage from *City of God* are found in Augustine's sermon *De Secunda Feria Paschae II*, 2-3 (*Sancti Aureli Augustini Tractatus sive Sermones Inediti ex Codice Guelferbytano 4096*, ed. G. Morin [Rome, 1930] 37-38).

[80] OA 8, cols. 1132-33.

[81] Maximinus notes in his *Collatio S. Aug.* 26 (PL 42, col. 739) that the Son was also seen by Jacob in the form in which He would someday come--i.e., in the form of a man. The wrestling is a symbol of Christ's passion; the name Israel means "a man who sees God." Very briefly, in *Contra Judaeos* 11 (*JTS* 20 [1919] 309), he mentions that Jacob saw Christ in the form of a man. See A. Spagnolo and C. Turner, "Contra Judaeos," *Journal of Theological Studies* 20 (1919) 293-310.

[82] Augustine notes the unbelief of later Jews on several occasions. In *Sermon 122.3* (OA 5.1, cols. 861-62) we read that this wrestling bout was a *mysterium*, a *sacramentum*, a *prophetia*, and a *figura*. Christ was prefigured in the angel's losing, a losing which was voluntary. In the same way Jesus was not angry at the Jews when He was crucified. Jacob remains lame in his unbelieving offspring, and so on.
In his commentary *On Psalm 44*, §20 (CC 38, p. 508) we read that the offspring of Jacob are blessed if they come to believe in Christ. In his remarks in *On Psalm 76*, §22 (CC 39, p. 1065) Augustine speaks of the ungrateful majority of Jews whose faith is vain and useless. Both these Psalm remarks are clearly based on the Jabbok incident.

[83]In his *Letter 147*.13-16 (CSEL 44, pp. 285-89) Augustine notes that Jacob and other holy persons have seen Christ at Jabbok and elsewhere

In Ps.-Augustine *Speculum* 2 (CSEL 12, pp. 299-300) the Jabbok account is cited, without further commentary, in a listing of biblical theophanies. This second chapter title indicates that the collected passages show the distinction of persons in the Trinity. Perhaps for the unknown author the Jabbok incident involved Christ alone, but we have no firm proof of this one way or the other. Another Ps.-Augustine work (*Testimonia de Patre et Filio Filio et Spiritu Sancto* 2.3 [D. De Bruyne, "Un Florilege Biblique Inedit," *Zeitschrift für die Neutestamentliche Wissenschaft* 29 (1930) 197-208; here p. 204]) has a similar listing with a similar title and no additional commentary.

[84]CC 39, pp. 1112-13.

[85]CC 40, p. 2163.

[86]*Sermon 122*.4 (OA 5.1, cols. 862-63).

[87]Much the same idea can be found in *Quaest. Gen.* 114 (CC 33, p. 42) and in his remarks on Psalm 77, §44 (CC 39, p. 1096).

[88]CC 39, p. 1158.

[89]CC 40, p. 2124.

[90]More allusions on this idea of seeing God can be found on Psalm 145, §11 (CC 40, p. 2113); on Psalm 49, §14 (CC 38, p. 587); and on Psalm 77, §7 (CC 39, p. 1071).

[91]CC 41, p. 31.

[92]CC 40, p. 2163.

[93]Matt 11:12.

[94]PL Supp. 2, col. 1077.

[95]Keyes, *Christian Faith and the Interpretation of History*, 118; Pontet, *L'Exégèse de Saint Augustine Prédicateur*, 318.

[96]Pontet, *L'Exégèse de Saint Augustine Prédicateur*, 585.

[97]Ibid., 379-83.

[98]PL 51, col. 752.

[99]*On Psalm 148* (PL 53, col. 567).

[100]*Interpretatio Evang.* 4 (*Sancti Epiphanii Episcopi Interpretatio Evangelorum*, A. Erikson [Lund, 1939] 5).

[101]*Sermon 54, Acta Conciliorum Oecumenicorum* 1.3, ed. E. Schwartz (Berlin, 1929) 150.

[102]*Psalm 43*.5 (CC 97, pp. 393-94).

[103]On Psalm 17:46 (English, Psa 18:45; CC 97, p. 167) and on Rom 11:25 (PL 68, col. 492).

[104]CC 142, pp. 232-33.

[105]In *Moralium Job* 4.67 (PL 75, col. 674) the example of Jacob's limping is related to the virtue of detachment. He who contemplates higher things does not know how to proceed with lower desires; he loses his bodily boldness as he gains in mental power.

[106]*Homily on Ezekiel* 2.3.21 (CC 142, p. 252).

[107]PL 76, cols. 292-93.

[108]*Moralium Job* 18.88 (PL 76, col. 92).

[109]Material rather imitative of Gregory can be found in *De Expos. Vet. ac Nov. Test. I in Gen.* 66-68, written by Paterius, a disciple of Gregory (PL 79, cols. 716-18). Julian of Toledo (d. 690) repeats the *Moralium Job* 18.88 statements in his *Antikeimenon* 1.20 (PL 96, col. 604).

[110]*Heptateuchos, Genesis* lines 1035-50 (CSEL 23, pp. 39-40).

[111]In Cyprian's *Coena*, 67 (PL 4, col. 1014) Jacob is described as being in an embrace; this could refer to the wrestling match at Jabbok, but the context does not offer any assistance for interpretation.

[112]CSEL 17, pp. 364-66. Owen Chadwick (*John Cassian* [2nd ed.; Cambridge University, 1968] 138-47) explains that the refutation of Nestorius' christological theories was the occasion for the composition of this work. Cassian used well known biblical arguments to prove Christ's divinity and individuality.

[113]*Instructionum* 1.24 (CSEL 31, pp. 73-74).

[114]*Homily 21 (De Pascha, 10)*, 3-4 (CC 101, pp. 248-50).

[115]In *Homily 35.4*, on St. Maximus (CC 101, p. 403), Eusebius notes that Maximus, like Jacob, sweated during his spiritual wrestling matches.

[116]CC 103, p. 364.

[117]See Marius Férotin, *Tractatus in Apocalypsin* (Bibliothèque Patrologique 1; Paris, 1900) §5, p. 58.

[118]*Liber de variis Quaest.* 16.2-3. A. C. Vega, A. E. Anspach, *Scriptores Ecclesiastici Hispano-Latini Veteris et Medii Aevi* fasc. 6-9 (Spain, 1940) 44-45.

[119]*Liber de var. Quaest.* 17.2, pp. 48-49.

[120]Ibid., 21.1, p. 57; has similar reasoning, as does *Quaestiones in Genesim* 5.27 (PL 83, col. 266).

[121]So *Quaest. in Gen.* 5.27 and *Etymologiarum* 7.7.6. See W. Lindsay, *Isadori Hispanensis Episcopi Etymologiarum sive Originum Libri XX* (Oxford: Clarendon, 1911).

[122]*Quaest. in Gen.* 5.27 and *Lib. de var. Quaest.* 17.2.

[123]*Quaest. in Gen.* 5.27.

[124]In *Apocalipsin Libri XII*, 2, Prologue, 5 (H. A. Sanders, *Beati in Apocalipsin libri 12* [American Academy in Rome, 1930] 110).

[125]In *Lucam* I (CC 120, p. 25).

[126]On *First Samuel*, 2 (in regard to 1 Sam 10:23), CC 119.

[127]There is a black and white photograph in Grabar's *Christian Iconography* (Princeton University, 1968) 336. The subject is located on the lower right edge of the right end panel of the casket.

[128]Black and white photographs can be seen in *Die Wiener Genesis*, W. R. von Hartel and Franz Wickhoff (Vienna, 1895). The plates are nn. 23 and 24, with an explanation on p. 153. Color photographs are in H. Gerstinger's *Die Wiener Genesis* (Vienna, 1931) pls. 23 and 24.

[129]I have not been able to find any photographs of this work. The description given here is from p. 705 of vol. 2 of Wilpert's four-volume work. Apparently the angel is badly damaged above the chest.

[130]The manuscript is Ms. Gr. 510, fol. 174, which is dated around 880 A.D. See Henri Omont, *Miniatures des Plus Anciens Manuscrits Grecs de la Bibliothèque Nationale du VI au XIV Siecle* (Paris: Champion, 1929), pl. XXXVII and p. 23. A black and white plate of this is in Goodenough, *Jewish Symbols*, ll. fig. 296.

[131]See S. C. Cockerell and John Plummer, *Old Testament Miniatures* (New York: Braziller, 1969) pl. 30. The manuscript has very vivid colors and dates from about 1250 A.D. This picture includes much more detail than most. We see Jacob's family and flocks preceding him and, further to the right, we see Jacob and Esau meeting amicably.
Reau mentions several church frescos and bas reliefs from the eleventh and twelfth centuries. I examined only the miniature in Cockerell's collection because it was easily available.

CHAPTER V

[1] Philo, Chrysostom, and Augustine emphasize repeatedly that Abraham and Sarah only gradually became aware of the other than human status of the three visitors.

[2] This threefold subdivision of rabbinic biblical citations is my own, but I would not have been able to arrive at it without Patte's efforts.

[3] In the short run, biblical scholars, students, and homilists need improved reference systems. The *Biblia Patristica* series is an important advance. It would be very helpful for everyone if Hyman's three volumes were updated and printed in English. If they were republished in this manner they, along with *Biblia Patristica*, would be the basic reference tool for the early centuries of the history of hermeneutic. The article by Townsend on ancient rabbinic sources, and a companion article on medieval Jewish writings in the second volume of the ADL series, are invaluable bibliographic aids for the non-specialist who wishes to track down specific Jewish writings. These should be updated every decade or so. Patristics scholars should see to it that a comparable set of directives be made available for those interested in the vast treasures of the ancient and medieval Christian world. Overviews of the history of hermeneutics such as Brevard Childs provides in his Exodus are ideal, but obviously very difficult to produce. Perhaps more experimenting can be done with the format of such presentations. The expositions which I made in this investigation are entirely my own and are most likely too *ad hoc* to be helpful in the field. I am convinced, however, that the only effective control or basis for scholarly, historical presentations lies in the consultation of all the references available for the particular texts and time periods. Perhaps historical studies of this sort could best be produced by small teams of scholars.

NOTES

APPENDIX I

[1]Remembering with Patte (*Early Jewish Hermeneutic*, 53) that "...in the Targum as well as in the Midrash the starting point of the interpretation is not necessarily the text in itself. Often it is the text as traditionally interpreted. In other words, what the Targum is expressing in Aramaic is not Scripture by itself, but Scripture as already interpreted in the Synagogue."

[2]H. B. Swete, *An Introduction to the Old Testament in Greek* (Cambridge University, 1902; reprinted, Ktav, 1968) 21.

[3]John Bowker, *The Targums and Rabbinic Literature* (Cambridge University, 1969) 5.

[4]According to Wever's apparatus, only a few manuscripts follow the MT on this point.

[5]More literal Greek Jewish translations from about 130 and 200 A.D., respectively; so B. J. Roberts, *The Old Testament Texts and Versions* (Cardiff: University of Wales, 1951) 123 and 126.

[6]According to Wever's apparatus, quite a few manuscripts follow the MT in regard to the position of this verb.

[7]"The living time" or "the time of living"; Speiser suggests "at about a life's interval," meaning at the end of a term of pregnancy. Cf. Speiser, *Genesis*, 130, and O. Eissfeldt, *The Old Testament, an Introduction*, trans. P. Ackroyd (New York: Harper and Row, 1965) 743, for further bibliography on this term.

[8]Bowker, *The Targums and Rabbinic Literature*, p. 9 and preceding.

[9]Ibid., 13.

[10]Bowker prefers the plural (ibid., 15).

[11]Ibid.

[12]A. Sperber, *The Bible in Aramaic* (4 vols.; Leiden: Brill, 1959) 4B.414.

[13]Bowker (*The Targums and Rabbinic Literature*, 16-20) discusses Díez-Macho's claims for *Neofiti* as a first or second century A.D. recension of a pre-Christian Targum tradition. Bowker himself opts for a third century date. The *Neofiti* volumes had not been published at the time of Bowker's book. See A. Díez-Macho, *Neophyti 1, Targum Palestinense*, Vol. 1 (Madrid: CSIC, 1968).

[14]McNamara, *Targum and Testament*, 198.

[15]Bowker (*The Targums and Rabbinic Literature*, 211) speculates that this might be a euphemism used to avoid any hint of idolatry in Abraham's gesture. His remarks were occasioned by a similar variant reading in *Fragmentary Targum*.

[16]Here and in *Onkelos* and *Ps.-Jonathan* the Targumists used
כסא (root II, M. Jastrow, *A Dictionary of the Targumim, the Talmud
Babli and Yerushalmi, and the Midrashic Literature* [New York:
Judaica Press, 1971] 653) apparently as a clarification or specification of פלא/פלי (1181).

[17]Bowker (*The Targums and Rabbinic Literature*, 20-21) discusses the two textual traditions involved but does not attempt to
date the material. Following Roberts (*The Old Testament Texts and
Versions*, 202), the *Fragmentary Targum* may be older than
Ps.-Jonathan.

[18]Again, the "vision" probably refers to this theophany; cf.
McNamara, *Targum and Testament*, 198.

[19]M. Ginsburger, *Das Fragmententhargum* (Berlin, 1899;
reprinted in Jerusalem: Makor, 1968) 95.

[20]Ibid., 77 and 95; Bowker, *The Targums and Rabbinic
Literature*, 209.

[21]Bowker, *The Targums and Rabbinic Literature*, 25. For text,
see A. Berliner, *Targum Onkelos* (Berlin, 1884; reprinted in
Jerusalem: Makor, 1968).

[22]Sperber, *The Bible in Aramaic*, 4B.3.

[23]Cf. Roberts, *Old Testament Texts and Versions*, 202; Bowker,
The Targums and Rabbinic Literature, 26. For text, see M. Ginsburger, *Targum Pseudo-Jonathan ben Usiël zum Pentateuch* (Berlin,
1903; reprinted in Jerusalem: Makor, 1968).

[24]Bowker, *The Targums and Rabbinic Literature*, 207, 193.

[25]Eissfeldt (*The Old Testament*, 699-701) dates the *Peshitta*
from 100-150 A.D. McNamara (*The New Testament and the Palestinian
Targum*, 51) cites five authors who believe that the *Peshitta* to the
Pentateuch was made from texts close to our Palestinian Targum tra-
ditions, as well as one opponent of this theory. Sperber (*Bible
in Aramaic*, 4B.415) says "The Peshitta belongs to the same family
of Aramaic Pentateuch-translations as the so-called Targum Onkelos."
On p. 416 he postulates that it represents an earlier stage than
Targum *Onkelos* of Targumic formation. Roberts (*The Old Testament
Texts and Versions*, 214-23) gives a general background and presents
arguments for and against Jewish provenance. For text see *Vetus
Testamentum Syriace*, ed. S. Lee (American Protestant Missionary
Society, 1914).

[26]Eissfeldt (*The Old Testament*, 695) sets the date of the
Samaritan Pentateuch as 400 years older than the MT, taking the MT
at 100 A.D. It is often close to the LXX. Roberts (*Old Testament
Texts and Versions*, 188) agrees on the dating. For text, see
August von Gall, *Der Hebräische Pentateuch der Samaritaner*
(Giessen, 1918).
    For the *Samaritan Targum*, T. H. Gaster ("Samaritans," *IDB*,
4.190-97; here p. 196) dates it in the fourth century A.D. and
notes that it is often similar to *Onkelos*. Roberts (*Old Testament
Texts and Versions*, 195) does not try to date it.

[27]Jastrow, *Dictionary of the Targumim*, 1347 (on noun forms).

NOTES

APPENDIX II

[1] Wevers notes several LXX manuscripts with causative verbs
(*Septuaginta: Genesis* [Göttingen: Vandenhoeck & Ruprecht, 1974).

[2] *Aquila* and *Symmachus* use forms of ἄρχω for שׂרית; we have
no evidence of how they rendered the rest of the verse.

[3] Could the LXX interpreters have been reading the verb נשׁה,
meaning "to forget"?

[4] *Masoreten des Westens* II.2, ed. P. Kahle (Texte und Unter-
suchungen series, vol. 4; Stuttgart: Kohlhammer, 1930) 10-11.
This is also called the *Palestinian Targum*. John Bowker (*The
Targums and Rabbinic Literature*, 21) considers these fragments to
represent a recension of the *Palestinian Targum* different from the
Fragmentary Targum mentioned above. Roberts (*The Old Testament
Texts and Versions*, 200-201) goes into more detail as to the
dates of the manuscripts and the significance of them vis-à-vis
Onkelos, *Peshitta*, etc.

[5] CG breaks off after v. 29, resuming at Gen 34:9.

[6] I.e., promise.

[7] Apparently referring to Gen 28:22.

[8] Possible misreading of מעבר?

[9] This is from Adolf Brüll (*Das Samaritanische Targum zum
Pentateuch* [Frankfort, 1875]), which is written in Hebrew script.
The *Samaritan Targum* edited by H. Petermann and C. Vollers in
Pentateuchus Samaritanus (1872) has עם אלהה ועם אנשה, and notes in
its apparatus instances of the ו being absent from עם. Petermann
also notes that the Samaritans did not properly distinguish gut-
turals in Hebrew and Aramaic in pronunciation, and did exchange
them in writing. Thus it is possible to explain Brüll's manuscript
reading אם as a variant for עם. All the information from Petermann
and Vollers' book was made known to me in personal communication
with Msgr. Patrick Skehan of Catholic University, Washington, DC
(since I cannot read Samaritan script). The *Peshitta* reading of
v. 29 is very close to that of the Targum of Petermann and Vollers.

225

SELECTED BIBLIOGRAPHY

Acta Conciliorum Oecumenicorum series. Ed. E. Schwartz, et al.
Berlin: De Gruyter, 1927-1971.

Albertson, Clinton. *Anglo-Saxon Saints and Heroes*. Fordham
University, 1967.

Armstrong, G. T. "The Genesis Theophanies of Hilary of Poitiers."
Pp. 203-7 in *Studia Patristica* 10. Berlin: Akademie, 1970.

_____. "Imperial Church Building in the Holy Land in the Fourth
Century." *Biblical Archaeologist* 30 (1967) 90-102.

Avi-Yonah, Michael. "Goodenough's Evaluation of the Dura Paintings: A Critique." Pp. 117-35 in *The Dura-Europas Synagogue:
A Re-evaluation (1932-1972)*. Ed. Joseph Gutmann. AAR/SBL,
1973.

Barnard, L. W. "The Old Testament and Judaism in the Writings
of Justin Martyr." *Vetus Testamentum* 14 (1964) 395-406.

Barthes, R., Martin-Achard, R., et al. *Analyse Structurale et
Exégèse Biblique*. Neuchatel: Delachaux et Niestlé, 1971.

Baur, Chrysostomos. *John Chrysostom and His Time*. 2 vols.
Newman, 1959.

Berliner, A. *Targum Onkelos*. Berlin, 1884. Reprinted in
Jerusalem: Makor, 1968.

*Biblia Patristica: Index des Citations et Allusions Bibliques dans
la Littérature Patristique*. Paris: Centre National de la
Recherche Scientifique. Vol. 1, 1975; Vol. 2, 1977.

Blackman, P. *Mishnayoth*. 7 vols. New York: Judaica, 1965.

Bloch, Renée. "Midrash." *Dictionnaire de la Bible, Supplement*,
vol. 5, cols. 1263-81. Paris, 1957.

Bovini, Giuseppe. *Ravenna*. New York: Abrams, 1972.

_____. *San Vitale, Ravenna*. 3rd ed. Trans. Basil Taylor.
Milan: Silvano, 1957.

Bowker, John. *The Targums and Rabbinic Literature*. Cambridge
University, 1969.

Braude, W. G. *Pesikta Rabbati*. 2 vols. Yale Judaica series,
1968.

Broda, Abraham. *Sefer Pirke de Rabbi Eliezer*. Antwerp, 1950.

Brooke, Alan E., and McLean, Norman. *The Old Testament in Greek*.
3 vols. Cambridge University, 1906.

Brüll, Adolf. *Das Samaritanische Targum zum Pentateuch*.
Frankfort, 1875.

Buber, S. *Agadath Bereshith*. Cracow: J. Fischer, 1902.
   Reprinted in Rome: Vilna, 1925; and in New York: Menorah,
   1958.

_____. *Midrash Tanchuma*. Rome: Vilna, 1913. Reprinted in
   Jerusalem: Ortsel, 1963.

_____. *Midrash Tehillim*. Rome: Vilna, 1891. Reprinted in
   New York, 1947; and in Jerusalem, 1965. The last includes
   Midrash Mishle.

Burghardt, Walter J. "On Early Christian Exegesis." *Theological
   Studies* 11 (1950) 78-116.

Chadwick, Owen. *John Cassian*. 2nd ed. Cambridge University,
   1968.

Chase, Frederick H. *Chrysostom, A Study in the History of Biblical Interpretation*. London, 1887.

Childs, Brevard. *Biblical Theology in Crisis*. Westminster, 1970.

_____. *The Book of Exodus*. Westminster, 1974.

Cockerell, Sidney C., and Plummer, John. *Old Testament Miniatures*.
   New York: Braziller, 1969.

Cohen, A., ed. *The Minor Tractates of the Talmud*. 2 vols.
   London: Soncino, 1965.

Colgrave, Bertram. *Two Lives of St. Cuthbert*. Cambridge University, 1940.

_____. "Bede's Miracle Stories." *Bede, His Life, Time, and
   Writings*. Ed. A. H. Thompson. London, 1932. Reprinted in
   New York: Russell and Russell, 1966.

Colson, F. H., Whitaker, G. H., and Marcus, Ralph, eds. *Philo*.
   10 vols. and 2 supplements (on the Armenian Commentaries on
   Genesis and Exodus). Loeb Classical Library series. Harvard
   University, 1929-1953.

Congar, Yves. *Tradition and Traditions*. Trans. Michael Naseby
   and Thomas Rainborough. Macmillan, 1967.

Constantelos, Demetrios J. *Byzantine Philanthropy and Social
   Welfare*. New Brunswick: Rutgers University, 1968.

Corpus Christianorum, Series Latina. Turnholt: Brepols, 1953.

Corpus Scriptorum Ecclesiasticorum Latinorum. Vienna: Akademie
   der Wissenschaften, 1866.

Daniélou, Jean. *From Shadows to Reality*. Trans. W. Hibberd.
   London: Burns and Oates, 1960.

_____. *Origen*. Trans. W. Mitchell. Sheed and Ward, 1955.

_____. *The Theology of Jewish Christianity*. Trans. John Baker.
   Chicago: Regnery, 1964.

De Bruyne, D. "Un Florilège Biblique Inédit." *Zeitschrift für die Neutestamentliche Wissenschaft* 29 (1930) 197-208.

Díez-Macho, A. *Neophyti 1: Targum Palestinense.* Vol. 1. Madrid: CSIC, 1968.

Du Roy, O. "St. Augustine." NCE 1.1041-58.

Eichrodt, Walther. *Theology of the Old Testament.* Trans. J. A. Baker. Old Testament Library Series, Vol. 1. Westminster, 1961.

Eisenstein, J. D. *Ozar Midrashim: A Library of Two Hundred Minor Midrashim.* New York, 1915.

Eissfeldt, Otto. *The Old Testament: An Introduction.* Trans. P. R. Ackroyd. New York: Harper and Row, 1965.

Elliger, Karl. "Der Jakobskampf am Jabbok." *Zeitschrift für Theologie und Kirche* 48 (1951) 1-31.

_____, and Rudolph, W. *Biblica Hebraica Stuttgartensia.* Stuttgart: Württembergische Bibelanstalt, 1978. "Genesis" fascicle by Otto Eissfeldt, 1969.

Epstein, Isadore, ed. *The Babylonian Talmud.* 35 vols. London: Soncino, 1935-52.

Epstein, J. N., and Melamed, E. Z. *Mekhilta d'Rabbi Simon b. Yochai.* Jerusalem: Mekitze Nirdamim, 1955.

Erikson, A. *Sancti Epiphanii Episcopi Interpretatio Evangelorum.* Lund, 1939.

Fausset, W. Y. *Novatian: De Trinitate.* Cambridge Patristic Texts. Cambridge, 1909.

Férotin, Marius. *Tractatus in Apocalypsin.* Bibliothèque Patrologique, 1. Paris, 1900.

Ferrua, Antonio. *Le Pitture della Nuova Catacomba di Via Latina.* Rome, 1960.

Field, F. *Origenis Hexaplorum Quae Supersunt sive Veterum Interpretum Graecorum in Totum Vetus Testamentum Fragmenta.* Hildesheim: Olms, 1964 (reprint of 1875 edition).

Finkelstein, L., and Horovitz, H. S. *Siphre d'be Rab.* Berlin, 1939. Reprinted in New York: JTSA, 1969.

Fischer, B. *Genesis.* Vetus Latina series of Bueron Abbey. Herder, 1954.

Freedman, H., and Simon, M. *Midrash Rabbah.* 10 vols. London: Soncino, 1951.

Friedmann, M. *Pesikta Rabbati.* Vienna, 1880. Reprinted in Tel Aviv, 1962.

_____. *Seder Eliahu Rabba and Seder Eliahu Zuta.* Jerusalem: Wahrmann, 1969.

Froidevaux, L. M. *Irénée de Lyon: Démonstration de la Prédication Apostolique*. Sources Chrétiennes, vol. 62, 1959.

von Gall, August F. *Der Hebräische Pentateuch der Samaritaner*. Giessen, 1918.

Gaster, T. H. *Myth, Legend, and Custom in the Old Testament*. New York: Harper and Row, 1969.

_____. "Samaritans." *IDB*, 4.190-97. Abingdon, 1962.

Gerstinger, H. *Die Wiener Genesis*. Vienna, 1931.

Gertner, M. "Midrashim in the New Testament." *Journal of Semitic Studies* 7 (1962) 267-92.

Ginsburger, M. *Das Fragmenthargum*. Berlin, 1899. Reprinted in Jerusalem: Makor, 1968.

_____. *Targum Pseudo-Jonathan ben Usiël zum Pentateuch*. Berlin, 1903. Reprinted in Jerusalem: Makor, 1968.

Ginzberg, Louis. *The Legends of the Jews*. 6 vols. Philadelphia: Jewish Publication Society of America, 1909-38.

Goodenough, E. R. *Jewish Symbols in the Greco-Roman Period*. 13 vols. Pantheon, 1952.

Grabar, André. *The Beginnings of Christian Art*. Thames and Hudson, 1967.

_____. *Christian Iconography*. Princeton University, 1968.

_____. *Early Medieval Painting from the Fourth to the Eleventh Century*. Skira, 1957.

Grant, Robert M. *The Letter and the Spirit*. New York: McMillan, 1957.

Die Grieschischen Christlichen Schriftsteller der Ersten Drei Jahrhunderte. Berlin: Akademie Verlag, 1897-.

Guillet, J. "Lex Exégèses d'Alexandrie et d'Antioch: Conflit ou Malentendue?" *Recherches de Science Religieuse* 34 (1947) 257-302.

Gunkel, Hermann. *Genesis*. 6th ed. Göttingen: Vandenhoeck & Ruprecht, 1964. This is a reprint of the 3rd edition.

Gutmann, Joseph. "Programmatic Painting in the Dura Synagogue." Pp. 137-54 in *The Dura-Europas Synagogue: A Re-evaluation (1932-1972)*. Ed. J. Gutmann. AAR/SBL, 1973.

Hanson, Richard Patrick Crosland. *Allegory and Event*. London: SCM, 1959.

_____. *Origen's Doctrine of Tradition*. London: SPCK, 1954.

Harkins, P. W. "St. John Chrysostom." NCE 7.1041-44.

von Hartel, Wilhelm R., and Wickhoff, Franz. *Die Wiener Genesis*. Vienna, 1895.

Hartmann, Louis N. "St. Jerome as an Exegete." Pp. 37-81 in *A Monument to St. Jerome*. Ed. F. X. Murphy. Sheed and Ward, 1952.

Hemmer, H., and LeJay, P. *Textes et Documents*. Vols. 8 and 11. Paris, 1909.

Hennecke, E. *New Testament Apochrypha*. 2 vols. Westminster, 1965.

Higger, M. *The Treatises Derek Erez*. New York: Debe Rabanan, 1935.

_____. *Massekhtot Kallah*. New York: Debe Rabanan, 1936.

_____. *Massekhet Soferim*. New York: Debe Rabanan, 1937.

Horovitz, H. S. *Siphre de'be Rab*. Leipzig, 1917. Reprinted in Jerusalem: Wahrmann, 1966.

Hyman, Aaron. *Sefer Torah Haketuvah Wehamesurah al Torah, Neviim, uKhetuvim*. 3 vols. Tel Aviv: Dvir, 1964-65. A reprint of the 1936-39 edition.

The Interpreter's Bible. 12 vols. Abingdon, 1952.

The Interpreter's Dictionary of the Bible. 4 vols. Abingdon, 1962.

The Interpreter's Dictionary of the Bible Supplement. Abingdon, 1976.

Jacob, Benno. *Das Erste Buch der Tora: Genesis*. Berlin: Schocken, 1934. There is a Ktav 1975 reprint of this.

_____. *The First Book of the Bible; Genesis*. Trans. Ernest I. Jacob and ed. by Walter Jacob. This is an abridgement of the 1934 work. Ktav, 1974.

Jastrow, Marcus. *A Dictionary of the Targumim, the Talmud Babli and Yerushalmi, and the Midrashic Literature*. New York: Judaica, 1971.

Jay, Eric G. *Origen's Treatise on Prayer*. London: SPCK, 1954.

Jenkins, Claude. "Bede as Exegete and Historian." *Bede, His Life, Time, and Writings*. Ed. A. H. Thompson. London, 1932. Reprinted in New York: Russell & Russell, 1966.

Kahle, P. *Masoreten des Westens* II.2. Texte und Untersuchungen series, vol. 4. Stuttgart: Kohlhammer, 1930.

Katzenellenbogen, A.E.M. *Allegories of the Virtues and Vices in Medieval Art*. London, 1939. Reprinted in New York: W. W. Norton, 1964.

Keyes, G. L. *Christian Faith and the Interpretation of History*. University of Nebraska, 1966.

Kittel, Rudolph, ed. *Biblica Hebraica*. Stuttgart, 1954.

Kominiak, Benedict. *The Theophanies of the Old Testament in the Writings of St. Justin.* Washington, DC: Catholic University, 1948. This is a compendium of his unpublished CU doctoral dissertation of the same title.

Kuntz, Kenneth. *The Self-Revelation of God.* Westminster, 1967.

Lampe, G.W.H. "The Reasonableness of Typology." *Essays in Biblical Typology.* London: Allenson, 1957.

Lauterbach, J. Z. *Mekilta de Rabbi Ishmael.* 3 vols. Library of Jewish Classics. Philadelphia: Jewish Publication Society of America, 1933-35. Reprinted in 1949.

Lee, S., ed. *Vetus Testamentum Syriace.* American Protestant Missionary Society, 1914.

Leroux, Jean-M. "Relativité et Transcendance du Texte Biblique d'après Jean Chrysostome." *La Bible et Les Pères: Colloque de Strasbourg.* Paris: Presses Universitaires, 1971, pp. 67-78.

Levin, S., and Boyden, E. *The Kosher Code of the Orthodox Jew.* 1940.

Lieberman, S. *The Tosefta.* New York: JTSA, 1955.

Lindsay, W. M. *Isadori Hispanensis Episcopi Etymologiarum sive Originum Libri XX.* Oxford: Clarendon, 1911.

de Lubac, Henri. *Exégèse Médiévale.* 4 vols. Paris: Aubier, 1959-64.

Mader, Evaristus. *Mambre.* 2 vols. Freiburg: Wewel Verlag, 1957.

Maimonides, Moses. *Doctor Perplexorum.* Ed. R. Samuel ibn Tibbon; rev. by Yehuda ibn Shmuel. Jerusalem, 1946.

_____. *The Guide of the Perplexed.* Trans. Shlomo Pines. University of Chicago, 1963.

_____. *Mishneh Torah.* Ed. David Arama. Jerusalem, 1965.

Mandelbaum, B. *Pesikta de Rab Kahana.* 2 vols. New York: JTSA, 1962.

Mann, Jacob. *The Bible as Read and Preached in the Old Synagogue.* Vol. 1. Cincinnati, 1940.

McGuire, M.R.P. "St. Hippolytus of Rome." NCE 6.1139-41.

McNally, R. E. "Exegesis, Medieval." NCE 5.707-12.

McNamara, Martin. *The New Testament and the Palestinian Targum to the Pentateuch.* Rome: PIB, 1966.

_____. *Targum and Testament.* Grand Rapids: Eerdmans, 1972.

Migne, Jacques Paul. *Patrologia Graeca.* 168 vols. Paris, 1857-1866.

_____. *Patrologia Latina.* 222 vols. Paris, 1844-1864.

Mirkin, M. A. *Midrash Rabbah.* 9 vols. Tel Aviv: Yavneh, 1956-
    1964.

Miqra'ot Gedolot. Jerusalem: Schocken, 1958-59.

Monumenta Germaniae Historica, Auctores Antiquissimi. Vol. 6.2:
    "Dialogi cum Gundobadi Rege" (Berlin, 1883) 1-15; vol. 9:
    "Liber Genealogus" (Berlin, 1892) 160-96.

Morgenstern, Julian. *The Book of Genesis, A Jewish Interpretation.*
    Union of American Hebrew Congregations, 1919; Schocken re-
    print, 1965.

Morin, G. *Sancti Aureli Augustini Tractatus sive Sermones Inediti
    ex Codice Guelferbytano 4096.* Rome, 1930.

The New Catholic Encyclopedia. 16 vols. New York: McGraw Hill,
    1967.

Nikiprowetzky, V. "L'Exégèse de Philon d'Alexandrie." *Revue
    d'Histoire et de Philosophie Religieuses* 53 (1973) 309-29.

Oeuvres de Saint Augustine. Bibliothèque Augustinienne series.
    Paris: Desclée, 1947-52.

O'Meara, John J. *Origen: Prayer.* Ancient Christian Writers
    series, vol. 19. Newman, 1954.

Omont, Henri. *Miniatures des Plus Anciens Manuscrits Grecs de la
    Bibliothèque Nationale de VI au XIV Siecle.* Paris: Champion,
    1929.

Oulten, J. E., and Chadwick, H. *Alexandrian Christianity.*
    London: SCM, 1954.

Ouspensky, Leonid, and Lossky, Vladimir. *The Meaning of Icons.*
    Graf: Olten-Switzerland, 1952.

Patte, Daniel. *Early Jewish Hermeneutic in Palestine.* SBLDS 22.
    Missoula, MT: Scholars Press, 1975.

Payne, J. B. "Biblical Problems and Augustine's Allegorizing."
    Westminster Theological Journal 14 (1951) 46-53.

Petermann, H., and Vollers, C. *Pentateuchus Samaritanus,* 1872.

Pontet, Maurice. *L'Exégèse de Saint Augustine Prédicateur.*
    Paris: Aubier, 1947.

*Preliminary and Interim Report on the Hebrew Old Testament Text
    Project,* Vol. 1: *Pentateuch.* London: United Bible Society,
    1974.

Quasten, Johannes. *Patrology.* 3 vols. Newman, 1950-55.

von Rad, Gerhard. *Genesis.* The Old Testament Library series.
    Westminster, 1961.

_____. *Old Testament Theology.* 2 vols. Trans. D.M.G. Stalker.
    New York: Harper and Row, 1962-65.

Ratner, B. *Seder Olam Rabbah.* Rome: Vilna, 1894. Reprinted in
New York: Talmudical Research Institute, 1966.

Reau, Louis. *Iconographie de l'Art Chrétien.* 6 vols. Paris,
1955.

Roberts, B. J. *The Old Testament Texts and Versions.* Cardiff:
University of Wales, 1951.

Robinson, J. Armitage. *The Philocalia of Origen.* Cambridge
University, 1893.

Rosenberg, Yodel. *Sefer Zohar Torah.* Montreal: Rothchild, 1924.

Rusch, W. G. "Some Observations on Hilary of Poitiers' Christological Language in *De Trinitate.*" Pp. 261-64 in *Studia
Patristica* 12. Berlin: Akademie Verlag, 1975.

Sancti Aureli Augustini Hipponensis Episcopi Opera Omnia. Benedictine monks of St. Maur, Paris, 1835-39. Du Roy, in the
NCE article, has a convenient table for locating specific
works in the Migne, CSEL, Bibliothèque Augustienne, and
St. Maur series.

Sanders, H. A. *Beati in Apocalipsin Libri XII.* American Academy
in Rome, 1930.

Sanders, James A. "From Isaia 61 to Luke 4," *Christianity,
Judaism, and Other Greco-Roman Cults: Studies for Morton
Smith at Sixty.* Ed. Jacob Neusner. Leiden, 1975.

_____. "Hermeneutics." IDB Supplement. Abingdon, 1976, pp.
402-407.

_____. "Hermeneutics in True and False Prophecy." *Beiträge
zur Alttestamentlichen Theologie: Festschrift für Walter
Zimmerli zum 70. Geburtstag.* Ed. H. Donner, R. Hanhart, and
R. Smend. Göttingen: Vandenhoeck & Ruprecht, 1977.

Sarna, Nahum. *Understanding Genesis.* Schocken, 1966.

Schechter, S. *Aboth de Rabbi Nathan.* Vienna, 1887. Reprinted in
New York: Feldheim, 1945.

Schildenberger, J. "Jakobs Nächtlicher Kampf mit dem Elohim am
Jabok." Pp. 69-96 in *Miscellanea Biblica B. Ubach.*
Barcelona, 1953.

Schrentzel, E. *Midrash Tanhuma.* Stettin, 1863. Reprinted in
New York: Horeb, 1924.

Shepherd, Massey H. "Liturgical Expressions of the Constantian
Triumph." Pp. 59-78 in *Dunbarton Oaks Papers* 21. Washington, DC, 1967.

Shotwell, Willis A. *The Biblical Exegesis of Justin Martyr.*
London: SPCK, 1965.

Simons, J. *The Geographical and Topological Texts of the Old
Testament.* Leiden: Brill, 1959.

Simpson, Cuthbert A. "Genesis." *The Interpreter's Bible,* vol. 1.
Abingdon, 1952.

Skinner, John. *A Critical and Exegetical Commentary on Genesis.*
International Critical Commentary series. Rev. ed.
Scribners, 1925.

Smart, James D. *The Strange Silence of the Bible in the Church.*
Westminster, 1970.

_____. *The Interpretation of Scripture.* Westminster, 1961.

Smith, Joseph P. *St. Irenaeus: Proof of the Apostolic Preaching.*
Ancient Christian Writers series, vol. 16. Newman, 1952.

Sources Chrétiennes. 220+ vols. Paris: Les Editions du Cerf,
1942.

Spagnolo, A., and Turner, C. H. "Contra Judaeos." *Journal of
Theological Studies* 20 (1919) 293-310.

Speiser, E. A. *Genesis.* The Anchor Bible series. New York:
Doubleday, 1964.

Sperber, A. *The Bible in Aramaic.* 4 vols. Leiden: Brill, 1959.

Sperling, Harry, and Simon, Maurice. *The Zohar.* 5 vols. London:
Soncino, 1933-34.

Swete, H. B. *An Introduction to the Old Testament in Greek.*
Cambridge University, 1902. Reprinted in New York: Ktav,
1968.

Talmud Bavli. Rome: Vilna, 1886. Later editions of the Babylonian
Talmud (including the recent Soncino *Hebrew-English Edition,*
1960) reproduce the Vilna edition exactly. Rashi's comments
are in the margins. My copy was printed in Israel in 1948.

Talmud Yerushalmi. New York: Talmud Yerushalmi Publishing, 1958-
1960.

Telfer, W. "Constantine's Holy Land Plan." Pp. 696-700 in *Studia
Patristica,* vol. 1. Berlin: Akademie Verlag, 1957.

Thackery, H., and Marcus, Ralph, eds. *Josephus.* 8 vols. Loeb
Classical Library. London: Heinemann, 1926-43.

Theodor, J., and Albeck, C. *Midrash Bereshit Rabbah.* 3 vols.
Jerusalem: Wahrmann, 1965.

Thompson, H. J. *Prudentius.* 2 vols. Loeb Classical Library.
Harvard University, 1949.

Thunberg, L. "Early Christian Interpretations of the Three Angels
in Gen. 18." Pp. 560-70 in *Texte und Untersuchungen,* vol.
92.

Tikkanen, J. J. *Die Genesismosaiken von S. Marco in Venedig.*
Helsinki, 1889.

Tisserant, E. *Ascension d'Isaie.* Paris, 1909.

Townsend, John T. "Rabbinic Sources." Pp. 37-80 in *The Study of
Judaism: Bibliographical Essays.* ADL, 1972.

Turner, C. H. *Ecclesiae Occidentalis Monumenta Juris Antiquissima*,
    I.2. Oxford, 1912.

Van Trigt, F. "La Signification de la Lutte de Jacob pres du
    Yabboq." *Oudtestamentische Studien* 12 (1958) 280-309.

Vawter, Bruce. *A Path Through Genesis*. Sheed and Ward, 1956.

_____. *On Genesis: A New Reading*. Doubleday, 1977.

Vega, A. C., and Anspach, A. E. *Scriptores Ecclesiastici
    Hispano-Latini Veteris et Medii Aevi*. Spain: Escorial, 1940.

Vermes, Geza. *Scripture and Tradition in Judaism*. 2nd rev. ed.
    Studia Post-Biblica series, vol. 4. Leiden: Brill, 1973.

Weber, Robert. *Biblia Sacra Juxta Vulgata Versionem*. Stuttgart,
    1969.

Weil, Gerard E. *Massorah Gedolah*. Rome: PIB, 1971.

Wevers, John W. *Septuaginta: Genesis*. Göttingen: Vandenhoeck &
    Ruprecht, 1974.

Weyer, P. H. "Novatian and Novationism." NCE 10.534-35.

Wilpert, Joseph. *Die Römischen Mosaiken der Kirchlichen Bauten vom
    IV-XIII Jahrhundert*. Ed. Walter N. Schumacher. Herder, 1976.
    This is a revision of part of Wilpert's four-volume 1916 work,
    Die Römischen Mosaiken und Malereien der Kirchlichen Bauten.

Woollcombe, K. J. "The Biblical Origins and Patristic Development
    of Typology." *Essays in Biblical Typology*. London: Allenson,
    1957.

Yalkut Shimoni. 2 vols. New York: Horeb, 1925. Reprinted in
    Jerusalem: Lewin-Epstein, 1951.

INDEX OF BIBLICAL CITATIONS

INDEX OF TOPICS